To PETE!

Best wishes.

Jerry

In the World:
My Journey from
Nowhere to Everywhere

In the World:
My Journey from
Nowhere to Everywhere

A Memoir

Dr. Gerard Brooker

Library of Congress Control Number: 2018900200
ISBN: Hardcover   978-1-5434-7594-4
                     Softcover   978-1-5434-7595-1
                     eBook   978-1-5434-7596-8

Print information available on the last page.

Rev. date: 02/05/2018

To order additional copies of this book, contact:
Xlibris
1-888-795-4274
www.Xlibris.com
Orders@Xlibris.com
772035

Contents

ACKNOWLEDGEMENT

NEAR THE END of 8th grade I was told that Monsignor Peter A. Kelaher, head of Our Lady of Mt. Carmel, wanted to see me right away. I was confused, as I had never met him.

"I do not want you to go to Bryant High School. I will pay for you to go to a private boys' school, Rice High School. Run it by your parents and let me know."

I have never understood his motive, yet I know his generosity changed the direction my life took, from nowhere to everywhere.

Here's to Monsignor Peter A. Kelaher!

PROLOGUE

I REMEMBER THE DAY she got angry with me. I was about ten years old, sitting in a drab classroom at Our Lady of Mt. Carmel grammar school in Astoria, Queens, with about 40 other 4th grade kids.

"Keep on looking," she blurted out.

"I am looking, but I can't find it," I said to her over and over.

If she had only looked for it, felt for it, just once, I might have found out a long time ago. She was a kind lady, a nurse, who came to our school once every three or four weeks to give us a one hour class on health, you know, how to brush your teeth, looking for cooties in your hair and how to get rid of them if you found any, how sitting up straight in class was good for the spine, taking a bath once in a while. That kind of stuff. Helpful, I suppose. At least it gave us a notion that our bodies needed to be taken care of on a regular basis, a useful habit.

She was, though, at a disadvantage because the school was run by Catholic nuns, a very strict and robotic sort of women who seemed to allow themselves only one of the many emotions available to us all. And that was anger, aided and abetted by the 12 inch ruler. You might think a small piece of wood like that wouldn't hurt much. Actually, it hurts more than a longer one which has more flexibility or bounce to absorb the energy, so less hurt. The 12 incher stings like a bee bite on the palm of the hand, or worse, depending on the sadistic impulses of each nun, on the back of the hand.

If water is soft and ice is rigid, my school was ice. In every way, ice. The coldness of the environment wrapped itself around every student and each teacher so that they, too, became rigid.

That is how our health teacher was at a disadvantage. As a trained professional, she probably knew that she could have put her index finger to the left side of my neck to locate what we were looking for. But, if she did, she might have been fired or reprimanded, depending on the mood of the principal, usually a nun steeped in the old school traditions of her order. And that would mean *no touching*. I never saw anyone touching anyone, and an accidental bump was followed with an exclamation of *I'm sorry*. When I look back on those days in that school, I have an image of the school as a molecule, and the teachers and students as atoms inside the molecule. The atoms would never touch each other, as that would create warmth that could produce consequences like affection and respect.

So, feeling about my neck by the health nurse was out of the question. We never did find what we were looking for. There was a reason for that: it didn't exist!

Fast forward now about 50 years, and I'm playing in an "Over 50" basketball league. As we shall see, I always loved sports, especially basketball and baseball. The game of basketball appealed to me. What I liked, and still like, most about it is that everyone is involved. Sooner or later, each player on the floor will participate, whether it be the star or the 5th man. I loved the flow of it. In many ways it's like a dance, a weaving in and out, with a lively ball that bounces and is subject to the whims of whoever possesses it in the moment, in the second, before it is directed once again on to another man. Every time it is possessed by a new man, the dance of the other four players changes. Each goes in a new direction, takes a new stance before one of them, ideally, is open to take a shot. If a choreographer with imagination would graph the moves of the players with the ball, whose moves also dictate the flow of those guarding them, they might have a new dance, a dance perfect for weddings. It can be a dance of 10, with an imaginary ball, with all men or all women or co-ed. I can hear it:

"Now, ladies and gentlemen, we need ten guests to take the floor to do a slow *B-Ball Dance*." It might be a slow dance like

Heatwave's "Always and Forever," or Elvis' "Can't Help Falling in Love." I'll take Patsy Cline's "Crazy." Maybe a fast *B-Ball Dance*. Say Lady Gaga's "Born This Way," or a Harlem Globetrotters' version of Cool and the Gang's "Celebration." In time, the B-Ball wedding dance could become as popular as the Chicken Dance or the Hokey Pokey.

Now and then during our "Over 50" games, my right eye would get weird, sort of black out, especially when I would take a difficult shot, a falling away jump shot, for example. It's a shot that takes lots of physical energy, especially if you are over 50 years old. The blackout would last only a few seconds, so no one ever knew and I never told anyone, except for my wife, Sheila. When it happened, I would just bend over to touch my knees, as B-Ballers do when they need a brief respite from the action, and no one would notice what had just happened.

After this occurred a few times, Sheila insisted I go see our family doctor, a most wonderful and talented young man, Dr. Sean McGrade. Sean not only finished first in his class at the Georgetown University Medical School, he is first in the most human ways he goes about the art of his science. He combines the science of medicine with the art of being human. He arranged for me to get an MRI to ascertain the problem. It revealed that there was nothing wrong with my eye or my brain.

However, a weird thing showed up on the MRI. They couldn't find my left carotid artery! A few doctors looked at the pictures, then sent me to the leading neurologist in the region, Dr. John Murphy. He looked at the x-rays and MRI, gave me a few perfunctory raps on my knees to see if I had reflexes, I guess, and had me follow his finger across my eyes before asking me to sit.

"One of your carotid arteries is missing," he said in a kind of routine way, as if he had told this to hundreds of his patients. "Which one," I asked. "Your left one," he replied to the question, a momentous one for me. I remember my first thought was wondering how I got along without it for these many years, and how much longer my body could get along without it.

"Is there an upside to this?" I asked, thinking I might be the next Albert Einstein.

"No," he answered curtly.

"A downside?"

"Yes. If you have a stroke on the right side, you have no backup. It is doing the work for you."

I learned that the body sometimes does extraordinary things to compensate.

Apparently, my right carotid artery had *in utero* built bundles of extra blood vessels that function in place of my left carotid artery by feeding the other hemisphere of my brain to my heart and back again. I have suffered no cognitive or other loss. Instead of dying or being severely retarded, I was born whole and intact, with a good brain. I did nothing to earn it, so I do not take credit. It was given to me as a gift, and I am deeply humbled to have received it. I do not know from where it came because, as I shall talk about it later, I struggle to find a God or, as some would say, a Higher Power. I have always tried to be responsible for the brain I was given. And I do not show it off unless I have to, or it is useful to do so.

CHAPTER 1

The Early Years

Age 1   **Age 3**

Mom and Dad

Sheila and I back in the day

When I was a monk

Athletic days

MY EARLIEST MEMORIES are of someone holding the nipple of a bottle of milk in my mouth. Another is of an overweight woman in a long black dress picking me up from a kitchen sink to dry me off. I remember, too, lying in a carriage while two girls, probably teen-agers, fussed over me. After that, no more memories until I was about five years old.

It might seem odd, and it is odd, but I don't have any background information about my parents or grandparents. The only certain bit of personalized information I have documented is that one of my grandparents was born in Nova Scotia. I do not know which one. Truly, I come from a closed-off, tight-lipped, non-communicative family. The one of us who had any family information was my older sister, Joan. She was, I think, the only one who had access to my parents' hearts. She is dead.

I really can't put the blame wholly on my parents, as I never was curious about such things and so never asked any questions. Except for the beatings, which I'll tell you about later, I think I always lived in the present when I was a kid. I went to school, did my chores later – bringing coal up from the basement, mopping the "dust bunnies" from under the beds, and then played sports. The school yard at P.S. 5 was my home away from home. I ate dinner, promptly at 6:00 p.m., or else I was grounded from my beloved sports activities, mostly basketball and baseball. After dinner I did some home work, listened to the radio or, later, watched a little television. I hardly ever thought of the next day's promise before going to sleep. I think that was my routine for years while growing up.

Much later in life I joined the National Geographic Genome Project and had my genetic background tested for both parents. There was little to probe about my father's background because his family tree was caught up in the vast centuries-long migration from northern Europe to central to western, probably landing in Germany or England.

The waves of people moving south wrought a vast commingling of blood and cultures.

My father's landing place is but a best guess. The "er" at the end of Brooker is German, and so it seems to suggest *from* or *by* the brook.

I did learn a lot, though, about my mother's background. I learned that I have perfect genetic markers with the Saami Indians of Finland. As the Saami people are an indigenous population that has stuck together for many centuries, much can be deciphered genetically about their progeny. They are stereotyped in America as reindeer handlers, yet in reality they are probably the most integrated of all cultures into modern society. In Finland, the Saami, unlike the American Indian, the Australian Maori, or the Amerindians of Argentina, are welcomed as doctors and lawyers, as well as regional chiefs.

I don't even remember walking in my sleep, which my father said I did now and then. We lived in a cold water flat that was heated by fired coal in one stove in the middle of our kitchen. My mother cooked on that stove, and heated water on it. I still remember the address: 26-09 Jackson Avenue, Astoria, Queens, which is now up-scale. Our flat was on the ground floor on the edge of a grassy lot that led to a major intersection to St. John's Hospital where I was born. It was in that lot that I first began to love birds, live ones to admire, dead ones to pet. The hospital is gone now.

Like so many other adventures in my life, I think someone was watching over me on these night-time escapades which could have been dangerous. I was a little old for a crib, maybe five or six, when the walks started. My father told me later in life that he could hear me make noise climbing over the side of the crib. I would go to the kitchen door, twist the lock to open it, then walk down an unlit hallway to the outdoors where he would get hold of me and put me back in the crib. I've always wondered if the sleep-walking was an attempt, even at a very early age, to leave an unwelcoming flat.

To give you an example of the general emotional climate in our place, I will use the crib as one of a hundred examples I could use. Our flat consisted of a series of about five rooms without doors to separate the rooms. As a consequence, there was very little privacy, and so I learned about sex quite early. At about ten years of age the crib was gone and I had a bed in one of the rooms by myself. I could stand on top of the headboard and look over a space of about 18 inches that would allow air to flow through the rooms, theoretically giving a little heat from the kitchen coal stove in the winter, perhaps a little cool air flow in the summer.

One morning, I heard the bed in the room next to mine making creaky noises.

So I got up on the headboard and looked over into the adjoining room. And there I got my first glimpse of sex in the flesh, as our two boarders, Grace and Arthur, were going at it hard and fast!

But back to the crib. Once, in the middle of the night, I woke up and there was a strange looking man standing at the foot of my crib, just staring at me with a sort of dazed look. I screamed so loud that the figure ran fast to my right and down the hallway that led to another exit door one, for whatever reason, we were not allowed to use. My screams woke my father who yelled at me, "What's the matter?" I told him about the mystery man. "Where did he go?" he yelled again. "That way," I said, pointing to the right. He jumped out of bed and ran to the right. He was a tough guy, as you will see. In retrospect, I am kind of grateful that he didn't find anyone, as I am sure there would have been hell to pay.

Now, he went into a tirade. "God-dammit, Gerard, you woke everyone up for nothing. What is the matter with you? Now, cover yourself and go back to sleep." He repeated several versions of this before going back to bed. I would have preferred a little kindness, a little comfort, mainly because I had just had the bee-jeezus scared out of me. To this day, I still believe there was someone there at my crib which, not incidentally, I peed in until I was about six. The way my father acted that night, berating me instead of comforting me, echoed the tone that prevailed in our house in the early years of my life. My father had rules for everything, and he was to be feared rather than loved.

I was a fragile kid, yet I've always thought that some of my afflictions were the projections of my mother's fears about her own health. She talked a lot about cancer and about the new vaccine for polio. I was among the first to get the sugar cube with the vaccine. I remember frequent nose bleeds and mad dashes on the IRT trains to New York City Hospital to find out the cause, which they never did. It was finally in my adulthood that I had a weak blood vessel in my nose cauterized. I had frequent ear aches, sharp pains, in what felt like a tiny ball in the back of my left ear. It was later diagnosed as a mastoid condition which, over time, gradually disappeared. I had a heart murmur and an enlarged heart, both of which became well over time. I was also diagnosed as being anemic, so my mother said. When I was in second grade at a Catholic school, I was placed in a wheel chair for a time. I do not remember for how long or why. Probably a polio scare. I do remember my mother wheeling me to see the school principal to ask her, beg her, to let me take the final exams which would allow me to enter 3rd grade. She adamantly refused, her rationale being that I was absent too many days. It was my first memorable encounter with the prescriptive ways of nuns. I felt then, and I feel now, that the exams would have been "a piece of cake" for me to pass, if only she would lighten up a bit and let me try. I thought that an injustice had been done to me. The sense of that injustice was more of a feeling of anger mixed with disappointment. Later in life, I thought that her motivation was a fear that if a kid could pass the exams without attending class for a while, this would place the efficacy of the 2nd grade nun's teaching in doubt. That would not do, as many of them seemed to have, ironically, a problem with pride.

I do not remembering my mother fawning over any of my brothers' or sisters' health. Perhaps they didn't have issues. I don't know, as I always had what I will call somewhat cold relations with them. There was the oldest, Bobby. Then Wallace and Joan.

I was next, in front of Kenny and the youngest, Eileen who was named after another sister named Eileen who died at the age of six before I was born. Another sister was still-born.

We also had a "sister" we called Aunt Gertrude as she grew older. I don't know why we began to call her that. Usually, we simply called her "Gertie." Perhaps it was an attempt by my father to hide her real identity from any snoopy authorities. You see, Gertie came to us in a strange way. One of our neighbors, a friend of my dad, was moving his family to Chicago. He told my parents that he didn't have the means to take care of all his children and would they take one of them, any one of them they wanted, including a newly arrived baby!

Far from being a family of means and with lots of their own children, my parents decided that taking the baby would not be feasible. So, they took Gertie who was, I think, about four years old. They did this without any official adoption process, no documentation. They just did it!

I often wondered about Gertie, whom I always loved and respected. I wondered how she must have felt being ripped from the bosom of her family into ours. I think it might have been the beginning of my ability to identify with others' suffering. I do know, as it was evident, that my parents did all they could to show her warmth and affection. I always loved being with her, even later in life after she married a man we called "Uncle Jimmy," who would play a significant role in my early years. Gertie always welcomed me into her home, always insisted on cooking a meal for me, whether it was sandwiches for lunch or a meal for dinner. Without my realizing it at the time, her goodness was an inspiration to me.

As I said, my relations with my brothers and sisters were distant, except for my brother Kenny with whom I became, let's say, friendly. We both liked school-yard stickball, and spent hours playing it against each other at P.S. 5, especially on Saturday and Sundays in the afternoons. The strike zone was drawn with a piece of chalk, and we following major league proportions as best we could. The strike zone was between the chest and the knees. I don't know why, but everyone who played this game drew the inside and outside of the "plate" much wider than the major league proportion, so that the chalk box drawn on the wall was pretty much a square. The school yard fence in back of the pitcher had three layers of metal mesh. Hitting the bottom third was a single, the middle a double, the top a triple, and over them all a home run. There were a few problems: an apartment building was behind the fence, and sometimes a home run ball, the pink Spaldings, would hit a window with a bang. We lucked out if there was no one home, and caught hell if someone was, usually the lady of the house. The window would open wide, she'd stick her head out and give us the *whatsis*, sometimes threatening to call the police. None of them ever did, but they scared us with threats so strong that we made a new rule: whoever hit a home run on top of the apartment roof was responsible to get the ball. That entailed going into the building, climbing about ten flights of stairs to the roof top, opening the latch door to the roof, looking around for the ball on tip-toes, finding the ball, latching down the roof door, and sneaking quietly back down the stairs. It was like going through a mine-field, the mine being any one of the explosive mothers who might pop out of their apartments to catch us in the act. It got so that a home run was unwelcomed by the one who hit it. Besides, it held up the game for about fifteen minutes.

As for the others, well Bob was twelve years older than I, and I was six when he went off to war to become a spotter/gunner aboard a PBY-4. I have spotty memories of him, all held together by the heroic status he held within the family, mostly by my father.

Though I picked up on the idolization that those in our neighborhood had for Bobby, my affection for him was real. When he came home from the war, he kind of took me under his wing. He taught me how to play baseball, playing many hours on a large abandoned lot with chards of broken glass, hitting fly balls to me while teaching me the proper ways to catch a ball. He played on a baseball team, and took me to his ball games, and sometimes let me hang out with him and his buddies, mostly in the neighborhood bars. He took me to Yankee Stadium and to the Polo Grounds. I remember that he always looked sharp, shoes shined. He often hung out with another vet who lived around the corner from us. I remember watching them on Saturday nights, leaving for their double dating, all shined up and looking fine. I wanted to be like them.

You see, Bobby's plane went down off Samarai, New Guinea on May 21, 1944 while testing a new engine. Only he and the pilot survived. He had many operations and spent over a year in Naval hospitals. I was not allowed to see him during that time, too young they said, though for most of it he was in a military hospital in St. Albans, Long Island, about a 45 minute bus ride from us. I would think about him a lot during that time, remembering the day that my mother received a telegram telling us that he was missing. I recall that she read it to me, the only one home at the time. She cried, while I went to one of the bedrooms, kneeling down and asking God to bring Bobby home to us. I did not know how to console her. We received another telegram, perhaps a week or so later, telling us that he was found, and that they would get back to us when there was more information. And they did. He later married Essie, and they had six children.

After he recovered from his wounds he would, now and then, be asked by my father to share his war experiences with the guys from around the block and the local bars. Although everyone was older and drank beer, my father allowed me to attend. We would sit in a large circle, and the men would ask Bobby questions about his experiences.

I learned much about the world and people during those evenings. How he woke up on a mattress in the waters of Milne Bay while a Dutch freighter made its way to rescue him and the pilot. How his heart stopped beating on the operating table and a young Navy surgeon, he learned later, refusing to leave him, opened up his chest and hand-pumped his heart back to rhythm.

He said that the nurses told him later about the raw obscenities he yelled while under anesthesia, and how they got lots of laughs out of that. I remember the story about the day his PBY almost took off with him on top between the two engines with a fire extinguisher in his hand, a regular procedure before take-off as the engines tended to flame, banging it on the metallic roof, hoping that someone in the plane would hear his emergency while it began to taxi down the runway. Mercifully, an air traffic controller in the conning tower did, and notified the pilot. And the day he was appointed the "shooter," the guy who stood on the highest spot to shoot at the sharks while his buddies tried to get in a refreshing swim in the sea.

He even told us, during one of his leaves, that he had fallen in love with an Australian girl. Her name was Vicky. He showed us a photo of her that he carried in his wallet. They decided to break it off, he said, because she did not want to move to America, nor he to Australia. I remember that she was pretty. And how sad I was to be introduced to the reality that love didn't always work out the way that I, in my idealistic, naïve, and romantic mind, thought it would. Nevertheless, he was my hero and would remain so unto his death, six months after he retired.

I never had much of a relationship with Wallace who was about seven years older than I. He was a bit of a recluse, and had no interests in sports, while I was playing lots of baseball and basketball. I think that and the difference in ages was just enough to keep us running on separate tracks. And, too, he didn't have the macho traits that my father appreciated. He liked photography and once set up a photo lab in his bedroom.

When our father found out about that, he made a big issue of it. "Get that stuff out of here right away. Now!" I remember him screaming at Wallace while the rest of it watched, kind of stunned, kind of afraid. My brother then committed the Big One. He talked back at my father, telling him that he had rights, too. That was always a NO-NO in our house, never talk back at mother or father. Without taking a breath, my father threw him out of the house.

I don't mean just leave for a bit. He meant forever! Wallace was just sixteen.

I was ashamed of my father for using his power that way. As I remember it, Wallace came back into the fold about a week later. I suspect that the essential goodness in my father, a goodness blunted by his own upbringing, brought Wallace home.

Wallace eventually joined the army and was sent to Korea at the outset of the war there. I remember that he was dishonorably discharged from the army and sent home. I never could find out why. I soon learned to stop asking.

My sister Joan was the one I could relate to while growing up. She didn't seem to have as many natural boundaries around the expression of herself as the rest of us did.

She could poke fun at my father, and get away with it. In fact, I think he liked it. She was a frequent companion of my mother. She was the only one who could get my mother to express herself about this 'n that, including her feelings. I remember one day when my mother severely beat me so that my nose and left ear were bleeding. She was in a fury, and drunk. Each time she hit me, for some trivial offense like not doing a good job at one of my choirs, I yelled back at her, "You stop that!" to which she replied, "Don't you talk like that to me," and hit me again. I would then say again, "You stop that!"

This would go on and on until my common sense prevailed and I shut up. It was a lose-lose proposition for me. If she did stop because I told her to stop, she would probably then tell my father who never hit me, but who came close several times.

After I finally gave in, Joan was there to console me. She wiped the blood from my face, and told me that our mother was now crying in the next room because she was ashamed of herself for hitting me. "If she is ashamed," I asked, "Why doesn't she stop doing it?"

"Because Daddy (which she called him) instructs her to do it. She has her orders."

This was all very weird to me. I felt a bit sorry for my mother. I felt ashamed of my father. I thought him to be a coward. Later in my life, I came to a different conclusion about his motives. Over time, I could see that he was a man who had many character faults at the same time that he was one of the most committed and generous men I knew. I think that he was caught between the prescriptions he grew up with from his own father, that is, there is a rule for everything and a way to do or not do everything, and his own most generous and good-hearted nature. I think he simply took the easy way out by telling his wife to do the dirty work. That he really did not have it in him to physically hurt his children. Strange. Different.

I did not call my sister Joan by her name. I always called her "Joannie" because it was an endearing name to me, although there were times when I did not find her endearing. I remember in the lead-up to Christmas, a holiday my father always celebrated with presents for each of us, when she began to whine at him that she wasn't going to get a Christmas present from him. You see, he bought her a fur coat several weeks before December 25th, the coat being her present. He worked two jobs around that season to make the necessary money. I remember going into the local supermarket during the holiday season and saw him stocking the shelves with canned goods. I left the store because I did not want to acknowledge that he was my father. Several of my classmates at the Catholic school I attended were from wealthy families, and I did not want them to know that I was poor, although they probably knew because the nuns would sometimes embarrass me for not having a white shirt and tie to wear each day. I wore what we could afford, a polo shirt, no tie. The harassment I took from the nuns about this took many forms, including not allowing me to be in class photos because I wasn't "properly dressed." I remember attempts to embarrass me in front of the class when I might challenge them, e.g, the day I insisted that one of the uses for hemp was for smoking, as in pot. She made me come in front of the class so she could scorn my answer as being a silly made-up story from a child who didn't even dress properly. When the nun wrote home about my polo shirts, my mother borrowed a tie from my uncle Arthur and put it on over the polo shirt. "You tell her," my mother said, "that we either eat food tonight or you get a white shirt." We ate food that night.

Back to my sister Joannie. I did not like that she pestered my father to compromise the agreement she had made with him by buying her an extra present.

I did not like that she started to date at fifteen and got pregnant at sixteen by my cousin who had a very distinctive bull-dog type face, so it was obvious who the father was. I always felt that the pregnancy bothered my father greatly because the immorality of it was transparent, and there didn't seem to be anything he could do about it. It was the first time that I saw his sense of a soft omnipotency challenged.

Over time, she and I almost lost complete track of each other. I left home at 17, and she married a few times to semi-shiftless guys, having babies, and then settled in Florida where I went to see her once with my youngest son, Jay. We spent an afternoon at her home by the canal in Pompano Beach. It was clear that she was not a happy camper.

She and one of her daughters, who lived with her and her husband, did not get along. The tension in the house was thick, outspoken disagreements filled the air.

It was not long after the visit that she began to call me regularly, asking for money. I became tired of that after awhile because by that time I knew that she was hooked on drugs, which she always denied to me. I told her that I would like to keep up our relationship, but that I would not be sending her money any more. We had a perfunctory relationship after that. Several years later, she simply put her head on her living room coffee table and slipped into a coma.

I flew to Florida to keep vigil with her two daughters. Her doctors told us that Joannie would never recover, that she was, in effect, brain dead. My job, they said, was to convince her daughters of this, so that they would sign off to "pull the plug" which they finally did. She continued to breathe for a week before letting go.

This might sound strange because of some disappointments I've expressed about her, yet I was deeply saddened by her early death. She was sort of heroic to me because she seemed to be the only one of my brothers and sisters to express her vitality.

She was a good and decent person. She took chances, and did everything a person with her disadvantages could do. Everything good and everything bad, or so it seemed. She was fiercely loyal to everyone, and full of potential. Sadly, she became another victim of drugs.

The youngest of us all is Eileen. She lives in Pennsylvania and is almost eleven years younger than I. Because of our age differences, we never did walk the same paths and only became close in the past ten years or so. She is one of the best people I have ever known, a true inspiration to me. She has had a difficult life, one filled with loss and disappointment. She is one of those people who manages to make gold out of dross.

Even when I disappoint her, as I sometimes do, she understands and accepts my reasons.

Recently, for example, she wanted me to write a letter on behalf of one of her sons in jail, guilty of manslaughter. I told her that my conscience would not allow me to do that. She graciously told me that she understood, even though the letter might have been quite beneficial.

Eileen was named after her much older sister who died suddenly when she was six years old from a sudden bout with rheumatic fever. My parents were not well–educated. My father dropped out of school in the 3rd grade, my mother in the 6th. I think that they probably knew very little or nothing about the signs or symptoms of this disease. My father told me that when he finally knew that there was something drastically wrong that he wrapped her in a blanket and ran with her to St. John's Hospital about two blocks away to the emergency room where she died the next day. I never knew her, but I sometimes talk with her, as I'd like to believe that there is a life after this valley of tears. I even would like to think that my still-born sister is alive somewhere.

It does not compute that a being who dies in her mother's uterus, is expelled from that place, gets wrapped up in newspaper and laid to rest by her father in a dumpster.

From my own experiences, education, and parenting, I am convinced that the way each of us is treated in the first years of our lives by our parents and siblings sets the tone of our psychic lives. I don't pretend that this is an insight. Hell, any modern text on early childhood confirms that. I am only saying it because what I am about to tell you about my parents truly did set the tone for my life.

Until I entered my teen years living in our apartment on the 3rd floor over the Roxy Bar and Grill, I had what I would call an "OK" relationship with my mother, though informed by an undercurrent of my anger. She was not a well-educated person, having dropped out of school in the 6th grade. I'm not even sure if she could read. Now and then, I would see her sitting at the kitchen table looking at the New York Daily News, our family news bible. She would look at the photos that were always abundant in the paper, then flip the page to look at the next set before flipping. She never seemed to be reading. I don't know if it was because she was disinterested or because she could not read. Sad to say, it didn't matter to me, I guess. I was kid, and a kid doesn't know much about love. I do remember the nights when my father would prompt us to say something nice to her after she would cook us a bountiful dinner, say at Thanksgiving. "Tell your mother how good the dinner is," he would direct us, releasing us to say what might have been in our hearts but never spoken in our uncommunicative family. Positive emotions were not in our vocabulary. Negative ones were, bountifully.

And I do remember when I was about nine years old saving my pennies so I could buy her a cactus plant that I had my eyes on for Mother's Day. I walked to the IRT elevated train station to go over to the other side of the street where the flower shop was. I put my pennies on the counter, and said, "This one." I remember that the guy behind the counter told me to pick a thumb-sized card from a pack of assorted cards. When I got home, I gave the plant and the card to her. I wondered why everyone laughed so hard.

The card read, "With My Greatest Sympathy." In retrospect, I think it might have been the perfect card.

Before she started to drink heavily, I would spend lots of time in the kitchen with her, mostly asking her questions about this 'n that. I was like a question machine, a machine gun spraying the questions like bullets one after another. "Gerard," she would sometimes say, "look at the clock," pointing to the one on the kitchen wall. "No more questions til the big hand gets on the 10." As it might have been 30 minutes after the hour, I would have to wait for about 20 minutes before I could go at it again. And I did just that, sitting on a kitchen chair and watching the clock for the punishment to pass while I thought about a new set of questions to ask. She would try to keep me busy by handing me a potato masher to cream up the spuds which I did so well that, after a while, the pot was full of dents.

Or she would have me pull out the feathers from a newly bought chicken. Yes, chickens were sold in the Day still dressed in their feathers. Plucked ones cost extra.

After plucking, she would have me cut off the chicken's feet. You could take one of the feet and pull back on its top skin so that the claws would move back and forth. I would take one of the feet and sneak up behind her and pretend that the chicken was scratching her neck. She would fake being surprised and scared. I loved it, as it all made me feel close to her, although she never told me that she loved me until much later in life when I practically forced the words from her.

She was old-fashioned in her ways, perhaps the way poor, uneducated women were in those times. She mothered eight kids, cooked dinners, great dinners, did the laundry, ironed, shopped, and made sure we all toed the mark with choirs and study habits. She took her orders from my father and executed the punishments declared by him who was both judge and jury. I don't remember her ever hitting any of my siblings, but I took it on the chin, so to speak. Mostly for answering her back, a major crime in the adjudications of the judge. She would sometimes bloody my nose and left ear by pounding me with her right fist until finally my desire to stop the pain trumped my refusal to give in.

I remember admiring her at a point in her life before drink took over when she was the mom on the block not to mess with. When there was trouble on the block, e.g., she would not hesitate to call the police. When any one, even another women, might use obscene language, she'd call the police who would actually respond and mediate the problem. She was a sort of rallying point for block problems.

If the rhythms of her life flowed between the typical mom of that time period and uber reinforcer, the constant part about her was her goodness. When she was sober she was sweet, even though I knew that word would embarrass her.

She could, though, be stubborn and didn't always know how to best negotiate her world. Unfortunately, I would sometimes get caught up in her world, as when the nuns in my Catholic grammar school would take me to task, as I've said, for not having a white shirt and tie, as was required. It was embarrassing enough, but she made it worse by sending me off to school with a polo shirt and my Uncle Arthur's tie. It looked silly and I felt silly. When the nun insisted on the white shirt, my mother sent her a note saying that it was either a white shirt or no dinner tonight and, by God, my kids are going to eat tonight!

As I look back on my relationship with her, I think the only sure way I got the affection I needed from her was when I would get sick, as I often did when very young.

I even cried and yelled out for her on my first day of school, as I reluctantly was seated in the first seat, first row. Whenever I got sick, she would constantly take my temperature, bring me soup and cheese sandwiches, which I loved. My favorite part was when she would bring me the New York Daily News that had the most comprehensive sports pages ever.

Yet, withal, she was never really emotionally warm. She was not someone I could confide in when anything was troubling me. And many things troubled me. I remember in first grade, for example, watching a bird's nest in a tree outside the second floor where our classroom was. There was a baby bird in it. I would watch it from my seat and pray that it would be OK. World War 11 had just started and I was always afraid that doomsday was around the corner. My father increased my fear when he would sometimes, while drunk, yell out into the night, "The Germans are coming, the Germans are coming." So, I was afraid for the baby bird. One day as I watched the baby's mother try to teach it to fly by pushing it out of the nest. I knew, I just knew, that the baby was not ready. I could see it drop like a rock. We still had about 45 minutes until school was over. I could hardly wait to see if the baby had made it, but I knew. When I ran down the stairs to see, there it was. On the concrete. Dead.

I was broken-hearted. Doomsday was coming, and the baby bird was dead. I really needed to tell my mom, but I knew that she was not available for this kind of intimacy. She was not equipped by her own upbringing to give comfort to the deeper parts of any of us kids.

I remember best the Friday evenings when she would take the three or four youngest children, which always included me, to dinner at the Chinese restaurant across the street. She would excite us by pointing out the many combinations of odd meals it was possible to order. After dinner, we would walk to the less expensive movie house where each of us would scramble to get one of the seats on either side of her as these were the best places to fall asleep against her stout arms after a hard week at school with the nuns.

I like to remember those wonderful evenings, the long walks home as it was closing in on midnight, and sometimes very cold. We were happy to be with her, sharing our thoughts about the night's movies and our dreams of the future. They were the good years when she had a certain and tough acceptance of life. She never asked for much materially, yet she was exuberant when my father bought her a fur-collared coat. I have no idea where the money came from. He did, though, gamble and I suppose that sometimes he hit it big.

It occurs to me now that I learned much about how I saw the world from being around her. Many times as a child I went with her on Friday evenings to the apartments where relatives lived. When we went to Aunt Dotty's place I had a choice to go in the back room with the rest of the kids whose moms would sit at the kitchen table, drink beer and gossip, or manipulate my mom to allow me to sit under the kitchen table. "If you use the coloring book I gave you and don't ask questions, you can sit under the table. Otherwise, I will make you go into the back room with the other kids."

I did not want to go to the back room, as it was the place where the older boys used boxing gloves to beat the crap out of each other. I tried it once and did not like the violence. If not boxing, then it was "spin the bottle." I was not yet ready for kissing.

So, I shut my mouth and pretended I was coloring, which I continued to do over many Friday evenings. They must have thought I was very naïve.

Their talk was free and gossipy, as they had nothing to hide from their husbands who, I presume, were also out drinking beer in the local taverns. I learned much about life during those times. I learned about sex and infidelity, about who was doing it with whom in the neighborhoods. I had always thought that my Uncle Jimmy's death at the age of 23 was way too young for anyone to die of natural causes. I learned under the table that he committed suicide. That information caused confusion and new feelings of shame about my father who always called Jimmy a coward for "shooting himself in the foot" after landing with the Marines on some Pacific island. Whether it was Iwo Jima, Guam or Saipan I do not know. But to call him a coward because the wound was in his foot, one of the ways to avoid combat, was to me a small boy, arrogant and shameful. I thought, right or wrong, that my father might have been responsible for Jimmy's death.

I learned, too, that another Jimmy, a dear family friend, was not killed by a laundry truck that fell over on him while turning a corner. I learned that he was mixed up with the mob in the city, and that he was stabbed to death.

I did not want to hear these things, as they made me sad. I just knew that it was too much for a kid to hear, too much to bear. I began to think that the world of adults was really screwed up. So, I stopped sitting under the table, and returned to the back room for a spell before I reaffirmed to myself that I didn't want to be there, either.

Yet, as I look back on those days, I realize that I was proud of her. She would exhort the other women to "take no guff from anyone," and to demand respect from every man. As a little kid, I was proud of her. She was a bit on the edgy side and she had a attitude of independence and a quiet determination to ask for what was right. I think that my father knew the line where soft and quiet ended and feisty began.

Between these days of my innocence and the end of her life at the relatively young age of 67 things changed between us, as I will tell you later, and not for the better.

Alcohol can do strange things to a person. I know. It took away her goodness, her truth, her beauty. Even at the end when cancer of the liver slowly claimed her spirit, she was angry when I tried to defend my father's love for her. She turned to face the wall of her hospital room, then crossed the Great Divide a few hours later.

Oh, my dad. It will be difficult now to separate the love-hate relationship I once had for him from the way I feel about him now. Time can do that, I suppose. As I have grown and matured, I have realized and accepted that he was at the center of my universe as a child, that he was one of the best men and one of the worst men I ever knew. Not the worst as in a perpetrator of crimes, but as in full of character faults. He was an alcoholic, and for years was in denial about this. He and my mom, when the addiction in them matured, so to speak, drank beer in the house the way some families drink soda, juice or water. As you will see, it had its effect on me later in life.

It was the way things were. Mom would often put the empty beer bottles in brown paper bags and tell me to take them down to the store where she had bought them for the 5 cent deposit on each, along with a note asking the proprietor to give me 2 bottles of beer with the deposit money.

As dad grew older, he would sit in his favorite chair with a gallon of Gallo wine at his side, waiting for the clock to strike noon, as his definition of an alcoholic was one who drank before noon. When the clock struck 12, he would open the cap on the Gallo and begin. By mid-afternoon, it was difficult to have a conversation with him, as he grew more and more aggressively opinionated.

Withal, he had a very tough life. In his prime, he was what was called a shop–steward, in charge of 250 men on the docks of New Jersey during the edgy time period when workers were unionizing and making their voices heard. He told me that his nose was broken twice in fights.

He stopped drinking when he was 86 years old. He simply stopped, without a support group. I went to Florida where he lived with my sister Joan to ask him why he stopped. "I was tired of it," he told me.

During that same visit, he spent several hours one night telling me about his life.

I felt like a priest listening to his last confession. It was a humbling experience for me.

He trusted me to tell me about some of the things he did in his life, failings that a dad normally would not want his son to know. I have chosen to let these die with him.

In many ways, the hard life he lived hardened him, though every once in a while his basic soft side would leak out. I remembered the evening after my mother was hospitalized for a few days with a stomach ailment. We were all having dinner together and, of course, the mood was different without her presence. He began to talk about her, about how the dinner was not as good without her cooking. He began to tear up, but could not hold back his sadness. He simply put his head on the dinner table and cried. Shamelessly cried, shoulders heaving. The love for his "Reet," his nickname for her, Rita, was there for us to see. Except for his sobs, the room was silent, as none of us kids knew what to do or say. It was a new experience for us.

To say his life was a hard one is sometimes an understatement. During that same confessional evening in Florida, he told me a story that I shall never forget. I couple of cases of liquor, waiting to be put on trucks for shipping, had been stolen off the docks.

Because the stolen cases were to be shipped by truck out of New Jersey, the theft came under the jurisdiction of the FBI. It became known that one of the men my father supervised was ready to reveal information about the theft. The day before the FBI was to investigate, the man disappeared. When the agents came to talk with the snitch, they were told that he had not shown up for work. As it was known in those circles that "snitching" was dealt with severely by the longshoremen, my father said the agents probably knew what that meant, that he had been *disappeared*.

Here is what actually happened to him: the men used docker's hooks to cut his arms off from his shoulders, and then dropped his body and the arms into the river. My father told me that he saw bubbles rising to the surface as the man helplessly drowned.

Humans are complicated, and I cannot fathom the anguish that my father must have felt about what happened, about the naïve and now dead young man, about himself, the men on the job. At his core he was a man whose goodness never had a chance to fully blossom. Poverty, lack of opportunity and education, can do that to a man.

He told me, too, that when my mom delivered a still-born baby in their bed that he did not know what to do with the fetus. He told me that he wrapped the baby in newspaper and put it in a shopping bag. He said that he did not know what to do, so he walked around endlessly before putting the baby in a dumpster. Poverty, shame, lack of education can do that to a man. I can only imagine the anguish he must have known in his life. At the end of his "confessional" to me, I was bursting with love for him.

I remember well his immaturity and silliness, and how these aspects of his character, when blended with his tough guy and intimidating nature, kept me and my siblings from an emotional intimacy with him. One night, for example, soon after the war with Germany started, there was what they called an "air-raid drill." All the lights in the house were to be turned off and the blinds pulled down. Searchlights lit up the sky, making it dramatic and scary. On the night I remember, he began to shout out, "The Germans are coming, the Germans are coming!" Needless to say, it made me very scared.

And because of his alcoholism, we never knew what side of the bed he would wake up on, or what mood he would be in when he came home from work, or on weekends when he had off. I really cannot speak for my siblings, but I know that his unpredictable ways stopped me on many occasions from telling him about experiences a son would like to tell his father, perhaps for consolation, perhaps for guidance and advice.

I remember, for example, the day I got into a squabble with a boy while I was delivering newspapers, for the Long Island Star Journal, a job I did 7 days a week for about $8-10 dollars a week, after school Monday-Friday, early afternoon on Saturday, very early on Sundays. As I remember the day of the squabble, I won the wrestling match with the kid and got in a few shots. He ran into his apartment building to get his dad, who was at me in a flash. He was a barrel-chested smallish man wearing a tank top.

To this day, many years later, I remember the hair on his chest sticking out. He slapped me around pretty good. I kept on ducking, trying to ward off his blows, but he got me pretty good. No one intervened. I cried a bit, and then went on to complete my paper route.

The beating messed up my head a bit for a while. He didn't really physically hurt me, but I felt humiliated that I couldn't do anything about it. It was plain wrong for a mature man to do that to a kid. I wanted to tell my dad. But I knew that I couldn't because he was so unpredictable. I was afraid that he would do nothing and I might despise him because of that. I was afraid, too, that he might get me to track the guy down and, at worst, do something really bad to him or get beaten up himself. I didn't want any part of these things so I just sucked it up.

And on the flip side of that, there was the day that I was bullied in my early high school days in front of our neighborhood friends. About a dozen of us were standing in a circle having a debate about something or another. I said something the big guy didn't like and he walked towards me and pushed me down on my back. I didn't know what to do and I was scared of him. So, I did nothing, just continued to lie on the ground while looking up at everyone.

Again, I felt humiliated. I was especially embarrassed that I had not retaliated in front of the girls who were a part of our neighborhood gang of friends.

A few days went by that summer when he met up with me again. This time with his two buddies who were as big as he was. I was lolling away the afternoon throwing a pink Spalding against a cement wall when he started to pick on me again. To this day, I do not know what came over me, some impulse to dignity that rose up deep inside me.

I would take no more of this, and my honor became more important to me than my body.

When he started to push me I came back at him. As his buddies cheered him on to execute the expected damage, they did not know that a rage was bubbling inside me.

I've had this come over me on another occasion when I was attacked by a mad dog. I might go down, I might be defeated, hurt, or dead, but the dog and bully would go down with me. I tossed him down by putting my left leg behind his right leg and pulling him off balance. I got on top of him, and pinned his upper body with my knees, pulled him up from the cement by his shirt collar while cocking my arm and fist to smash his face.

Lots of thoughts ran through my mind. I realized that I was a bit crazy at the moment and could break his nose, or severely hurt him. That his buddies might get into it. At 3:1, I would certainly lose, perhaps more than my dignity. That there would be the retribution from the bully at some unexpected time. That I would get into trouble with my father for causing him the inconveniences from the fallout consequences. Perhaps the police would be involved. Who knows what else?

So, what did I do? I let him go and ran. I ran and ran and ran, more so I think to run from myself and what I had almost done. I was afraid of them, and I was afraid of myself. In retrospect, I think the anger I had stuffed inside myself was beginning to show. When I was out of breath, I went into one of the apartment houses, sat on the steps in the hallway and cried. I was bewildered by it all, a potpourri of feelings that made no sense. So I decided to do something that would affect me for many years. I would no longer trust anyone since no one, or so I thought at that moment, could any longer be trusted. I painted an imaginary box made of ice around my heart, a box no one would ever be allowed to enter without my permission. I remember soon after the bully incident when one of my teachers, a Christian Brother at Rice High School in Harlem, New York, stopped me on the stairs of the school to ask me what was wrong. I guess he could tell that I was troubled. "Why don't you just mind your own business," I answered his overture of kindness. Without my permission, he would not enter.

What I really wanted and needed was to be able to tell my father what had happened. Yet, he was too unreliable in what he might do, from overkill to nothing.

His presence in my life was more theoretical and conceptual than it was tangible and real. I remember only once that he threatened me. When I was about fifteen, I chanced on smoking a cigarette one day in our bathroom after school was out. It was about 3:30 in the afternoon when I heard him pounding on the door for someone to let him in. He had come home early that day. As I remember it, he never carried a house key because he did not want to lose it, or because he thought someone of us all would always be in the house. I knew it was him because he began to yell. In a panic, because smoking implied a pact with the devil for him, I opened the bathroom window, pulled a towel off the rack and began to fan out the smoke. As I was doing this, he began to pound harder and yell louder. I just had that sense that something bad was going to happen, that he was agitated and, if he knew I was having a smoke, it might very well be the end of my life as I knew it.

I waited as long as I could to give the cigarette smoke a chance to escape before I went to open the door. The blood vessels in his neck were about to explode. "If I ever catch you masturbating, I'll cut off your dick." That was all he said, a real confidence builder, if anyone ever said so.

Because he never really gave any of us guidance about relationships, or showed us by his actions how to relate except for the "guy thing" with bar-room friends, our own rapport with each other, except for Joan in whom I could confide once in a while, was always irregular and twitchy. By *twitchy* here I mean not warm or affectionate, perhaps even odd. My brothers, from time to time for example, would tie my hands and feet with rope, tape up my mouth with duct tape and put me in a closet and close the door to leave me in the dark. I would try to yell but because of the tape, I could only mumble a murmur.

Although I would think at these times how close to death I would be if any of them got really stupid by plugging up my nose, I would not tell my father simply because I thought he would not know how to behave reasonably with them. I could only think that he didn't want to know anything about what had happened, or that he might exact an unfair and disproportionate price on my brothers.

He was not a nurturing kind of dad, and was prone to make fun of us whenever we might react to anything romantic, in real life or on T.V. I remember when I thought it was time for me to ask a girl for a date. And a kiss, I might add. I came to this realization at the time I was contemplating becoming a monk. I guess I thought it a necessary experience for me to kiss a girl at least once before I entered the closed–off life where I would take a solemn vow of chastity. I didn't think it was right for me to take this vow before I could even know what I was missing.

Because I was afraid to let my father know that I would be having a date, I walked six blocks away from where we lived to use a pay phone to call the girl of my choice,

Agnes DeRose. I called her because she was always sweet to me during our years at Our Lady of Mt. Carmel Grammar School. I thought if I used our land-line, for which we needed our mother's permission, he might find out and make fun of it all.

Agnes said yes, and I took her to a Broadway show. We took the IRT el train home to 30th Avenue and I walked her home, my heart thumping in my chest. How do you kiss a girl? kept racing through my mind. When we got there, she stood on the first step of the entrance, her face level with mine, which made my mission easier.

I took her by the shoulders and touched my lips to hers so lightly that it probably barely met the definition of a kiss. But, I was satisfied. I did what I had to do, and my father would never know. Little did I know then that I would not kiss another girl for over seven years.

One of the character defects he had was the way he treated our dog whose name was Kiki. Yet, it was seeing the brutalizing ways that he treated Kiki that first made me aware of love. You see, my father would sometimes beat the dog over the head with a rolled-up newspaper. For no reason. Just for kicks. So, I figured early on that there was something wrong with my father. I do believe that he might have been beaten as a child and that this was his way of "doing unto others."

He would laugh while our dog would cringe. She was so scared of him that when he came into the apartment she would hide johneath the stove.

"Why do you do that?" I yelled at him one day, a dangerous way to talk to the man. "She's a dog, a good dog. Stop it."

"If you don't shut up," he responded, "you'll get some of the same." I was about ten, so there wasn't much I could do. I think, though, that he did let up, at least when I was around.

I could never understand why a man would do that to a helpless animal. My heart aches for my dog even now as I write this. I thought my father was a coward to harm a defenseless animal who couldn't fight back. Kiki was a fragile girl, and I began to feel her fear and dread of him. And I began to know a few things about love and affection, about the needs of others. When she would come out from under the stove for me to pet her, this mutt with the sad eyes that beckoned to be loved, I began to understand my own needs for affection that weren't being met.

To this day, when I think of her and that needy look of anticipation to be loved, I think of the helpless and unloved children everywhere who are abused by those more powerful.

One day, they would become my Kikis.

I think that now and then the goodness, truth and beauty with which my dad was born would sometimes leave his spirit, especially when he was drunk, the days of horror for me. The days when he would laugh with my mother when I was about eight or nine years old as they hung me out of the window of our 3rd floor apartment, she by one foot, he by the other. As I would scream in terror and panic, they would roar with a kind of weird laughter before making it worse as one of them would let go so that now I was hanging head down by one foot, helpless.

When they would finally haul me back in, I would vent my pent-up anger at them before running away from them to the back of the apartment because I was ashamed of them and I was afraid of them. What hurt most was the realization that my parents, the ones I most expected to protect me from harm, had become the ones who might do me harm. I could no longer count on them. Perhaps it is why I do not automatically trust others until they have passed the high bar I set for them.

I did, though, make overtures of filial friendship to him, and he fatherly affection to me after that. I remember the day, not long after the window hanging, when he told me that he would take me to see a movie with him, which was big deal to me. As it turned out, it was the only time we ever went to the movies. It was a war film, starring William Bendix. That I remember. Not incidentally, he would often read me the news of WW II battles. For some reason, he always picked me, perhaps because he could tell that I was interested in these matters.

The walk home after the movie, from Steinway Street to Grand Avenue and 31st Street took about 20 minutes. I felt close to him that day. I looked up at him and said, "Can I hold your hand?" It took a lot of courage for me to ask him that, as he did not show outward affection. He was very "old school" about that. But, he answered, "Yes," with a look that suggested it was okay, yet awkward. I remember feeling so proud that day as we walked home holding hands.

I find it curious as I look back at my life and the relationship I had with him, and how I never really got to know my mother. As we have seen, I don't have a lot of memories of her. Maybe that is why I left the life of a monk. To find out, to know, this beautiful creature called Woman.

But, back to my in and out, up and down, love-hate relationship with my dad, this union and breaking away, this identification with him and rejection of him. And how the amalgam of the parts was in some big way critical in shaping who I am. When I was about seven, I wasn't allowed to leave the block where we lived in Queens, or even to go across the street by myself. I knew only the block I lived on, and that only to the left of the flat we lived in. To the right there was a broad, four-lane road which, in the eyes of my wary mother much too dangerous to cross unescorted.

To the left was a very long block, ending near what is still today called Queens Plaza, a gateway stop connecting the IRT elevated trains to a variety of places in New York City. At the time, knowing nothing else, I was satisfied with my boundaries.

The neighborhood was nothing more than endless boxes of cold-water flats with a single bakery shop as its centerpiece. But it was my block, my world, the only world I knew.

That shop would play a special role in my life on the day I learned a little about myself, about a sense of place, about purpose.

You see, Thanksgiving was a big deal in my family. My father would always bring home a very large turkey, fitting for a family the size of ours. On the holiday I remember here, the bird he got, probably from the union boss, was especially large, maybe 20-25 pounds, too big for my mother to cook in the oven.

My initiation into the adult world came one day before Thanksgiving.

"Gerard," my father said, "I want you to go down to the bakery shop and make arrangements with them to cook our turkey tomorrow." It was the first important assignment of my life. I wasn't sure, though, what was expected of me. I think my father could sense that. "You go down there and tell the man that George wants his turkey cooked tomorrow. He'll know who I am. Tell him it's a big one, maybe twenty pounds and that we plan to have dinner at six. Ask him two things . . . ." Before I braced for the two big ones, he said, "How many things are you going to ask him?"

"Two," I said with pride.

"Ask him what time you should bring the turkey there, and ask him how much he wants to charge."

I think I ran to the bakery shop right then. "George is my father and he wants me to bring the big turkey to you tomorrow to cook it. We will eat at six and he wants to know how much money." I got it right, or so I thought.

"Well young man," I think he said, "tell your father that I need to know how big it is, how many pounds, before I can tell you when to bring it, and how much I will charge."

Filled with a sense of purpose, I ran back to the flat. "Dad," I said, "he wants to know how many pounds it is, and . . . then he'll tell me how much money and how long it will take."

"Your mother says it is about twenty pounds. I already told you that."

I ran back to the store, intent on getting the rest of it right. "It's about twenty pounds," I told the baker.

"Okay, now tell your father it will take a little over four hours, but I can't be sure. You'll have to check back. And tell him it'll cost three dollars." I think he paused before he asked me if I could remember all that. "Ask him, too, if it'll be stuffed.

It made me feel important that I knew the answer. "Yes, my mother stuffs things."

We didn't have a phone in those days. I was the messenger, and I felt grown up delivering the word.

The next day was the "Big" day for me. I pestered my father to get started. "I think we'll bring it down about one o'clock," he said. "That'll give it plenty of time to be ready for dinner. It's a big bird, so you'll have to help me carry it." It made me feel so important to be helping my father. I know now in retrospect that my father must have known my enthusiasm for being given a central role in our annual Thanksgiving dinner.

By one o'clock my mother had already fit the turkey into a long metal pan with handles. When the stuffing began to pop out, she sewed a few more stitches into its stomach. I could tell that my father was strong enough carry it alone, but he let me take one of the handles for the walk to the bakery. I was helping my dad, on *my* block!

"My boy here will be back in four hours. Please let him know how it's going," my father told the baker.

I remember the day as a series of walks to and from the bakery, starting after the four hours had ended. "Tell your father it'll take a while longer," he kept repeating, and then finally, "Tell your dad it will be done in fifteen minutes."

I couldn't wait to deliver the good news. I ran home. "Dad, fifteen minutes more and we can bring it home," I blurted to him, nearly breathless from running.

Finally, we got to bring the big bird home, covered by a wet cloth. "Careful," my dad said, "she's still hot and sizzling. We've got to keep her steady in the pan."

Without incident, we put her on the coal stove. "She's a beauty," he said to my mom. I could tell by her smile that she was pleased. I yearned for my dad to acknowledge my role in the whole affair. He never did.

You might infer that his failure to recognize me that day meant that he was indifferent to me. Again, as I write this now I think that it was just his way of saying to me, perhaps without knowing he was saying it, that a man doesn't have to be recognized for bringing home the turkey. He just needs to bring it home.

Perhaps the reason that it has taken me so long to really appreciate my father is that, maybe like most kids, I wanted him to be perfect. I thought that other kids had perfect dads. I knew that in my grammar school, one or two of the boys had dads who were doctors, others dads who wore a suit and a tie to work. I remember walking into a grocery store one day when I spotted my father wearing a white apron while he stacked canned goods on a shelf. It was during the pre-Christmas season and I know now that he probably was working a second job so he could buy each of us presents. I was ashamed then and left the store, mostly because I thought it would embarrass him to know that I saw him in a menial job.

I know now, also, that he had an unusual way, or so I think, of liking me. I was the only one of us, for example, that he would read the news to on Saturdays and Sundays; the only one of us he let attend the grown-up sessions, sort of debriefings, with my brother Robert after he came home from the war; I was the one he asked to make a record at Coney Island of the song "Anchors Away" so it could be sent to Bob in the Pacific somewhere. He even gave me advice, trivial advice though it was, when I first married. "Don't ever tell your wife that you like a sandwich she might make for you to take to work. If you do, she'll give you the same goddamn sandwich for the rest of you life. And remember when you've seen one pussy you've seen 'em all."

Even when I was being found out at the end of what I call my "felonious period," during my early teen years, he did not complete the threat that I knew he might. Perhaps it is the nature of a threat to keep you scared. I was going through a very rough patch in my life during the winter of 6th grade, and I started to act out. My dear friend, Albert Occelli, died suddenly of a burst appendix. Our teacher, a nun, simply said, "I have bad news for you, Albert died last night. Now take out your history books and read chapter 8." As it was, I was not getting along with the nuns who made fun of me in front of the class. Again, the dress code included a white shirt and tie for the boys. I wore a polo shirt, and now and then a tie with it, which was embarrassing. It was my experience that some of the nuns compromised their mission by being small-minded and ungracious.

As I've mentioned, I got no sympathy at home when Albert died. It was as if no one knew how to handle it. I was devastated. As Albert was the first person in my life who showed me love, the air was taken from my psychic balloon. He would buy me penny candy, and we would vie for the # 1 spot in the class for highest average. He'd be 94.2 one quarter to my 92.8, and I'd be 95.1 to his 94.6 the next. As I remember it, he was the winner more often than I was, yet I didn't mind it. I remember once when I tried to show him a deck of cards with photos of nude women on them that I had taken from one of my older brothers' stash, Albert simply said to me, "I don't think we should be looking at these." And that was the end of it. No reprimands, no lectures. We never spoke about the episode again and resumed our relationship as if nothing had happened.

I know now that Albert's death was traumatic for me. I would walk about a mile each night to the funeral home to be with him. I would talk to no one, and no one talked to me. The only consolation I had during that time was playing with Kiki's puppies under Eileen's crib. I think they were reminders of life for me.

It was a time period in my life when I felt abandoned. So I turned to acting out, probably to get attention. My first in a series that lasted about a half year, was when I decided to launch a firecracker crusade against the Italian Men's Club which was around the corner from where we lived. I first practiced tying clumps of firecrackers together in precise proximity so that the blast on one would lead to igniting the next one, and so on. I practiced this in the local public school yard at night. Once I achieved some measure of expertise with that, I began to practice sneaking up the twelve or fifteen steps leading up to the meeting room so that I could peek in and see the old men talking. By doing it over and over again when they weren't there, I learned how to go down the stairs using only the right-angle points of each step to slide down as fast as humanly possible in order to get away after I would light the first firecracker, throw the stack into the room under the table and hear the first one go off. As soon as I heard the old men shout and scream curses, I would "fly" down the staircase, run to the right into the darkness, which I also practiced, then run across the street to the other side before crossing the street again into a well-lit avenue. At this point I would stop running and would take up a nonchalant walking pace like any other person would. At this point, I felt safe so even if the cops began a chase after me, I would seem like all the others out for a walk or to shop in the evening.

After each time doing this, I would wait about a month before doing it again.

Little did I know that the old men were catching onto my game.

When I wasn't getting my "fun" out of shaking up the men's club, I would do something more insidious several blocks away at the underground garage where cars were repaired. I noticed that a pipe came up from the garage, probably to let out carbon monoxide and let in fresh air.

Again, I went to twining the firecrackers together and tied them to a string about 18 inches with a small rock tied to the string. The weight of the rock would pull the firecrackers down the pipe and into the underground garage. I would put the rock end into the pipe, light the firecrackers and let them go. Once I heard the *boom* start and the men shout their anger, I would run to the left before making the first right turn possible and begin to walk the walk of the innocent. I don't think that I realized the damage I could have caused those men, although I think I had an inkling because I turned to water by way of acting out.

I would go up on rooftops of apartment buildings, each time with two balloons filled with water. Only two because I could not handle any more than that. I would look over the roof-top ledge, spot a group of two or three people walking together, gauge the time it would take for the balloons to fall along with the speed of their walking and, like a bombardier, drop the balloons on them. Even if I missed a direct hit, the balloons would burst on the concrete and splash all over them.

All of this was stupid and dangerous, and it took me time to realize it, mostly with the help of my father and the Christian Brothers of Ireland, my father in his own frontal and intimidating way, the Christian Brothers of Rice High School in more spiritual, though not totally un-intimidating, ways.

My felonious period ended abruptly when my father sat me down one Saturday afternoon. "Gerard," he said in a somber tone, "a few of my *dick* (detective) friends told me the other day that someone has been throwing firecrackers into the Italian American Men's Club. They told me that he has been spotted running away. That he is a young man and matches your description."

It was as if a death sentence was about to be cast upon me. What he said next surprised me. His tone was even, I would say understanding, when he looked me in the eye and said, "I want to tell you, Gerard, if that young man is you that you will be sorry that you have ever been born."

Wow! I remember being kind of psychically knocked out when I heard this. Lots of thoughts and emotions ran through my mind. The death sentence had just been commuted, but only if I stopped being a super jerk, which I decided right then to stop.

I had just been given a lease on life. Momma didn't make no dummy.

I think, though, there was more to it than that. I had finally been taken notice of by my father. I had finally been acknowledged, though in a strange sort of way. And I saw a side of my father that renewed my confidence in him. He could have jumped to conclusions right away and found me guilty of the crimes, deserving of punishment.

His words to me that day said a lot about him, his intrinsic goodness which he would later belie as his drinking grew in frequency and depth. I began to understand why he threatened so much, but could not lay the wood to us, so to speak, but would delegate the punishment duties to my mother.

After Albert's death and at the end of what I call my unpunished criminal period, I began to grow inward, and became a bit of a loner, and very introspective. In the first winter of my aloneness, I would sometimes go at night to the outdoor basketball court at P.S. 5, the public school about a ten minute walk from our apartment, and shoot around in the darkness by myself. I remember several nights going there in a heavy rainfall and taking jump shots until I couldn't see fully because of the rain blowing into my eyes.

I always wondered what the guys I played with here during the day were doing. Exciting things, I thought. Always more exciting than what I was doing, a loner playing in the rain by myself. I began to think of myself as being odd.

It was during one of those nights in the rain that I began to wonder why no one else spent time like this, though spending time like this did instill in me an inchoate sense that I really wasn't wired the way many of my acquaintances were.

I bought a pair of roller skates with my paper-boy money, and spent many hours that winter on those skates shooting a roll of black tape with a hockey stick against the garage doors on the block behind us. Although there was an organized roller–skating hockey league in our neighborhood, I did not have the confidence to join it. As it was, I seemed to have been developing a way with the puck that would serve me well later when I played ice hockey.

As I said, my inner life was becoming introspective, I think overly so. I began to wonder about the ways of the world. Why, for example, our government would drop A–bombs on Japan, killing thousands of children. I became fearful that the Russians would do the same to us. In my little boy's mind, the only thing that would protect us from such an event was the combination of Mickey Mantle and Stan Musial, special Americans that no one, not even the Russians, would dare harm

Let me explain. I was becoming a heavily invested baseball fan, even creating, as part of my growing loneliness my own baseball league. All I needed was a blue booklet, a pen or pencil, and a pair of dice. And my bedroom to be by myself.

Here's the way the game was played with the dice. A 2 and a 12 were home runs.

3 was a double play, 4 a walk. 5-6-7 and 8 were outs. 9 was a single, 10 a double, 11 a triple. Each game lasted 9 innings except, of course, for extra innings. At the time, there were eight teams in the American League and eight in the National. Each team had 25 players. I knew almost all of the names of the players on the reality rosters, so I would just list the starting lineups in the blue book

Let the games begin! Each team had about a 50 game schedule, so my league had standings, and a World Series. At the end of the season, I had an enormous chore, which I enjoyed. In retrospect, figuring out the batting averages for all the players, as well as who led the league in home runs, runs batted in, doubles and triples and batting average.

You can imagine: 16 teams each with a starting lineup of nine players, and a 50 game schedule. Lots of math. I enjoyed it so that I became an expert on numbers. I was always fascinated when my work was over and the results were in to let me know the name of the players who led the league in each of the designated categories. As I remember it, they seldom matched reality. That was part of the magic in this for me – every man had a chance to shine!

I never told any of my contemporaries about my league, as I thought they would not understand why I would do this when I could be doing normal things. I thought they might think I was an odd-ball, which maybe I was at the time. Really, I think I was just in the pits of a very difficult period, and was more comfortable being alone.

One of the experiences I had around this time was with a young black kid about my age. You see, my father was also prejudiced about blacks. The young man I'm talking about here sold newspapers and cigarettes from a kiosk at the end of the block where we lived. During the week, I had to walk past him to use the stairs, my mother's directive, up to the el train walkway which kept me safe from the morning rush hour traffic. I hated it because it made me feel so childish, yet it was the way I had to go to and from my school until I was twelve.

He was the only Negro I knew. Sometimes, we'd exchange a few words, mostly about the Dodgers or the Yankees. I always liked him, probably because he was about my age and he treated me with kindness, something I received little of at home or in school. I always wondered why he didn't go to school, but never asked. In fact, I didn't even know his name.

Looking back on that day that I will always regret, I realize that my father's prejudice had rubbed off on me, a young boy who thought, as most young boys, that my father was a torchbearer for truth. Yet, he regularly used the N word, and the mosaic of his racism included many colors not white. He probably learned these things from his father whom I never knew, so I cannot say for sure.

Here's what happened on that day. It was a summer morning and I had my baseball gloves and a ball with me as I went down to the corner to ask the Negro boy to play with me. He was walking away from the kiosk on his way somewhere, perhaps home. "Do you want to have a catch with me?" I yelled. He looked stunned that I would ask. I will always remember the tenderness in his eyes. He said No, that he had to go. I responded, "OK, little 8-Ball, go home to your momma."

The way he looked at me changed my life. I had never seen such hurt in anyone's eyes. It was as if they spoke of the oceans of hatred that had washed over his people for centuries. I had betrayed my overture to play with words of mockery and denigration.

He looked as if he wanted to say something back, but his lips were sealed.

He turned and ran. I turned inward, where the grip of prejudice, over time, released its hold on me.

After that, I avoided him, but I would peek to see if he was still there, until the day he disappeared and never came back.

I still think of him, even now a lifetime later. I sometimes wonder where he is, and if he is happy. Or dead. I wish I could take back the day. To speak with him as I would now. And to call him by the name his mother gave to him.

Most everything I did during those days I did by myself. As we didn't yet have a TV, I got a pair of cheap binoculars so I could watch television shows in the open windows of the apartments across the alley-way. I could only imagine what the characters were saying, but I could tell from body movements and context what was going on.

I kept having dreams during that time of falling out my bedroom window into that same alley below. I would never die in the dreams. I would hit the ground and, like a pink rubber ball, bounce back up again to the window. I learned later about the dreams is that there was, and is, a resilience in my spirit that I would let no one ever snuff out. I would always bounce back.

During this time, too, I built a small transistor radio for myself that I could listen to under the covers at night after we were told to go to bed. As I remember, I could get five or six stations, one or two of them hosting deliberations about issues. Between the television shows and the radio programs, my imagination began to soar. My curiosity about the world was being tickled.

When I look back at that time of my life, I know that I lived in the shadow of my parents' negativity. Yet I know, too, that if it were not for the excessive drinking as they got older, if they had not cashed in, so to speak, their poverty, lack of education and experience to the numbness that alcohol can afford, they still were parents who made me toe the line about school and doing my chores about the house – cleaning under the beds for "dust-bunnies," putting out the garbage, washing my own clothes, getting my own breakfast. All of these things were helping me to be a responsible person. And for that I am grateful.

In the way of being grateful, I will always think of my Aunt Priscilla who in many ways took over the role of her sister, my mom. She often took me to Madison Square Garden to see her son, Norman Diviney, play hockey with the New York Rangers farm-team, the Rovers. She would buy me candy and ice cream, and cotton candy because she could afford these things, which my mother could not. Her husband owned "Diviney's Bar" around the corner from us, so I assume they had money. I cried at her funeral.

As I began to move along the road towards graduating from grammar school, I was happy that I would no longer have the nuns in my life. It was never a good fit. They were cold and demanding, I needed warmth and trust. I remember the "battles" I had with them, the lies I told to them as I stood up to what I perceived to be their immaturity, their prescriptive training, their self-righteous ways. I would not give in to them. Once, our 4th grade nun called me up to her desk and asked me what hemp was used for. I said, "It's used for smoking it." She didn't like this, insisting that it was used for making rope.

"That may be so," I answered, "but it's also used to smoke."

I some ways, the beginning of a new journey was on the horizon. I yearned to know the ways that life could be different for me. I remembered the policeman from the 114th precinct in Astoria who gave me and the other kids each a small brown envelope with 38 cents in it – a quarter, 2 nickels, and 3 pennies, and how that spurred my imagination that there was hope and possibility, that I could move someday into a more stable and supportive environment, that there were people out there, like the policemen in our neighborhood, who really cared. That there might be days of consistent behavior, unlike the time my father took us all to Lake Ronkonkoma for a week where we kids had a great time. I still remember the freedom we were given. Ironically, what I remember most is that we were not allowed to go into the water. All meals were a part of the deal, so we could go off with our little buddies – I still remember Eddie and Bucky.

We were very sad to leave the freedom we had those days, from morning 'til dinner when we had to meet again to eat together before watching a big screen movie with snacks. We were sent to bed by ourselves while our parents enjoyed the company of their own peers, probably while drinking beer. Yet, at the end of the week, while waiting for the Long Island Railroad to take us back to the city, my brother Wallace cried, prompting my father to go into a tirade about how ungrateful we all were after he had worked so hard to get the money to take us on a vacation. There was no sympathy for my brother's tears.

What I was beginning to learn was that my mother and father were drinking beer like normal people drank glasses of water or cans of coke. It was what you did.

It was what everyone did, or so I thought. My thinking would have profound consequences for me down the road.

One day, at the end of that summer before going to high school, my father re–affirmed to me that I was, in some ways, his favorite, perhaps one of the last times I had a real, yet brisk, feeling of affection for him. An inverse equation was being built in my mind: the more beer he drank, the less I liked him.

On the day in question, he asked me to pick a horse for him to bet on in the Roxy Bar and Grill below us, a hangout for locals like my father, as well as "dicks," bookies, and an assortment of Runyonesque characters. I picked the first one in a card of eight, and it won. Before you know it, a few of the locals were standing at the bottom of the 3rd floor staircase where we lived. Apparently, my father had told the men at the bar that I had picked the winner. So now, with the men at the bottom of the stairs, he asked me to pick again. I did, and the horse won. This continued for six races in row, all winners picked by me. I remember that day well, and my feeling of importance.

I was a psychic. I was the guru who dispelled the darkness of not knowing. By now the staircases were crowded with men who, like Wall Street brokers, had insider information.

My 7th pick lost, and when I looked down at the staircase for the 8th race it was empty. Although I got six in a row, I thought I would get some kind of comeuppance from my father for failing him. That is the kind of relationship I had with him. I don't remember him saying anything, a plus for me. At least I wasn't out of favor for the day.

I learned a few lessons from that experience. Mostly, that everyone loves a winner, and how fast and easy it is to fall from on high. One minute I was "The Man," the next Gerard.

When I look back on my life, I sometimes wonder why certain things happened to me, and why I could make certain decisions that, looking backwards from the perspective of Now, seem beyond my capacity. Perhaps someone is watching out for me, nudging me, so to speak, in a certain direction.

One of those events or experiences that happened to set a direction for my future occurred on a July evening at the empty lot by my grammar school, the same place where my brother Bob and my father taught me how to catch a baseball. I was riding my bike when I saw a crowd of boys my age trying to organize a baseball game. I could tell there was confusion.

"What's going on?" I asked one of the boys. "We can't start the game because we have only one catcher and no one else will do it."

"I'll do it," I said. And so I did, with my fielder's glove and someone's face mask.

I did okay, as I remember it, though I was disappointed that my long fly ball fell short of going over the wall where it might have crashed through a window in the nun's house in back of the wall.

That game marked my introduction to organized sports which would play a critical role in my development. It would bring me out of my shell. I gained new friends, and it filled up the spaces of my loneliness with a sense of belonging. I would no longer seek the drama of getting into trouble to be noticed. I had sports to gain acceptance and recognition.

And I discovered that I had skills. Not major league skills, but enough to stand out in the in the local leagues. I became an All-Star baseball player in the CYO (Catholic Youth Organization) league and an All-Star basketball player. I played in two leagues, the CYO and the PAL (Police Athletic League). To this day, I am grateful to the men who ran these leagues. Most especially, I am indebted to Mr. Cobert, an Astoria taxi driver, who taught me the intricacies of baseball and the skills of basketball.

I also learned to play football, yet had enough sense to drop out of that before whatever sense I had left might be banged out of me. I also learned to play ice hockey when I became a monk. I always loved the competition, and went on to play Over-50 basketball and Over-40 softball for many years.

I was planning to go the local public high school at this time. It was called Bryant High School, about a 15 minute bus ride away. That's when the monsignor who was the head of Our Lady of Mt. Carmel grammar school called me into his office. Over the years of going to school there, I had see him about three times when he would stop by our class to say hi. I did not know him, nor did he know me. I was puzzled when the 8th grade nun told me that the Monsignor, Father Peter A. Kelaher, wanted to see me in his office. I thought I must be in trouble.

"Sit down," he said in a sort of imperious way. "I do not want you to go to the public school. I want you to go to a private boys school in Harlem. It's called Rice High School, and it's run by the Christian Brothers of Ireland. It's a good school."

He directed me to run the plan by my parents, and told me that continued tuition funding by him would depend on my getting good grades. I was to show him my report card each quarter and, if it pleased him, I would get the cash for the next quarter there and then. Only once over the years did it get a little edgy when I showed him my report card in the dark as he was on the run.

"These marks are terrible," he yelled at me. I started to cry, as I did not understand because the marks were not terrible. "Please put on your glasses," I requested. He did, looked at the card again, apologized and gave me the cash. "Oh," was all he said.

His relationship with me continued to be impersonal, while his generosity marked a way that would go beyond a change in me. The years ahead would become transformational.

CHAPTER 2

The Teen Years

**600 year old mummy
in New Guinea**

**At base camp,
Mount Everest**

**Belly dancing
in Jordan**

**Being stupid on Tarawa.
Never do this**

**Blessed by a Shaman
in Peru**

**Blowdarting
in Amazon village**

"SOME DAY I am going to see the world," I said to myself as I stood in front of our doorway in Astoria, Queens. I would soon enter the doorway of Rice High School at the end of that summer, and I realized that the sum of my travels up 'til then was a one–day visit to a friend of my father in New Jersey.

We had gotten a television set that year. That, along with a wide array of reading at the local library, was making me aware of the wider world. I was curious about mostly everything, so curious and annoying to my mother with my questions that, yes, she would ship me off to the library on Saturdays. This lasted until I discovered the world of sports which then occupied most of my spare time.

I loved going to the library where I could wander about its shelves to pick any book that aroused my curiosity. I would read it until I got bored with the subject matter, then put it back on the shelf before stalking the rows for the next book that would excite my mind. I would read randomly until it was time to go home for dinner at 6 p.m., the exact time always for the family dinner. If any of us dared come home late, privileges were taken away. Grounding after school was the worst.

When I finally retired after acquiring five earned degrees and years of mandatory reading as a teacher, it was a great and constant joy for me to once again read whatever I wanted and whenever I wanted. My mind had become eclectic in its interests, and I could pamper it once again.

In order to get to Rice, I had to get up early enough to wash up and dress, eat a piece of toast, and walk 15 minutes to the bus that would take me over the Triborough Bridge to 125th Street in Manhattan to Harlem, a Negro neighborhood, to the school.

School started at 9 a.m. but we had to enter the building by 8:45. Beyond that time, the door was closed and would not open until the late-comer knocked. Thereupon, one of the monks would open the door, jot down the culprit's name and assign him to JUG the following Saturday morning for an hour, sometimes standing up while reading for long stretches, depending on the sadistic tendencies of the monk in charge that day.

When the time standing and holding a book grew long, the book, too, grew heavy.

As I was a teen in love with sleep, as teens are wont to be, I timed getting up to do the necessaries before walking to the bus without a minute to spare, literally without a minute to spare. If I missed the 8:10 bus, I would cross a very wide and dangerous road, Queens Boulevard I think, to get to the other side for the same bus which got there at 8:20. If the 8:20, everything – the bus ride over the bridge, the walk from 125th Street to the school – would have to be exact to get me to the door by 8:45.

If a little off, let's say the traffic over the bridge, I would be late. So, I knew JUG, and JUG knew me. Incidentally, JUG meant Justice Under God. It sounds horrible, but it taught me some discipline about being under the gun of time, which we are more or less slaves to in our culture. I needed real discipline.

I was afraid of the neighborhood because at the time I was prejudiced, something my father taught me, as is the way that prejudice passes on from one generation to another. It took me a long time of being open to experience to rid that poison from my way of being, to know that the color of one's skin is a genetic adaptation to the climate where one's ancestors were born. Nothing more, nothing less!

It wasn't so much that being without discipline didn't have consequences for me.

I knew discipline at home. And I knew consequences. I began to realize, though, that rules and expectations were for a purpose, a way for people, especially in places crowded like New York City, to get along, to have some order, a touch of peace, a way to be.

Rice High School was a crucible of growth for me, and the intellectual gifts of birth allowed me to pass its many tests, both mental and physical. The monks who taught us set the bar high. Even though I stuttered when I read aloud, I still had to take a wide variety of subjects. I remember years of Latin, Spanish and French, and different kinds of math. I especially remember algebra in which I was at first a real dumbbell, and geometry which I loved. Go figure! We were given, too, a wide array of science classes like biology and physics. I remember boasting to a classmate, a smart–assed showoff guy, or so I thought, whom I disliked, on my left while taking a piss in the men's toilet at school that I had gotten the highest mark in the class on the New York State Regents exam in physics. I was so shy that I never spoke up in that class, so he seemed stunned that such a quiet kid like me could outdo him. I took it that he thought I was lying. I do remember getting such a kick out of that.

We had to take all kinds of history, too. I never embraced these classes because of the lifeless ways they were taught, dates and facts mostly. They never really lived for me until I began to travel widely years later. I liked the literature courses that analyzed the meaning in poetry, the short stories, creative writing, the novels. I remember wrapping the cover of "The Young Lions," a brilliant story set in the Germany of World War II, with brown paper from a shopping bag so I could read it on the train which I sometimes took to school on a rainy day. It had allusions to sex in it, as well as a provocative cover, so I thought it must be a "dirty" book, and everyone would think I was a "dirty" boy for reading it.

I'll always remember Mr. Gilson's history classes, most especially the days when he talked about his own personal experiences. How he went many times to the Gettysburg Civil War battlefields, sometimes to simply sit on a promontory that over–looked a certain part of one of the many battles that took place there. He told us how he would spend time just imagining what had taken place about a hundred years ago. He alone made American history live for me.

And the day he told us about his Army time, coming home from overseas, his ship pulling into Hawaii as the sun was going down. To this day, I can see him sitting on the classroom desk, telling us about that evening. His description of the island was so rich in its details – how the setting sun washed the green hues of the island into colors less and less vibrant until he could only see the lights of the hotels, homes, and restaurants. He imagined what must be going on in those places, things he, too, longed to see after his service was over and his life normalized again. December 7, 1941 lived then for me. And the seed to see the world was planted.

He did not simply teach facts. He did not see us as repositories of knowledge.

I knew in some inchoate way that I wanted to be like him who experienced each of us as people first, young men quite capable of receiving his heart as well as his knowledge.

I now know that many years later when I too became a high school teacher that I allowed myself, over time, to reveal my own heart to my students, helping to make my literature and writing classes live. As I understood that each of my students was a unique person, my classes became more powerful. I still remember the day in class when I really understood the efficacy of joining my brain with my heart. It was a Friday afternoon, last class before school was out. I was teaching a class called "Readings and Writings in Contemporary Issues," a course for seniors. They were not on their "A-Game" all week long, and I was really dissatisfied with them, especially as the unit that week was taking a hard look at world hunger issues.

Just before the bell was to ring, I told them how upset I was. "I'm thinking about giving you a weekend assignment to make up for your lack of effort this week." I paused as they waited. The room got very quiet. "I'm also fighting a battle myself. Should I go with my head on this one and give you the weekend work, or should I go with my heart, knowing what a great group you are and that next week you will do better."

Their reaction was somewhat thunderous. In unison, they pounded fists on desks with a kind of sing-song rhythm of *Heart, Heart, Heart.*

And so it was. My heart would prevail that Friday afternoon. They were really on their game after that. They got the message. Heart trumped head. I knew that it was the better way for me.

Adolescence was a difficult time for me as for anyone. My body was growing, its hormones flowing. At the same time I was attracted to girls, yet, my extreme shyness allowed me to show my real interests just once.

Before I let you know about my first love, I want to tell you about a theory I have. I think that every person is born with a template in his or her genes of the perfect love. Even as we lie, wrapped in swaddling clothes, in the comfort of our mother's first embrace, the archetype of the person who matches the template is in the gene that conveys the spirit of that person to us, male or female, depending on our sexual persuasion. If we are lucky, we will one day come across the path of the one who *is* the template. Maybe that is what we call love. I think, too, that more than one person can match the template. And so we might fall in love more than once.

The tricky part of this is that the discovery can easily be conflated with infatuation, as they have the same starting point. I have been infatuated many times, in love three times. I have found that one of the ways to distinguish the difference is to let time go by as we get to know the person who seems to embody that which we have always sought without really knowing what it is. Of course, the person must show up. Before that, we can only guess at it or romanticize about it. This is where we are lucky or not. Remember, you can not invent the archetype. It is in your genes as much as the color of your skin is. And don't forget, to complete the circle, she must say yes to you, while there are lots of reasons to say no: wrong time, one party is married, age differences, etc. I have only once seen template meet template and know quickly that this one goes beyond infatuation.

I think the distinctions between the template and infatuation leak out over time.

Another way to say this is that the model includes infatuation, but infatuation does not include the model. My point of view is limited to male hetero. When I am immediately taken with someone, the signals are there: her smell, subtle as that may be; skin; smile; quality of her voice; her spirit of adventure. Her intellect. In another word, the connection or, as some would like to say, the chemistry. Yet, these signals can be like a thin film or mask that hides undesirable qualities. The signals can lack the depth that those who bear the template have.

I remember, for example, a woman I was infatuated with when I was a young man. She and I would talk casually now and then, mostly on the block where we both lived in New York City. When I finally asked her out, we had a nice day at the beach.

That is, until I decided to kiss her. I found out quickly that her breath could stop a five–wheeler in its tracks. Not the template, end of infatuation.

On the other hand, the woman who *is* the template has few or no "undesirables," and her "desirables" have a lasting quality. That is not to say that she is perfect. Who is?

Nor does it imply that we don't have to work at the relationship. It only suggests that the special person has the possibility to endure in the attraction she has for the one who is lucky enough to find her.

The presence of the template can cause problems. You see, sometimes it can happen that a second bearer shows up after we have committed to the first. I've always thought that a pursuit of the second is a losing proposition. If real, you stand the chance of losing your first discovery. As it is the same template, why bother?

Now let me tell you about my first love. I was fifteen. It was the summer before my sophomore year at Rice. Her name was Amy. She was in the same grade as I was, and she lived in New Jersey. I really only remember the way it made me feel when I was with her, living for the summer with her aunt who lived on our block. Even now, I sometimes think of her when I drive the New Jersey Turnpike, and hope she is happy.

At first she started hanging out with a group of about seven or eight of us. We played hop-scotch or skipped rope, and now and then played "spin the bottle." I was happy that we didn't play that game when she was there that summer. I think if the bottle ever connected us I might have died at the enormity of kissing her. Or if she had to kiss one of the other guys in out little group, my jealousy might have exploded.

As it was, we would sit on the side of the long curved steps that led to the front door of a restaurant at the end of the block. I would ask her to sit there with me because I hoped she would take it as something without an agenda, unlike walking to the Astoria park, about fifteen minutes away, which might have seemed like a "date." I couldn't risk that she might say no.

I remember how the guys on the block would pass us by would sing "Once in love with Amy," and then as loud as they could, "Always in love with Amy." I think they wanted to embarrass us. At other times, they would say, "Makin' out, makin' out."

Actually, it made me feel special that maybe, just maybe, Amy and I were a pair.

As I look back on it now, I think I know why Amy was so special to me. I think that when I was born I had the template of the perfect girl in my heart. And it was Amy!

Maybe three or four times in my life I've had the "bonne chance" to meet the imprint made flesh.

Amy was the first time.

I was dazzled by her face. It was so beautiful that I couldn't take it in unless I stared, which might have revealed my feelings for her, so I never did that. What I mean about her face is that I couldn't understand it. Or comprehend it the way I could with, let's say, the girls in the neighborhood clique, or my mother's. I mean, I could look at any one of them and I would see a face, just a face. With Amy, though, each of the parts of her face was so magnificent that when I tried to see the harmony of them all, it simply wouldn't happen. I tried the quick glance. I even tried squinting my eyes when she wasn't looking at me because I thought a blurry peek might reveal the fullness of her magnificence. Neither of these worked. And so she became mysterious to me.

Like I said, I could only take in the parts. The short hairstyle seemed to make her playful, even puckish. I remember that her eyes were sort of almond shaped, giving them that perpetual glow that artists dab into eyes. Her jaw was square, but in a female sort of way that seemed perfect to me. I wondered why her lips appealed to me so. They were thin but they were, I don't know, nice? I sometimes felt like licking her nose, especially when she would sweat. A friend once told me that this might indicate homosexuality but hey, like the man said, sometimes a nose is just a nose. You must not analyze the template. It is what it is.

Mostly, though, I loved talking with her, probably because her ideas were different from those of my friends. She was sort of a dreamer. I remember the day she told me about a story she had read in a magazine about the poor children of Africa. It drew me to her like an iron filing to a magnet, especially when at the end of the story she giggled in a sort of self-effacing way. I would give anything to hear that giggle again.

Before she left to go back to New Jersey, we traded addresses. "See ya" was all we said. I wrote to her two times. She never wrote back.

I have many memories of my three years at Rice H.S., some fond ones, some not so. I remember how I stuttered, and how none of the boys in my classes ever made fun of me. That was big for me.

Though I was a quiet kid, I never took any crap from any of my classmates, though most of them were tough city kids. I remember that one of them was shot in the leg by what they called a "zip" gun, put together with wood and rubber bands. He came back to school in a few weeks and was a bit of a hero for awhile.

And the day in the cafeteria at lunch when I was hit in the chest by a small bit of food. I didn't know who did it, but I did know that it had to have come from the section in front of me. I had just sat down with a plateful of spaghetti. I stood up with the spaghetti in my hands, grasped the plate with my right, balanced by my left, then flung the contents of the entire plate across the room, hoping to get the culprit by splattering the many. I know now what I didn't then what they mean by collateral damage.

It was not only a kind of stupid thing to do, yet also an untimely thing to do, as just then the principal of the school, Br. Dennis Wright, who later became a good and dear friend, entered the cafeteria. He saw what I had just done.

He immediately blew his whistle which was a command for everyone to stop whatever he was doing and wherever he was, frozen in time. I looked at him, he looked at me, raised his right-hand finger commanding me to come to him. And then gave me the beating of my life with a large leather strap he carried in his cossack, a black robe. He hit me on the palms of each hand so many times that after a while I could not feel the pain any more. My hands began to feel like rubber as the strap continually bounced off them. He then made me bend over so he could strap my behind, which he did over and over. In the macho atmosphere of city kids, I was a star who could take it without uttering a sound. If he did that today, he would have been put in jail. But it was a different day.

I remember, too, the day when my friend, Charlie, from Our Lady of Mt. Carmel School and I were walking on 125th Street on our way to the high school one morning, when a young man stopped us and said, "Give me your money." We just looked at him as if to say, "Were you born stupid, or do you work at it?" Angered by our inaction and refusal to hand over our lunch money, the guy showed us the handle of a gun in his right pants pocket. If nothing else, this kicked Charlie, a really tough kid, into action.

He took the change he had in his pocket, held it out in his hand and said, "This is my lunch money. My mother worked hard to get it, and you're not getting it." He put the money back in his pocket, grabbed me by the arm and yelled, "Run." And so we did. I think we were more afraid of getting "JUG" than we were of the guy's gun.

It was around this time that I began to realize that I was a smart kid. I didn't think much of that, though I began to see and appreciate how committed my teachers, mostly monks, were to their profession. Their lessons always seemed to be highly crafted and purposeful. I was getting a really first-rate education at the same time that I was beginning to understand the quality and nobility of leading a life of purpose, as compared to the drifting life I had been leading. What I was seeing on a daily basis in school began to impress me more and more as the days went by though I was still very introverted.

I remember one day when I was walking up the stairs to get to my next class when one of the monks, Br. Columba was his name, stopped me and said, "You have been looking lately like something is bothering you. Would you like to talk about it?" I stopped and looked at him. "Why don't you just mind your own business," I answered. He looked stunned.

Besides keeping too much company with my own head, I think I said this to him because no one had ever expressed a concern for me, and I simply did not know how to handle his overture. To reveal myself at the time was out of the question.

Ironically, at the same time as I was being rude to Br. Columba, I was getting an itch to becoming one of them. I was actually thinking about joining the order to become Br. Brooker.

Yet, even to this day I mull things before I make major decisions, thinking of the alternatives. So I continued going to school, and playing lots of sports. I wanted desperately to try out for the Rice baseball and basketball teams, confident that I could make the baseball team as a starter. However, I needed to work to help pay for my clothes and incidentals such as lunch money and recreation, and the New York City egg–creams which I loved. At ten cents a glass, I got one on many days after I finished my paper route. There was no egg in the drink, nor cream. Only milk, seltzer water, and syrup, either chocolate or vanilla. My favorite was vanilla.

I was becoming interested in clothes at this period of my life. I remember stopping often at a men's clothing store to look at a jacket in the window. It was brown and had a snappy look on the mannequin in the window. I decided to save money to buy it. It took me a while and I finally got it. I wore it about three times when I realized that the shoulders were padded, so much so that I thought I looked like a football player with shoulder pads. Although I gave the jacket away, I bought a Rice High School jacket without the words. I had to iron on the words. They kept coming off and I kept ironing them back on. I loved that jacket, as I did the dungarees I bought extra long so I could roll up the bottom of the pants to show an extra large white cuff.

The longer the cuff, the more stylish one was in those days.

I wanted so much to be like the others, but I never felt like I fit in, though I did what I could to be one of the guys. I played all the macho games. "Johnny Ride a Pony" was one of the games. For the most part, it was played with about 5-6 guys on a side.

One of the guys, usually a bigger kid, was the post set against a wall. He stood up straight while each of the other five bent over locking his shoulder against the legs of the guy in front of him, while holding on to his waist. When everyone was connected, each one of the other team would run across the road as fast as he could, then jump as far as he could to land on top of the connected pile, usually aiming to fall in front of the "post" man to weaken him Then the next guy would jump into the middle while each one after that would, in turn, try to crush the middle of the pile. If it collapsed, the real pain would then come to the guy in the pile who collapsed first. If they did not collapse, the game was over, no winner, no loser. Then we would switch sides.

Now, if the chain was broken and collapsed, the guy who "broke," usually the one in the middle of the pile, would have to brace his hands against the wall while bending over and spreading his legs so that his privates were unprotected. Each of the winners was allowed to take two "shots" from the other side of the street with a pink Spalding ball. As the distance was far, hardly anyone ever scored a hit. But when he did, I think you could hear the laughter around the neighborhood as the poor stricken kid ran in circles to get rid of the pain.

I also played another macho game called "Knucks," usually on a rainy day when there wasn't too much to do. I don't remember the details except that it involved two guys. The winner was allowed to take the deck of 52 cards, if it was a "big" win and stack the deck either fully like a brick or with the cards together yet spread or splayed in a closer win, so that they would do less damage. If the winner decided to use the brick formation of the cards, I think he was allowed to strike his opponent's fisted knuckles twice. If splayed, about triple that number.

Over time on a given day, one's knuckles could be damaged, even raw and bloodied. I remember sometimes calling a time out so I could run home to my mother who would clean the wounds with a brownish tincture before band-aiding them. I would then go back to my opponent and use the knuckles on the other hand.

Crazy, you say. Yes! But a badge of honor that we were tough guys.

Probably more crazy than that were the nights when we would go to P.S. 5, the local public school where I learned to play basketball. One or another of the guys would buy .22 caliber bullets which we would take to the school yard late at night when no strangers would be endangered. We'd build a small wood fire in one of the arched entry ways into the school. When the fire seemed hot enough, everyone would go about 20 yards from the fire except one volunteer whose job it was to go to the fire with a handful of the .22's and place them into the middle of it before running to hit the concrete deck and cover his head while waiting with the rest of us for the bullets to go off in the fire. Sure enough, they would go off in a few minutes, much to our collective delight and celebration. Stupidly, we would sometimes go to the fire when the bullets did not go off so we could see what was preventing it from happening. Usually the cause was that in the rush to get out of the line of fire, the bullets were not well placed. Fortunately, no one was ever hit.

We played stickball in the streets, usually on one that was not crowded with cars coming through, so as not to be interrupted. A street that had the IRT El train in the background was best as a ball hit on it was an automatic home run. The home run hitter could then trot around the bases like a major leaguer.

In the summer, there was always a game of "pitch the pennies" in the evening.

There was an organizer who would find concrete that stopped against a flat wall so that the designated players, let's say three or four a game, would toss maybe 5-10 pennies against the wall. The one closest would win all. A "leaner" was almost a sure thing. The winner took all the pennies. If the penny closest to the wall was not evident, the "organizer" made the call. He made his money by bringing tons of pennies that he sold, making a handsome profit as you got 8 pennies for a dime. Now and then, he upped the ante to throwing nickels or dimes. That version was not popular.

Though none of us had a sex life at that age, we did keep track of each of our "coming out" party, so to speak. That was the day when we told the group that we had an orgasm the day before, accompanied by an emission of sperm. I guess we though it a rite of passage, that we had become men. Little did we know at the time that it took much more than this to be a real man.

At some point in all of this, my father began to take me to Yankee Stadium now and then. I might have been his companion "by default." My older brother, Bob, the only other son who cared about baseball, was by now married to Essie, on of my all-time favorites, leaving only me for the ball games. We had a certain kind of ritual, my dad and I. When the train got to "161st Street," the stadium stop, he would give me my seat ticket. I'm sure that going to ball games gave some excitement to his otherwise uneventful life. "I'll see you later," he'd call to me, "and remember, show your ticket to an usher if you get lost." I would run to the ball park where I entered the first possible gate to then run to the first possible ramp to see the field. How I loved that – to see the green of the outfield grass and the smoothly kept dirt of the infield! And then to actually see the players I read about – the great Yankee players, Joe D., The Scooter Phil Rizzuto, Yogi. Ah, yes, a boy's dream.

Joe Dimaggio entered my life on one of those winter Sundays when my father took me to Yankee Stadium to see a football game.

There was a new league called the American Football Conference that had a team called The New York Yankees, starring Buddy Young, a very fast "scatback" who could sweep the ends like no other in those days. I remember, too, the name Bruiser Kinard, not because of anything he did on the field, but because of his wonderful football name, "Bruiser." And there was Spec Sanders who seemed like an old man to me.

I don't know how my dad did this, but he scored two box seats at field level.

I remember how cold it was that day when, in the second half of a good game, a large hulk-like shadow holding a kid's hand loomed in front of me. He had on a long and dark winter overcoat that filled up my entire field of vision. I waited politely, a bit. When I couldn't wait any longer, I tapped him hard in the small of his back, saying in the best New York words I could find, "Are you made of glass or somin?"

He turned around and didn't say anything. He just glared at me. It was Joe DiMaggio! I was too awestruck to say anything, as he looked down on me, a little boy not worthy of a response. As he walked away, still clutching the boy's hand, I turned to see if it really was him. Or, had I imagined it? Yes, it *was* the Yankee Clipper and I had made contact.

I didn't think my father would believe me, so I didn't tell him until a little time went by. "Dad, did you notice the man who got in my way a while ago?"

"I think so."

"It was Joe DiMaggio," I responded in a most pleased way as if being cast in the shadow of the great Number 5 was something that might excite him, make him proud.

"Okay," was all he said.

No one believed my story about Jolting Joe. I thought that taking it up a notch would help. So I made up the Big One. I told my classmates how this mountain of a man got in my way. It was Joe D. One of my mates asked me what I did.

"I punched him in the back."

What I remember also about that day was how DiMag held his son's hand, something my father did with me just once. And how sad I was many years later when I read that DiMaggio and that same son had become estranged as Joe grew older.

Of course, like every other kid, I continued to grow and develop during that period. I remember clearly going to a movie one summer day, probably for no other reason than I had nothing else to do. It turned out to be a day to remember. Strange as this might sound, it was while watching the movie that the aesthetic gene in me came alive.

Before seeing this movie which was called, I think, "The Red Shoes," I had never thought of love as being an intense fluttering of the soul, as the awakening of the heart to the spiritual beauty of a woman. What I mean is that it was the first time that I was *aware of* it, and the beginning of a self-monitoring process that would continue to expand in me.

It was a time when I knew that love between a man and a woman was not simply an infatuation, or how the other looked, but as a deep stirring that would forever change the way I would see the world.

I did not fall in love with the dancer in the red shoes of the ballerina. She was much older and too mature for me to create an identification or a yearning. Yet, the way she seemed to me to have s complete fulfillment of her being stirred something new in me. The music, the colors, the aesthetics of her profession, being the object of jealousy – all these aspects of the film together sparked a new inner me.

Mainly, I think, it was the first time I experienced the unique in-born template in my heart that matches the perfect person which for me is, in part, the woman who possesses an inner completeness. It is not a thing that one analyzes in his head. Rather, it is intuitively known by her admirer. This sense of things can be quite powerful in me, powerful enough so that being in the presence of this person can satisfy my deepest yearnings. It is as if a magic and spiritual circle is drawn around our beings and inside that circle is everything I need in my life. In this experience, in that movie that day, I discovered that there is a woman who contains in her being a complete world. Not a perfect one, just a complete one. By complete I mean that through thick and thin she keeps intact her birthright, that is the goodness, truth and beauty that was hers at birth.

It is the lucky man who has such a woman in his life. It is not simply a gift full of wonder. By its nature, it is infatuation proof. In time, infatuation wears off. It is the reason why so many get an early divorce. There is a quiet as well as a fundamental acceptance of her in this circle I became aware of in me that day at the Loew's Triboro Theater. In the acceptance of strengths and frailties, I became aware that love can grow, though it took many years for me to practice that awareness. Because of "The Red Shoes," I became ready and lucky to meet the woman who lived in my soul. In fact, as I write these memories I am married to her.

By this time, my inner self was astir. Rice High school was giving me stability and I was beginning to feel that I fit in. Of course, my participation in sports, especially baseball and basketball, gave me the context to meet and accept new friends. I especially remember the Saturday nights when I would go with a few friends to the movies at the big movie house in Astoria, the already mentioned Loew's Triboro, since demolished.

There was a certain sense of belonging when I would meet the guys in this magnificent movie theater that seated about 3000 and had a ceiling of stars that twinkled so that I felt as if I was in a special place. The theater had a balcony but we mostly sat in the main floor, snug as bugs in a rug. I think it most accurate to say that the theater was colossal.

Besides a starry sky, it had huge velvet drapes, large statues, huge chandeliers, two candy counters, and several bathrooms. Usually, there were two movies on Saturday nights, a feature and a B movie, with a 10 minute break between the two for bathroom and popcorn. Including the coming attractions and Movietone News, it was always a full and fun night, especially at the break time when the guys who played different sports would gather in the lobby to say hi and share scores of the games they played in that day.

I've always enjoyed as an adult belonging to groups that I felt kinship by way of having common goals that were and are important in some way to me. When I was a juvenile at the Loew's Astoria, I felt that I belonged, perhaps for the first time in my life.

It didn't hurt that I was a good athlete and could brag about my accomplishments like the others. We did the bragging in an inferential sort of way. In answering the question, "How many did you score today, Gerard?" with the answer "Sixteen, I think," you were bragging in an acceptable way. "Sixteen, I think," really meant *sixteen* exactly. The "I think" part was intended to mean that you really didn't keep count. But you did. Always!

On the surface it might seem silly for me to say that I have never felt that I belonged more anywhere than I did on those Saturday nights. Yet, that is the truth of who I am. I even began to ask my buddies for the help I needed. I was deathly afraid of the water, for example, and wanted to learn how to swim. So I asked two of my friends if they would come to the big pool at Astoria Pool to help me. "I'm going to jump in," I told them, before asking them to jump in to save me if I seemed to be drowning. "If I'm drowning, I'll yell to you." So, I jumped in and, sure enough, I began to drown.

They were good mates and saved me, each on one of my arms. "I'm going to do it again," I said, "right now, right away. Will you help me again, if I need you?" They agreed, I jumped in and came up, my arms jigging forward and back. Lo and behold,

I stayed afloat!

I found out, from this and a few other experiences, that it was the beginning of the way I would face *all* my fears in life, by confronting them head on.

So the days of my high school years moved along steadily. I was more in the world of my peers that in the world of my family from which I was slowly moving apart.

I don't even remember a cut-off time to be home. I would just leave in the evening, do something or another, then go home, seemingly without ever being missed.

Once, for example, when I was sixteen I decided to go to Times Square by myself to celebrate New Year's. I naively thought I would find friends, really strangers, in the crowd to find joy and togetherness. No one even said hello to me for the entire time waiting for the celebrated ball to drop, marking the New Year. Nor did I say hello or try to embrace anyone else. In the midst of a hundred thousand people, I was alone.

And then I tried to do something, anything, to mark the occasion. So, I decided to go to the Palace Theater to see Xavier Cugat and Abby Lane where I sat in the middle of older people, only to be embarrassed by the "blue" jokes that made them laugh. I remember getting home about 3 in the morning, no questions asked. I was disillusioned.

I was needy for affection. Yet, the place where I looked for it, the well of my parents' affections, was empty in the ways that I needed it. In looking back, I am certain that they did the best they could, truly. They came from poverty and were uneducated, and the graces to show affection were never sown into their own souls, so how could they ever give it to others?

In an inchoate sort of a way, a desire to grow and develop began in me. I wanted to get away from a home that seemed to be smothering me. In time, I realized that the way to do that was right in front of me every day, Monday through Friday, the Christian Brothers of Ireland, the monks who were my teachers at Rice. I wanted, too, to be a person of commitment, and this was exactly who they were. I could see in their daily teaching how each was a stand for excellence in the art and craft of teaching. I wanted to be like them. I wanted to have something that I could totally throw myself into.

I told my parents about my intentions and they were quite pleased. I think even proud that they would have a son devoted to the Church. It seemed to give them a kind of bragging rights in our extended family that I was to be a member of the Christian Brothers of Ireland, a congregation founded in Ireland in 1802 by a merchant named Edmund Ignatius Rice. Their mission is to teach the poor, and they now have many schools around the world. Edmund Rice will perhaps soon be canonized in the Catholic Church as a saint.

In order to be accepted, I had to take many steps, including a physical and dental exam at my family's expense. Our family's health habits did not include dental hygiene, and I had to have 16 cavities filled! I asked the dentist if he would fill four each week, and I wanted the work done without Novocain, as I did not have enough money for it, and I also wanted to see how much pain I could endure. I wanted the drilling to get to the very center of pain to see if my mind could accept it and not run away. I did it, something I could not do today.

The psychological exam was painless, kind of mundane. The doctor asked me if I liked men. "Sure I do," I answered, "I have lots of guy friends." I think he was poking around to see if I was gay.

It was in August of that summer that I left for West Park, New York, about 60-70 miles north of New York City, along the Hudson River. Ironically, although part of my leaving was to get away from home, I became profoundly homesick for a few days. It's hard for me to explain homesickness. It was as if my soul was sick, longing to be back where I knew my surroundings, people and places. I wanted to pack and go home. An analogous way for me to describe the feeling is what happens when we fall deeply in love and are rejected. For awhile, we just yearn for the presence of that person.

It takes time to let it go. And so it was with me, as I embarked on a new journey that not only changed me and my life. It transformed me.

CHAPTER 3

My Years As a Monk

**Boa Constrictor
in Cambodia**

Classroom in North Korea

Climbing Mount Fuji

Cuba

**Flying the family
flag on Iwo Jima**

**Grand Ayatollah
Imami of Tehran**

S O HERE I was, 17 and at St. Joseph's Juniorate in West Park, New York, the beginning of a seven year journey as a Christian Brother of Ireland. As in so many crosroads in my life, I don't know how I made the decision to leave home.

It takes a bit of courage to do that, yet I never considered it a brave thing to do.

I just did it.

From the moment the homesickness left me, I felt satisfied that I had done the right thing. My entire being felt refreshed and excited. Here I was leading a purposeful life. I was going to be a teacher, and my mission was to teach the poor around the world. I would be doing something that mattered.

The juniorate was a place set up for young men who aspired to be a monk to finish high school and to get a start on their religious training. I was entering my senior year of high school, so I would have one year there before taking my first vows, five of them, as a monk.

I loved it! I absolutely loved it from the start. I had meaning and purpose.

I was receiving advice on this 'n that, something I needed yet had never received in a way that was palatable. I never thrived from fear. Of course, I would do as expected under its threat, but I never did grow under its umbrella, not even through my years getting a doctorate when I had to tell my Mentor that my work was not growing under his prescriptive ways, that I really needed encouragement.

During that one year at the juniorate, I was discovering parts of me that I did not even know existed. My stuttering soon was a thing of the past, and I could participate in the give and take of the classroom. I was happy to get out of the big city.

I loved the smell of the trees and will always remember one of the first days on the porch of this large mansion-type house, painted an optimistic yellow, when my entire self, body and soul, noticed that the surrounding woods seemed to be holding me in its arms, protecting me against the noises and smells, rudeness and edginess of New York City.

I knew right then that I would thrive here.

If I remember accurately, there were about 50 of us in all, 12 of us seniors, and the rest spread among sophomores and juniors. I don't think freshmen were allowed.

Too young, I suppose. They came from the many high schools that were run around the United States by the monks. They were good and trustworthy young men, some of whom I still have contact. Over time, a comparative few remained and took what was called their Final Vows: poverty, chastity, obedience, perseverance in the Congregation, and free instruction of youth. I never got to Finals, though I did take the same five vows annually.

No matter, I think. In the long run, I continued to do in the secular life many of the things I was taught in the Brothers.

Oh, how I did thrive! I came to West Park with very little sense of myself, of who I was. I think it is called self-mage. I never thought about these things, so I didn't know that I didn't know that I had a poor self-image. It was only when I was encouraged during that year to express myself in a variety of ways that I began to realize that I had talents, that I had character flaws, that I had to work at my confidence in some of the self-expressions that I knew, more intuitively than anything, that would be important to me as time went by.

For the first time in my life, I loved getting up in the mornings, quite early as I remember. It was not difficult because we also had to go to bed early. 10 to bed, not a minute later, 6 a.m. up, not a minute later, lest we missed brushing our teeth and shaving, if we had to. I did that year, every second day.

The routine was fairly regular, so much so that when the head master now and then deemed it a sleep-in day or a visit to the Baseball Hall of Fame in Cooperstown, it was deeply appreciated.

We first went to the chapel where Mass was said, prayers prayed and meditation tried. I say *tried* because that is what it was for me, an attempt, something I could never master. Oh, I did try but spent most of the time trying to figure out which of my courses needed this or that attention. I remember once trying to figure out the answer to a most difficult math problem that I had spent a huge amount of time the night before trying to solve. The answer came to me during the meditation period. I felt both elated and guilty that I got the answer when I was trying to commune with God. At one point I was so bad at meditating that I thought about leaving the monks.

After all these prayers, we had breakfast, always a very hearty one, especially in the winter when hot soup and biscuits were served before the main meal, usually fit for young men growing at a fast rate. I remember, too, that there always was a large bowl of peanut butter and lots of bread on every table. It brought me some inner delight that three meals a day, good and healthy meals, were served to us each day, something I did not, with the exception of dinner, get every day at home.

After breakfast, we had to do clean-up chores. I remember the one I liked the most, cleaning up the billiard room. You see, I loved to play billiards, so I would do my chores – dusting the walls from the chalk dust, sweeping the felt table with a special brush, emptying the garbage pail – as quickly as I could, then spend the rest of the time playing billiards!

We had a little time before going to classes the rest of the day, with a break for lunch, of course, until 2:30. After that, we dressed in play clothes for games, baseball in the warm weather, flag football or soccer in the cold, as well as ice hockey. We had a few young men from Newfoundland and they were excellent hockey players, so that game took on a certain prominence with us because of their "star" quality and generosity in showing us city kids how to play the game. I never knew how to ice skate, yet took to it quickly. In fact, the principal of the school, a wise and older monk whom I loved, asked me if I would be the "guardian angel" to three of the Newfoundlanders who didn't know much about American culture and were not terribly fluent in the language. Of course, I felt honored.

They were required to sit at my table for every meal and to make inquiries about this 'n that. They had different words for some of the ordinary objects in our way of speaking, lots of different idioms, too. *Boots* were *stocking vamps*. Dried fish were *faggots*. You can imagine how funny it seemed to me the first night we had dried fish when one of them exclaimed, "I love faggots."

Breakfast porridge was *mush*, and their mom was a *mutter*. It took time, but we got by, having many laughs along the way.

After sports, which I loved, we cleaned up, went to chapel to say the Little Office of the blessed Virgin Mary and The Office of the Dead, both in Latin, before going to dinner where we were allowed to talk to each other. I was often made the head postulant at the table, an honor and a duty, mostly earned simply because I was a senior.

My job would be to keep the conversation going and in the right direction, as well as to ask for more milk, something that always reminded me of a Dickens' novel. I would have to take the milk pitcher, stand in the middle of the refectory, hold up the pitcher so the principal could see me bow for milk ("More milk, Sir!). If he deemed it OK, he's flick his finger which meant OK. I'd then hop to the kitchen refrigerator and get more milk.

After dinner, we had to study, collectively, for another hour before having a half hour of recreation, which consisted of playing billiards, talking with others, listening to records, ping pong, then more prayers, then teeth brushing, then bed.

I thrived on the routine. I loved that I won the speech contest. From stutterer to winner! I was given a lead in "No Room at the Inn," a Biblical play about Christmas in the Holy Land. I couldn't imagine that I could ever have been in a play, and here I was on stage. The success I felt inside myself about acting in a play stirred me on to get into acting a bit more. Over time, I acted in "Mr. Roberts," "Arsenic and Old Lace," and in the novitiate, that is the first rigorous year of training with vows, I was given the lead in "The Life of Edmund Ignatius Rice," the founder of our congregation. There was a keen competition for that role, a prestigious one for obvious reasons. The success had nothing to do with my acting ability. I had no idea if I was good or mediocre. It was the inner joy that came to me simply because I had the nerve to tryout for a role. I was beginning to seek out opportunities for experiences with self-expression which, unknown to me at the time of being in the Juniorate, would help a great deal in my future.

My grades were good, and the sports were fun. I was even given the lead altar boy role in the Easter Mass, a big deal. I still can smell the lilies that decorated the altar.

I remember that I prepped so much that I began to move the celebrant here and there around the altar, as it was a lengthy and complicated ritual that I knew by heart Truly, I was discovering myself. I was happy for the first time in my life. I had teachers who were talented, supportive and kind. Sometimes, I felt as if my spirit were dancing a happy dance as I discovered this new way of being, this new purpose and commitment.

The year went by quickly, and soon spring and then summer were upon us.

The juniors and sophomores, now seniors and juniors, were sent home for the summer in order to make room for a new wave of young men who had just finished high school in various places around the country, and who now wanted to be monks.

It was fun and uplifting to receive these men. Some of us "old-timers" were put in positions of leadership on the fields of play as well as in the rooms. We showed the newcomers how to make a military bed, and how to do their chores. We never, though, had to do our own laundry. In a clumsy method, we each had a laundry box, usually made of aluminum, which we sent home every two weeks, I think, to our parents through the mail with our dirty laundry. They would clean the clothes and then mail the box back to us. We must have been a really smelly bunch, as we changed our underwear and socks about twice a week, our pants rarely, and took a shower once a week on Saturday nights for six minutes that was monitored by one of the professed monks, that is, monks with final vows. After five minutes were gone, he would bang on the shower door and declare, "Five minutes are gone. You have one minute left!"

We took classes for a month that summer. Typing and economics. The typing classes did not help me, as to this very day I still type with two fingers. The economics class, though, was my first exposure to the working world of big-time money: theories, supply and demand, marketing, recession, capitalism, etc. I remember the teacher, a Br. McMullin, a fabulous teacher, so well prepared. He wanted us to get off on a good start, as every course we took from this point on would count towards a degree from Iona College, an all-male school at the time of about 3000 students, located in New Rochelle, New York. He made up a system of bonus points we could get that went something like this: for each extra project, from a list, we would do we could get one extra point added to whatever final grade we accumulated from quizzes and tests. I think my final score was about 110, an A+. I was so elated to get a high mark, so proud of the way it made me feel about myself, that I decided to set the bar very high for the next four years. In fact, for those four years I did nothing more than pray, study, pray and study some more. I became obsessed with marks and a grade point average, so much so that I went to talk with a very old brother named Angelus Lynam to ask him if graduating *summa cum laude* ("with the highest honor") was hard to do. He said, "Yes, it is. You've got to study as much as you can. You've got to sacrifice." I replied, "I'm going to graduate *summa cum laude.*"

As soon as summer school ended we were shipped off to a little town north, still in New York, called South Kortright. It was there that we were prepared to "take the habit," a strange term, indeed. The habit was a reference to the kind of special outer garb that we would wear for the rest of our lives. It had a slim white collar, a black robe that went a little above our shoes, and was centered by what was called a cincture, a kind of black wrap-around the waist.

Our preparation for receiving the habit was mostly in the form of spiritual readings, lectures from the white haired monk who would be our Novice Master, praying, college credit classes in religion, praying, meditation, and sports which, at this time of the year was baseball, occasionally softball.

Each Sunday morning we were required to write a letter home to our parents while listening to classic music which the novice master, deemed holy by his superiors, chose. I liked writing home, yet I never liked classical music. Apparently, I did not have a soul for it, and it never touched even the surface parts of me, much less the infinite spaces of my heart.

I always felt guilty that I did not like the novice master. I thought he tried too hard to seem like a holy man. He had a kind of distant personality that young men could not easily identify with, though he once did break out of that mold when he called us, about fifty or so, to a meeting. "Men," he started, "some of you have been coming to see me about the guilt you are suffering while going up at Mass to receive Holy Communion.

"It seems as if some of you are getting erections at Mass while, at the same time, receiving Communion." Then, in what he must have thought to be a hilarious and somewhat serious joke, if that is possible, he said, "Remember, Brothers, that the habit covers a multitude of sins," a reference, I suppose, to the biblical saying that "Love covers a multitude of sins."

I remember how in his spiritual lectures to us, he would close his eyes, head tilted up, and go on. To me, it was just "blah, blah, blah, blah, bla."

Most memorable, was the day of my "Exit Talk" with him in the days before we left the novitiate for what was called the Scholasticate, located off Route 9W along the Hudson River. I think he said something along the lines of how I would some day make a fine monk. Then came the "kicker," about how intense I seemed to him. He opened the top drawer and pulled out one of those long red rubber bands that is usually used for holding bundles together. He took it in both hands and stretched it almost as far as he could, then asked me, "What will happen now if I tried to stretch it some more?" I quickly answered, "It'll snap . . . I guess."

"Yes, it will," he said. Then came the kicker: "You are like this rubber band, and you will snap if you don't let up. You are too intense." I kind of had an inclination about that quality of mine, yet I never thought much about it. I just considered it a kind of drive towards excellence that was a part of my makeup. What angered me as I left his office was that he kind of diagnosed something he thought of as a character fault, an illness of the spirit, and then shook my hand *goodbye*. I kept thinking about his words, wondering what I was supposed to do about this flaw of mine. It was as if he said to me, "You have a ticking time bomb inside you, and some day it might blow. Good bye and good luck with that."

In all, though, it was a year of growth for me. I will always remember the beautiful August day when we received the habit. My parents, little sister Eileen, and two of my brothers were there. The fifty of us young men wore the habit for the first time. We were placed in a large semi-circle on the great lawn that was guarded by a white statue of the Blessed Mother of Jesus. Our relatives stood behind us, while the Novice Master and his assistants took places of prominence, along with many older visiting monks from here and there. I took the name Liguori that day.

There were hugs and kisses, and plenty of food. I remember that there was a sort of sad finality to it all for me. As I said good-bye to my parents, I realized that I would only see them "now and then" for the rest of my life, and possibly only "then" if I was sent to a far-off mission, say Africa.

Each of us novices had to produce a sort of term paper religiously themed. I chose the life of Christ as he lived it in Nazareth. The time of researching this theme would change my ideas about organized religion for the rest of my life. The Jesus I found during my investigation was a man of the people, a man who wore sandals, and dusty robes, the Son of God who gave his very soul, his life, to his constituency.

Indeed, I personally found the Son of Man.

Because of my findings, the first seeds of disbelief were planted in my mind, though I did not know it for many years. The trappings of religion did not match the unreconstructed Jesus. The organized version was transparently a fraud. I wanted the real Jesus. And he is difficult to find.

Without my realizing it, that year marked the beginning of my search for a personal God, one who knows us and cares about each one of us, from the socially and financially lowest to the highest. I longed to find a God who was good, omniscient, omnipotent, transcendent and personal, one that some day I might find infinitely appealing, way beyond even the spiritual feelings I have found when I ever experienced a deep love for a woman.

As I said, it was a year of growth, in the end a very good year, in a way, a simple year of prayer, study, introspection, sports. I was finding out more and more who I was, who I am. I discovered, too, that I could make others laugh, as I did one night on stage. I could act, and was given the lead to play Edmund Ignatius Rice, the Founder. I was a better than average athlete, a really good student.

What I didn't find out was that I wasn't really cut out to be a monk. Praying was hard and sort of rote for me. Meditation was just about impossible, as I would spend most of that time fighting sleep. I thought that I ought to have an inner goal to be spiritual, even holy. I was neither one, yet didn't even know that I didn't know.

And so, we moved on to the St. Gabriel's Scholasticate, a place, as the name might indicate, where we would really emphasize a full load of college courses, while at the same time grow spiritually, though the spiritual part was not as emphasized as it had been the previous year.

I loved that year, a time when I truly felt as if I was becoming a man. We were given more independence and knew that if we simply kept our five vows that we could be responsible without strict supervision. If I remember right, I took courses in history, math, French, English, philosophy, science and theology. I loved them all, especially philosophy, eventually majoring in it. For me, philosophy was truly a love of wisdom.

It was a way to look into the inner and infinite spaces of the human mind, as it searched the whys, ways and wherefores of life, though in some ways, as time went by, my attempts to discover the nature of things and people caused me more angst than peace, especially as I tried to figure out the origin of things. To this day, it is still difficult for me to simply accept things as they are. I want to know why they are as they are. I want to know why a supreme Power, if there is one, made the world the way it is, and why not better, easier, not always a quiz, a test, a mark. And why there are so many bad people in the world, why so many temptations.

I know the classic answer is that we were given free will to exercise in order to be whoever we want, in the extreme good or bad. I think that we will never know, at least in this lifetime. I am trying to accept that.

This beginning of deeper thinking that started at the Scholasticate continued into the developing life of my mind. I began to wonder, as I pasteurized cow's milk, about many things, the world, good and evil, the Holocaust. I began to want to know what could motivate men to enact these crimes, I wanted to know what ideas could nurture a frame of mind, a hatred so great that it would kill millions of people. My mind was especially numbed at the reality that over one and a half million children under the age of 15 were killed by the Nazi regime. How could this be? Over time, I read as much as I could about that period of history. Then, years later, I decided to see for myself. I visited Dachau first, then several years later, Auschwitz and Birkenau. Frankly, the visits made me even more confused. I embraced the idea for many years that everyone was born in goodness, truth and beauty, although I am now at a point where I no longer believe that.

I think that some men are born without a conscience and/or are so weak in their convictions that they can be easily swayed to do evil things, as millions of Germans did under the Nazi regime.

I do not point an accusing finger at all of these people, as I found out one day in the Scholastic year how without a developed conscience I, too, can lose my goodness. I was nineteen that day when I asked permission to go into the woods with the group's .22 rifle to hunt crows. It was the manly thing to do, I thought, at that time in my life. I spotted a crow high up in a tree and shot it.

It fell right in front of me. I could not find the wound until I turned up its left wing to discover a clean bleeding hole in its chest. I was confused as I bragged about this to my peers at supper that night. I knew there was something wrong with what I had done.

Yet, the gravity of it did not stick, as a few months later I killed a woodchuck with the same rifle, from about 100 yards. The distance made me proud of my shot and again I bragged.

Years later, as I began to build a life-time love relationship with all animals, mainly through the influence of my wife, Sheila, I felt very guilty that I had killed two beautiful sentient and intelligent creatures. What gnawed at me mostly was that I was stuck, really stuck, with what I had done. For many years all attempts to reconcile myself with the killings failed. I had taken two lives and nothing, absolutely nothing, that I could, or would, do could ever bring them back to life. Killing them was irreconcilable.

It was years later that a Buddhist monk in Bhutan gave me the key to some peace about what I had done. You see, there are lots of ravens in Bhutan, and they are considered to have the sanctity of a temple. I look at them like being the big brothers of crows. As I was alone, I was blessed that a monk named Tenzing was my guide who taught me much about his religion. I did not tell him about killing the crow, but I did ask him if it was considered a sin in Bhutan to kill a raven.

"There are two ways to look at it," he said. "If you kill it as a thinking, mature person with deliberation, you can never be forgiven. But if you are immature and not yet fully aware of the grievous nature of killing a live being, you can be forgiven, but only if you make amends to it."

I interpreted his words to mean I could one day be forgiven, as I thought back how immature I had been at the time of the killing. I found a way that I could make amends to the crow while I was taking a walk one day. There, in the gutter, was a dead crow. It didn't have any marks on its body, so I assumed it had died some kind of natural death. I put it in my car and took it to the woods where I buried it.

There was no way I knew about how to make it up to the woodchuck. So, I went to West Park, N.Y., to the exact spot in the field where I had killed it. The landscape had changed a bit, but I found the spot, overgrown. I stayed there a while and thought about the day long ago. I expressed my sorrow for what I had done, and asked for forgiveness, whether to the Spirit of the Universe or the woodchuck, I do not know.

It was the best I could do. I have given up the guilty feelings that had haunted me for so long, knowing that I had done what I could do to be forgiven. Carrying it around any longer would be psychically and spiritually fruitless, and unhealthy.

Carrying around unhealthy habits, especially in my thoughts, was never a good thing for me, as I was naturally inclined to think that any sign in my body that was out of order was an omen of death for me. It got particularly bad in this regard during the Scholasticate year. I was ordered once, for example, to be the coach of one of the not so talented basketball teams in an in-house tournament, when I noticed a red blotch on my leg. I fast concluded that it was cancer! I didn't share my concerns with anyone, and I was sure that each game I coached would be my last. Until one day the blotch disappeared. I never thought of myself as a hypochondriac, yet I knew that I had excessive concerns about my well-being. Probably from the wounds of my childhood.

Things were happening fast, perhaps too fast for me to absorb them. Subjects that I was once poor or even bad at were coming to me with ease. From being a complete bust in algebra at Rice H.S., for example, I became king of the hill. I was beginning to feel also in a way I had never before done. I cried, for example, on the day that my father turned 50 years old, thinking it marked the end for him.

I was becoming self-sufficient. Perhaps the vow of poverty had something to do with that. Perhaps it was a realization that I didn't particularly care about material things.

When you're nineteen years old and have to ask for permission to take a new tube of toothpaste from the closet and you are not embarrassed by that, then maybe you are indifferent about the whole idea of things coming your way. I was beginning to realize that I was more caught up in the things of the mind, in the spiritual aspects of being.

Mostly, though, it was the feeling of belonging, of being attached as a way of living to something that was bigger than myself. I was becoming somebody with a future that meant something to me. I would be a teacher, a teacher of the poor. And I was preparing for that in many ways. Most notably for me was that I was being given a brilliant education, a great curriculum taught by extraordinary and committed teachers.

I loved each day walking up the hill to the building where the classrooms were. I loved our tiny classrooms and the realization that each day my mind was being opened to the bigger, wider world. Little did I know that one day I would see so much of that world that I came to think of myself as a citizen of it.

When classes came to an end we trudged off to Lakewood, New Jersey, part vacation, part work, to ready a new Scholasticate for those finishing their work as novices. It was sort of one day on, one day off. I guess you could say that I was given shitty days "on," as I was assigned to keep the top layer of the septic system clean. The top of the system, a sort of large sweeper that would keep the top layer fluid with sprinkled water would be shut down as I did my work. I wore high boots and worked alone with a shovel that had a long and lean blade. I had to dip the blade about one inch into the "crust," then slide it along to he end of the blade before tossing the contents into a wheel barrel. Each time the barrel was full, I had to dump the contents into a pile. I was told that a commercial truck would come to take away the piles to wherever.

The master monk told me it was good for me, a way to enhance humility.

The "off" days were good. There were bicycles available, and I would sometimes take one to a pond to fish for catfish which I would give away to other local fisher-men, as we were told, erroneously I think, that they were filthy fish because they would eat anything at the bottom of the water.

There was a rule. Of course, a rule. One of the reasons I left organized religion is because of the many rules it has, intended to govern my behavior, as if I could not do this for myself. In the context of rules and friendship in the monks, the rule was *No PF's* – that is, *No Personal Friends*. It is perhaps a good rule if its intention is to turn humans into robots. It is, too, a rather contradictory rule: how can one train to be a teacher of the poor if one doesn't know anything about personal friends, sometimes the life-blood of the poor?

Even in the use of the bicycles, we were not to have personal friends. Without really realizing the rule, I would go with Brother Placidus to fish. He soon became my fishing buddy and a friend, a personal friend. We would talk about this and that, usually grave matters, and later became philosophy majors. Years later, we are still pals.

From Lakewood, we were sent to New Rochelle, New York, the home of Iona College, a small school of about 2000 men. Years later, the school became co-ed. It was a "safe" school for us to mingle with the secular students, a safe place for young men with a vow of chastity. We were allowed to talk with women if the subject matter was decidedly not casual. Relevance to something serious was needed. I should have taken it as another sign that I was not cut out to be a monk when I would go to see a young secretary, I think her name was Miss Pride – who could forget that name – regularly to see if my GPA had changed. She must have known that I liked her, as one's GPA changed only two times a year!

It would be two years of hard work, alas, not as a monk trying to get more *spiritual*, but as a student trying to graduate *summa cum laude*. We were required by our vow of obedience to get five hours of exercise each week, and that was to my liking. I played lots of handball on the campus outdoor courts with my friend of a lifetime, Ralph Santalis, whose name at the time was Brother Savio. In season, I played basketball and tag football. And, of course, baseball, my first love. Most memorable about that time was pitching a 9 inning shutout, and showing my intensity when I increasingly yelled "I got it, I got it, I got it." The older monk in charge of us, a serious guy in his own right, tried to call me off. I got even more intense with my call, and caught the ball. He yelled, "Take it easy," and I yelled back, "I told you I had it."

It was bad form to yell at your superior, and I knew it, though nothing came of it. Funny how we remember certain things.

I prayed when I was told to pray, usually in the morning after getting up, and in the evening before going to bed. But, I still could not meditate. I could hardly get up in the morning as I was always tired from my studies. In fact, one winter I was put in charge of waking up all the young monks in the morning. I was given an alarm clock and a very large bell. As I remember, we rose at 6 a.m. and had a half hour to clean up and get to the chapel that was about 400 yards away.

My assignment was to go about the house at 6 and ring the bell like a crazy man to wake up everyone throughout every room and each floor. I did not always ring the bell on time, as I liked to roll over for another wink or two. I was constantly embarrassed as my cohorts and I got to the chapel 10 or 15 minutes late. Finally, I went to our superior, Brother Scanlan, to ask him to relieve me of my responsibility. He refused, nicely I might say, and asked me to continue to work at getting up on time. I don't remember the rest of the story, though I suppose it was another signal that I wasn't cut out to be a monk.

As I look back on that time of my life, I realize that it was another perfect setting for me to continue my love for learning.

Everything I needed was given to me: tuition, books, room and board. I was not distracted by work responsibilities, except once a week as a senior I was required to cook dinner for all of the monks, seniors and juniors. One night, I decided to go to a basketball game, but not after I prepared meat loaf in the oven on a timer. When I got back from the game, the meat loaf looked more like a very large potato chip, totally burnt. I went right away to see Br. Scanlan to tell him of my negligence and to ask him what I should do. "I've heard you cook a pretty good coffee cake. Why not make as many of them as you can, get out plenty of ice cream. Tell the monks when they come for dinner that it will be an hour late, confess your dereliction, and make it appealing." I ran back to the kitchen, and when the monks showed up, I fessed up that I had gone to a game in the college gym to see Kevin Loughery, an NBA star, play and blew it on the timer. Dinner would be an hour late, so "Why not tend to your studies." I wanted to put some fluff on my excuse, so I added, "I am making some of your favorites tonight, lots of coffee cakes and lots of ice cream. See you in an hour." They gave me a round of applause. I never knew if it was because they felt sorry for me, or that they were just a very good bunch of guys, or that they really liked my coffee cakes which they had before received small sizes of for dessert. In any case, I took some ribbing for it.

My memories, though, are mostly what an extraordinary man was Br. Scanlan, who transformed my screw-ups into something that would benefit me, gold from the dross of my being human. He never once made me feel "less than." Long dead now, he has always remained for me the template of how to be a really good, loving and generous man.

It was during this time period that I started to feel a little deprived of female companionship. Looking back, I realize that at 20 years of age this was natural. At the time, I got over these feelings by wanting to honor my vow of chastity, and by sublimating my needs with studies and an intense desire to graduate with high honors.

In order to study the way I wanted, I needed to find a very quiet place where I would not be interrupted. I found two.

One of them was in the basement of the house where we monks ate our meals and prayed in the chapel. I don't remember why I explored the basement where I found an outlet for a light bulb. Somehow, I got a lightbulb, and set up a chair and a tiny desk.

I would go there when I could to study. I was never discovered, though I had a hard time staying away from this spot during our annual 7-day retreat when we were not allowed to talk or study and prayed a lot, both in community and alone. I was always tempted to go down there and study which I resisted because I wanted to be true to my vow of obedience. I remember that my addiction to books and excellence pulled me down there one afternoon when the 7 day retreat was over and we were once again allowed to talk with each other. When Br. Scanlan said the code words that gave us permission to talk, "Live Jesus in out hearts," I ran into the basement to once again open my beloved books.

I don't remember how I discovered the other place, which I found late in my senior year. For some reason, I opened a cellar door by the side of an old, tiny chapel, on campus, one that was hardly ever used. Lo and behold, I found another basement.

I struck gold! It had a shower in it, as well as a ceiling light that worked. I made a make–shift desk down there and kept a towel on a line so I could use the shower when I wanted.

It was nice to luxuriate in its waters beyond the expected 6 minutes. So I now had these two places and my room, which I shared with two other monks, to study.

It was during this time, too, that I began to be outspoken to the other less diligent monks about their behaviors. I learned later in reunions with those who had also left the monks that I was gathering a sort of reputation as a "know it all," a "holier than thou" sort of person. For example, I noticed that the two monks in my room were spending lots of time talking with each other, not allowed in the rooms, and scheming to rip off others' term papers. I couldn't take it any more. "Do you guys realize that if you spent as much time doing the work as you do trying to figure how you can avoid doing it, you'd both probably be top-notch students. And besides, you're cheating. How can you be good monks when you are like that? And you're not supposed to be talking in the room. I'm trying to get some work done here!"

They didn't say a word. I was happy that at least they didn't plot anymore in my presence.

On another occasion while we were on a week's vacation, thanks to Br. Gus Galway, I was asked one evening by three other monks if I wanted to go into town to pick up a few girls. I was stunned. "Do you guys realize that you have chosen to be monks with vows, including chastity. The vow, I am sure, precludes picking up girls." I was working up a full head of steam, as I was angry with them. "You are either a monk or you are not. If you don't want to be, why don't you just leave!" I don't think I struck the right note. They did not answer, turned, and presumably went to pick up girls. To this day, I cannot figure out why they thought I was a "know it all." As I grew older, I realized that I cannot figure out, except in an academic sort of way, why some people are the way they are.

I cannot, for example, grasp a frame of mind that would organize millions of people to hate the Jews to the extreme of killing millions of them, including children.

I cannot imagine why extremists in the world are raised to kill others. How could one accept that it is his/her mission in life to kill others who disagree with them? How could one believe in a god that wants them to kill others, and rewards them for the killing?

Perhaps they are born defective, perhaps the gene that governs compassion is incomplete. Perhaps the average IQ is not 100, a convenient round number, but more like 85-90-ish. All of this gets in the way of my attempt to find a God that is transcendent, full of wonder, Love itself. I want to know why the world that we live in is so defective, while at the same time honoring a god, if there is one. It is a delicate psychic lode to carry.

I must tell you, my dear readers, that when I was going to school at Iona College as a monk that none of these thoughts ever entered my mind. I am ashamed to say that I accepted whatever I was taught and did whatever I was told to do. In retrospect, this way of being gives me some idea of how millions are led to do what they are told. If there was a song to echo my behavioral ways during that period, it would be easy to record the words. One would simply a gather a hundred sheep together and record: *Baah, Baah, Baah!*

In a very real way, those two years were a potpourri of enigmas: stunted social growth along with academic development. It was as if I were put in a box with an everlasting supply of secular and spiritual books, good food and my material needs.

I realized, as I was heading towards graduation and my mission to teach the poor that I was beginning to lose interest in being a monk. The excitement and drama of it was fading. I would have been content to stay at Iona working towards my bachelor's degree for the rest of my life.

With about six week to go before graduation, I realized that I still had eleven term papers to complete, with little or no intention to do so. There was something terribly wrong going on with me. All I wanted to do, or so I thought, was to get on a bus to Albuquerque. Why Albuquerque? Your guess is as good as mine. So, I went to see Brother Mark Eagan, a psychology professor I had had that year.

"Br. Eagan, I don't know what is wrong with me. I am supposed to graduate soon and I still have eleven term papers to do. I want to stay here at Iona forever, and I want to get on a bus to Albuquerque, New Mexico.

We talked for awhile about these contradictions. I told him about my quest to graduate with honors, how I had proclaimed that to Br. Angelus Lynam years ago.

"You are about to graduate *summa cum laude*. You will be throwing away your degree if you don't complete those papers," he warmly lectured me

His interest in my well-being flipped my thinking. I completed the eleven papers with room to spare and had my degree with honors. One morning, too, while I was walking up a staircase to go to a class, I took the weekly school newspaper, *The Ionian*, from the pile on the side of the staircase and there was my picture, the soon to be recipient of the Philosophy Award. I think it might have been my senior thesis called "The Philosphy of Evil" that was being acknowledged. Or maybe the class near the end when our philosophy professor asked if anyone could sum up the sequential set of courses in Thomistic philosophy that we had been offered. Much to my own surprise, I offered a summation, a good one I might say.

Needless to say, my family attended my graduation. I was especially proud that my dad was there, as I always knew how much pride he took in my academics. When I was called to the stage, "Gerard T. Brooker, *Summa Cum Laude*" I was, perhaps for the first time in my life, proud of myself for accomplishing something that was difficult because it took effort and vigilance over a long period of time. I knew, too, that my dad was proud of me, and that my big brother, Bob, whom I always took pride in, reciprocated those feelings for me that day.

We still had that summer to take post-graduate courses before being assigned to our missions. It was the custom to assign missions annually, so none of us, old or new in the congregation, knew from year to year where we would be. Most assignments. though, lasted for at least a few years.

I took three courses that summer and spent many hours in the basement of the old chapel. Our superiors did not pay much attention to us. As long as we kept busy and out of trouble, there wasn't much supervision. We were expected to eat meals together and to pray together maybe two or three times each day.

And then came the day when we would be given our first mission assignment.

I really wanted to be given an assignment in a foreign land. The thought of that excited me. Africa or one of the poor islands in the Caribbean would do. We ate breakfast at the usual time, and then the Provincial General took center stage. Our names were called alphabetically, and so I was one of the first ones.

"Brother Liguori Brooker, please come forward. You have been assigned to St. Cecilia's Grammar School in Harlem to teach 6th grade. Congratulations!"

I gave the expected smile as I received the piece of paper with the words "St. Cecilia" on it. In fact, I was deeply disappointed. I wanted the romance of Africa, and I got Harlem. I was so inexperienced about world affairs, so naïve, that I didn't see the connection.

I was given a weekend with my parents in Astoria, Queens, then I was taken to a brownstone tenement in the middle of Harlem where I would spend the next year with 6 other young monks, two older ones, and the principal, Br. Gus Galway, one of the best men I have ever known.

It was a very busy year, one in which I found the work of being a teacher fatiguing. One day, for example, I sat on my desk while reading aloud to my students, all male, African-American and Latinos, mostly Puerto Ricans. Sleep overcame me and I fell off the desk onto the floor! You can imagine the hail of laughter.

I loved those boys, most of whom came from difficult families. I always cleaned up my classroom after school on Fridays, you know the blackboards cleaned with wet rags, the desks wiped, also with wet rags, before turning each one of them upside down to clean the underside. Once in a while, we'd mop the floor, hang new posters.

I would invent things to do as the majority of my 40 + boys wanted to stay and help.

Along with the other young monks, we realized that, with one exception, we were really good basketball players. So, we played a lot, even beating the varsity team of one of our brother schools in the Metropolitan area.

Br. Gus got us lots of tickets to Madison Square Garden to see the best college teams play. Theoretically, we were not allowed to smoke or drink alcohol until we had taken Final Vows, usually, I think, after seven years of annuals.

"Brothers," he would say, "we all know that only Ben, Iggy and I are allowed to drink and smoke. However, I might allow it. If I throw a pack of cigarettes on the table, feel free. Now, the drinking is a little different. We will have what is called a *gaudy* (from the Latin word "Gaudeamous" meaning Let Us Rejoice) on Friday afternoons before dinner and other special times, when I might allow you annually vowed monks to drink. Let us be careful, though, as I might get into trouble by allowing this.

"You must never drink unless I say so. If there is a visiting monk that I might invite, wait until I say so to pour yourselves a drink." It depended on how liberal the visitor was, or if he was big shot in which case there was no "Pour yourselves a drink."

Ben and Iggy were two older and kind of eccentric monks who provided lots of laughs for us younger guys. Ben liked to go to funerals in Harlem and take photos of the dead in coffins. He would ask the bereaved if he might take the watch from the dead person's wrist and keep it. When he was re-assigned to the west coast, I was directed to clean up his room, and found several cigar boxes full of watches!

Iggy was a bit weird. When he would buy a new pair of shoes, he would always cut off the toe part above the sole. I asked him why he did this. "So my feet can breathe," he answered. As he couldn't get around too well, he was allowed to have a car, a very old one at that. He would turn on the ignition and let the car warm up, but would not drive it until the *I* on the *OIL* gauge was reached. Why? Because the *I* stood for Iggy, his nickname.

I once went to see him teach his 4th grade class. He was sitting behind his desk with his shoes and socks off, his feet soaking in a bucket of warm water. He asked his kids to "Show Br. Brooker how Jesus does it." In unison, they stretched out their arms as if they were being crucified on a cross. It was really spooky.

Several negative things, though, happened to me that year in Harlem. I slipped into a depression around Christmas time and asked Br. Galway if I could spend a week on the farm in West Park to get away from it all. He let me do that. I suspect now, looking back, that I was beginning to feel the hard work it took to be a teacher of excellence and I was somehow weighing the pros and cons of it. I felt, too, as if I was being smothered. I am not blaming the monks for this. It was simply a realization that for me the life of a monk was essentially boring. We were at rock bottom asked to live a life of dedication to loneliness. As I've mentioned before, we were not allowed to have any personal friends, and I think I was beginning to understand that I did not want that in my life. I decidedly wanted to be connected with others, especially women as, almost ironically considering my mother's sometimes harsh treatment of me, I've always thought of them as being more open to intimacy than men who, too often, are competitive in their relations with other men.

In the first week of my mission in Harlem, I would begin what would be for me a 23 year relationship with alcohol which would become my best friend and worst enemy.

It has been theorized by those who study alcoholism that its genesis might be genetic or due to a certain temperament prone to its addiction. I think I had both. You see, alcohol was used in my family of origin much the same as other families I knew drank soda or juices. As I grew older, I thought of it as just another normal thing to do.

Starting at about the age of 12, I used to plead with my dad at the Thanksgiving meal to let me have a small drink of wine. Within minutes of drinking it, I would get dizzy and have to go to bed. I always asked the next morning how the rest of the night went. In fact, I was an alcoholic waiting to happen! And didn't know that I didn't know.

Both my mom and dad began to drink excessively as they got older. In fact, my dad's definition of an alcoholic was one who drank before noon. Given this description, he would sometimes, as he grew old, sit in his chair with a gallon of Gallo wine, waiting for the wall clock to strike noon, Magic Time, when he would open the bottle cap to begin the day's journey into Never-Never Land. As the hours passed, he would become more talkative and so opinionated that there was no longer a conversation but an avalanche of opinion, a monologue, that went in one direction only. He would become a first-class bore.

I reacted to this by staying away from him after I left the monks. I remember during that time period when he asked me one day why I didn't come around much any more. I told him that I was very busy. In fact, I was in some ways turning into a self–righteous snob. Every time now when I hear Harry Chapin's *Cats in the Cradle* I feel guilt come upon me.

It would be fairly accurate for me to call this and the next year as "The Unconscious Period" about my drinking. I remember the first time that Br. Galway allowed the young monks to drink on a Friday to mark the end of our beginning week as teachers. I asked someone what was the drink of choice in Harlem. I was told it was rum and coke. So I poured a 12 ounce glass ¾ full of rum and the rest coke. Soon enough, the room began to spin faster and faster, so much so that I couldn't get out of my chair to go to dinner. Everyone found this quite funny. And so did I, not realizing that within a few years I would have a problem.

At the end of that year, I was assigned to a new mission, Bergen Catholic High School in Oradell, New Jersey, where I was to teach religion to 10th graders and English to juniors and seniors. It was there that the stress grew. I am not an effective disciplinarian, and it would take experience to find my own identity, my own effectiveness in commanding a class without losing my authentic personality which found joy in teaching. I knew very little about the craft of teaching, and I was just getting a peek into the art of it. To do this, I needed to be in touch with my emotions as well as my intellect. It took me a while, but I began to be present to my students, and wanted to be worthy of their trust. I wanted to be authentic, and I began to realize that I must never pretend to be what I was not. I began to allow myself to learn from my students by really listening to them, by giving up the mask of knowing it all. The techniques of how to do this were beginning to come to me, slowly I admit. For example, when I didn't know the answer to a question, I now began to say, "I don't know. Would anyone like to look up the answer for us and bring it in tomorrow?" Hands would go up, and I would pick one, usually someone who could use the recognition of contribution. Alas, with today's technology at their fingertips, most would give me the answer in a few seconds.

Nevertheless, I was beginning to understand that teaching is an art as well as a craft, that the craft without the art is just OK, and that the art without the craft can be pretentious and boring. I wanted to know how to do both, and I needed a more comprehensive way.

I began to think about leaving the monks. It wasn't that I was drinking too much.

In fact, after the experience of the room going round and round in Harlem, I realized that I had to moderate my drinking. And I did.

Yet, I was beginning to feel lonely in the life I had chosen. I began to wonder where I could find a richer, more full, way for me to go about my work in the world.

Being in the monks was beginning to stifle me, in many ways. On weekends, most of the monks in my community were gone by mid-afternoon. At first, I wondered where they would go. Finally, I asked, and was told that they were invited out to one or another of the parents in this well-to-do community, and sometimes to Broadway plays.

The togetherness in community that I sought was not there.

As I was the assistant athletic director, a combination water boy and equipment manager, I had keys to all of our facilities. On Saturday nights that winter of my discontent I would open the gym and get a rack of basketballs out of the equipment closet and play ball by myself. I remember practicing half-court hook shots, a la the Harlem Trotters! Sometimes, I could hear music coming from the large ballroom next to the gym where community dances would be held. Now and then I would sneak a peek to see what was going on. I noticed the women, and had a soft yearning to be there with others and not by myself playing basketball.

As time went by, I began to accept a few invitations myself to attend parties.

I noticed, too, that as soon as I got into the party, I would view the room like a scanner to pick out a woman I would like to meet. I would take advantage of my white collar and black suit, knowing that it would get me an audience. I was being drawn to women like an iron filing to a magnet.

As I started seriously to think about quitting the monks, I was getting very anxious, as I had read somewhere that if any of us turned our backs on a vocation asked of us by God that we could lose our immortal soul. So, the decision to leave might have consequences. Heavy stuff!

I continued to teach, and volunteered to coach the freshman baseball team. I loved the game and I loved teaching the young men how to play. We had a good team, finishing 13-4. We even beat the J.V. team at one of our rival schools.

One of the ways I dealt with making the decision to stay or leave was to walk the streets at night. And for the first time in my seven years as a monk I had my own room where I finally found a way to reduce the tension that was building in my body by getting on all fours on my bed. For some reason, letting my stomach hang down would take away the anxiety I was constantly experiencing.

I began, too, to have nightmares. Scary? Yes. But also fraught with a bit of comedy, too. I would sometimes wake up in the middle of the night screaming at the imagined rats that were crawling all over me. My screams were so eerie that I thought I would wake up Bergen County. Not so! But I always woke up an old Irish monk named Br. Bradley who would gently knock on my door and ask if he could come in. He would sit with me for awhile to keep me company while I composed myself. I was always grateful.

Every time I had the nightmares, I would go to breakfast hoping that the principal monk would not say the words, "Live Jesus in Our Hearts," which allowed us to talk with each other. It seemed like he would always say the magic words on the mornings after my screaming fits. Immediately, the table talk turned to the night before. "Did you hear the screams? Who screamed? The screaming woke me up." Br. Bradley would look at me across the table and wink at me. Only we knew. Once, a young monk turned to me and asked me if I had heard the screams. "No, I didn't," I answered. "In fact, I had a good night's sleep," I said.

Finally, I thought I could use some help in making the critical decision to stay or leave. So, I told my superior at the high school, Br. Dave. I asked for permission to go to see Br. Mark Eagan, a professor I had at Iona College for two courses. I liked Mark because he trusted me. At the end of one of his finals, I went blank. Although I had studied hard and was ready for the test, I could nor remember a thing I had prepped for.

I got up from my seat. "Br. Eagan," I said, "I'm sorry but I cannot remember a thing about the course. I have studied hard, but my mind is a blank."

Perhaps the warning from my white-haired Novice Master that I was ready to snap like a rubber band was beginning to happen.

I was ashamed that Eagan might think I was trying to scam him. "I'll tell you what," he said, "why don't you go for a walk on the campus for a bit, and when you are ready come on back. Maybe go to the statue of the Blessed Mother and ask for her help."

I did as he asked, but it didn't help. I went back to my desk and tried to remember, but I was still blank. I wrote him a long note in the exam booklet mostly, I think, about my good will towards him and his course. I waited until all the other students left before I handed him my blue book. I thanked him for his kindness and expressed disappointment in myself.

For about a week, I thought that my desire to graduate with honors had just gone down the drain. When I received my report card, I looked immediately to his course. He gave me an A!

He trusted me. I trusted him. So, I would go to see him weekly for a few months.

I was allowed to use the community car for the trip over the George Washington Bridge to New Rochelle. Mostly, he listened. I remember telling him that I had missed many of the prayer sessions with the community because I was working with the football and baseball teams. But I was keeping track of the hours I missed so I could make them up.

Yet, I knew that was impossible, that I felt squeezed between a rock and a hard place, as there would never be enough time. He told me to take the small notebook in which I kept track of the hours, tear up the pages and flush them down the toilet bowl, and then never to keep track again. Never. It came as a great relief for me and opened the space to make a decision with freedom, not one fraught with guilt.

I also told him about my fear of losing my eternal soul if I left. He told me that that was nonsense, old school fear-bearing talk. "Do you really think that a loving God would do that?" he asked me. The answer became self-evident in the question.

Finally, he said to me one day, "It's time for you to make a decision. I'm going to ask you a question. When I do, I'd like you to stop thinking and answer me immediately with one word, *Stay* or *Go*. Do you understand?"

"I understand."

"OK, here goes," he said. "Do you want to stay or go?"

"Go," I answered quickly. I could feel the pressure in me being released. I had finally made the decision with a freedom that I knew would change the course of my life.

He immediately got on the phone to call a man named John Nolan who had also once been a monk, had left and was now married with several children. The chairman of the math department at Memorial Junior High School in South Huntington,

Long Island, he did whatever he could to help others who were leaving. I went to his home a few weeks later to prepare for an interview. As I didn't have a civilian suit, he lent one of his to me. I was offered a job to teach grade 8 and 9 English. I accepted and was given a contract immediately. I remember carrying that contract in my pants pocket for several weeks as I was reluctant to tell any of my fellow monks about my decision to leave.

I finally told my principal, then word got around. At that time in the development of the Congregation it was not well-received to leave. I have heard it is different now, and that they have a farewell party. However, at the time of my leaving, you were treated somewhat like a defector. No one ever said goodbye.

I still had about 6 weeks to complete my teaching responsibilities at about the same time as my five annual vows would expire. Poverty, chastity, obedience, free instruction of youth, and perseverance in the Congregation would be no more for me.

I remember it was with a certain amount of trepidation that I knew I could now talk with women. Perhaps date with women. Perhaps do the deed with women. I didn't have a clue.

Soon after making my decision to enter civilian life, I went home to tell my parents. "Mom and dad, please have a seat, as I have something important to tell you."

The solemnity of the request seemed to fill up the room, or so I thought. "I am going to leave the monks at the end of this month" is all I said.

My mom broke the ice. "I'm not surprised," she said. "I see the way you look at girls when you visit." It was as simple as that. Well, almost, as I thought I had just stripped them of a certain prestige in the neighborhood of having a son who was a religious.

The last month or so was weird for me. Teaching like a monk, but no longer being one, wondering if any of the monks in my community knew that I would be leaving.

I didn't feel like I had a right any more to discuss the usual matters, especially when one or another of them might theorize about the next assignment. No one ever talked with me about leaving, even though I was certain that they all knew. Looking back on it, I see that it was all quite robotic and dysfunctional.

So it was with a sense of dread and relief that I was ordered by the Provincial General, head monk in the North American Province, to come to his residence in New Jersey to see him. His name was Brother Loftus, a man for whom I had a great respect. He took the religious name "Austin," though he might as well taken the name "Integrity."

I was scared about meeting him, as I thought I had kind of let him down.

Turned out, it was a great meeting for me. He told me that he understood how I felt, my loneliness and sense of not belonging. He graciously accepted my decision.

I will always remember the strong and positive way he ended the meeting. He said,

"Remember, when you are at the bottom, there is no way to go but up." You wouldn't believe how many times in my life those words have given me consolation.

He gave me enough money to buy a second-hand Ford that I needed to go round–trip each working day from my parents' apartment in Queens to my new job in South Huntington, L.I., about 120 miles each day. He also gave me a sort of credit card that I could use at a department store to buy to buy civilian clothing. "Get whatever you need, he said, "and when you are done mail it back to me." He shook my hand, wished me good luck and blessed me. Now, there was a man!

And then the day came. I ate breakfast with the others in silence. I was very weepy because no one would talk with me as I left, except Br. Hubert Vaughn, a middle–aged monk we called "Blondie," because he had blond hair. He walked me to the car where my brother Bob was waiting to take me home to live with my parents.

As soon as we backed away from Bergen Catholic High School, I began to cry.

"Why are you crying?" Bob asked.

"I don't know," I answered. "I think I'm going to miss them. Many of them have been together with me for seven years," is all I could think of.

CHAPTER 4

The Learning Years

**Hiroshima Peace
Conference**

Hiroshima, Japan

Hurricane Katrina

I was once a Medici (see book)

In the Arctic

In the Caribbean

WHAT I REMEMBER most about being home again was how noisy and crowded everything seemed. I was used to quiet surroundings for years, so I found it difficult to go to sleep at night. The cars seemed to belch outside my window, and the motors of the busses that ran up and down the street beneath that window seemed to roar. And then there was O'Reilly's Bar immediately beneath my room. I could hear the music from the juke box, especially late into the night on Saturdays. And I heard the laughter of the patrons, mostly older people. I seldom went into the bar, mostly because I was never a bar person. The conversations there did not meet my interests.

My Uncle Arthur was a bartender there. He died a long time ago, but he was the model of a good and generous man to me during those days of my re-orienting myself to the civilian world. Whenever he saw me, he'd ask me if I needed any money, which I usually did, as I couldn't keep any of the menial jobs I tried before the start of my teaching job in September. He's put his hand into his pants pocket and pull out a wad of bills before peeling off a few for me.

And when I did go into O'Reilly's Bar when he was tending, I'd put down a dollar bill for a ten-cent beer. He would go to the cash register, put in the One, and give me 4 quarters change. On the next beer, he'd take one of the quarters and give me 2 dimes and a nickel for change. If I had 5 beers, I'd eventually have 8 dimes and 4 nickels on the bar. When I was ready to leave, he'd scoop up all the change, put it in the cash register and give me the One dollar bill back again!

On the first Saturday home, I went to the apartment of an old friend of mine who had a sister named Rita. I got up the courage – yes, courage was needed – to ask her if she would like to go to the movies with me on the next Saturday.

A nice-looking woman, she was enthusiastic about it. Then when I began to think about it, I wanted to run, go back to the monks, go to Albuquerque, go anywhere but to the movies with

Rita. Every time I think of Alec Guinness in "Bridge Over The River Kwai," moaning, "My God, what have I done?" I think of me that night in Rita's apartment.

So, I took the coward's way out. I stood her up. The most embarrassing part of the experience was that I never saw her again, as I avoided her any way I could.

Sometimes, I would cross over to the other side of the street or, worse still, go around the block when I would see her, just to avoid her.

I was really a clumsy oaf during those days. I tried several menial jobs. One was going from door to door in apartment houses in the Bronx to sell kitchen knives. I was given a brief instruction on how to do this: "If a man opens the door, just say *Can I talk to the misses?*" My instructor gave a few boxes of knives to me and his phone number to check in at the end of the day.

My first job lasted about five minutes. I was told to start on the first floor apartments of any apartment house, and ring the bell of the first door. I did as I was told. A fat man wrapped in a white towel opened the door. "May I talk to the misses?" I asked. "There aint no misses here," he growled and slammed the door.

It kind of spooked me. So I went across the street and called the number I was given.

He came to the same diner where we had just met, and I gave him back the knives.

I really struggled for awhile. A friend of my Aunt Gertrude tried to teach me how to dance. She was about nineteen years old. But every time I tried to learn a few steps and she got close to me my manhood would rise up and I would get embarrassed. So I had to stop that.

My ineptness with the ways of the world began to show. I got fired from my second job that first summer. I was hired to drive vacationers from the Bronx to various summer rentals in the Catskills. My boss would give me a pickup and delivery address, nothing more. To save money, he would have me pick up two, even three, sets of people in the limo. In those cases, I'd have to find two or three homes in the Bronx, then the same number of resorts in the Catskills. I was not very good at finding the addresses and was often late, especially to the last pickup. I soon got fired after a succession of complaints from customers.

I couldn't even go out to dinner without screwing up. A group of the guys from the old days heard that I had left the monks, and invited me to have lunch with them and their girlfriends in New York City. When the sommelier popped the cork on a bottle of wine and poured a bit into my glass I thought I would help the guy. I took the white napkin from his arm and the bottle of wine, and began to pour the wine around the table.

Of course, everyone began to laugh as they thought I was trying to be amusing. Then the reality of what I was doing set in. Total humiliation!

And then there was the time that I went to the Majestic Theater in New York City to see "South Pacific." I got into my seat and lit up a cigar. As soon as I started to puff on it and watched the white smoke float towards the ceiling, those far and near began to fan the air with their programs. I quickly realized that once again I didn't know the rules of this new world I was in.

I was so used to bending on one knee, genuflecting they called it in the monks, whenever I entered the pews of a church or chapel, that I would do this out of habit when I would enter an aisle at the movies. It was a monk habit that was hard to break. I just figured it out on my calculator that I had probably done this over 10,000 times over seven years. And now it had to stop. As I look back at this eccentricity, I wonder what people thought I was doing.

And then there were the Irish girls my old friend James took me on Saturday nights to dance with in New York City. He told me that they were new to America and wanted to meet American men. I was an American man who wanted to meet them. I remember the red hair and their beauty, and how good they smelled. They were the epitome of wonder, the essence of my inner mythology of women.

There was, though, a problem! I could not understand what they were saying to me. No matter how many times I tried to understand, the brogue was too strong. I told James that I wouldn't be going with him any more. He told me to keep on, that in time as the girls got acclimated their language would be more to my liking. "No," I said, "I can't wait that long."

And then I met Kathy who was in a master's program in a psychology class that I was taking at St. John's University in Jamaica, Queens. She was a beautiful Italian girl of about 24. Every time a class ended, about six of us would go to the cafeteria to have a cup of coffee and talk about the class that day. I never paid much attention to her. You see, I was a realist, so I thought she was entirely out of my league. It was nice, though, to be a part of this group, as it gave me a chance to learn some social skills, especially how to have easy conversation.

One day in the after-class session, Kathy left the group to get a cup of coffee.

A few of the men started to talk about how beautiful she was. "Don't you think she is beautiful, Jerry?" which was the name that I asked new friends to call me. I thought at the time that *Gerard* was old-fashioned, though I use it now as an author.

Back to Kathy: "Of course, I think she is beautiful," I replied.

"Then why don't you ask her out?" one of the guys asked.

"Are you kidding, she wouldn't go out with a guy like me!"

"Haven't you noticed, Dummy, that you are the only one in the class she lets look at her notes? Haven't you learned anything in the class? It means that you are the only one she trusts to take a peek at her inner being!"

I think the guys were a bit too Freudian, but I didn't care. I only heard that a beautiful women would think enough of me to perhaps say Yes if I asked her for a date. A new me was being born. Maybe I *was* good enough.

So I waited one day to ask if I could talk to her alone. "I wonder if you might be interested in having a cup of coffee with me some time?" I kind of tucked in the belt of my heart to take the rejection. Certainly, she must have a boy friend, I thought.

"I'd love to," she said. I couldn't believe it. She didn't even hesitate. She just said, "I'd love to." I felt as if I was bouncing when I walked to me car to go back to Astoria.

I was going to have a date with a girl like that. Oh my God!

She gave her phone number to me and told me how to get to her apartment in Brooklyn. When I called, I told her that I had a problem, that I didn't have enough money to have a regular date, but that I would have money in a week or so when my teaching job would begin. "If you want to wait?" I said, but I never had a chance to finish.

"No," she said, "let's do something. I have money," she continued. Letting a woman pay for a date was out of the question for me, so I got creative.

"How about this?" I said. "There's a drive-in theater in Huntington out on the Island where I'll be teaching soon. We can park across the street where we can see the screen and try to figure out what's going on. Then we'll find a diner and have a cup of coffee. I do have enough money for a cup of coffee."

I held my breath, thinking this would be the end of Kathy.

"It sounds like a really fun idea," she said. And so we drove to Huntington, and had a bunch of laughs trying to figure out what was going on in the film. I think it was about a couple of guys who were opposites sharing an apartment. We then nursed two cups of coffee each for about two hours talking about the movie, the fun, our ambitions. She wanted to be a teacher. I still remember how excited I felt being with her that night at the diner, how happy she seemed to be with me. She even laughed at my attempts at humor. I first thought that she was just being polite, but I found out that it was real, that she really liked being with me. I was kind of amazed that an extraordinary person like her might like a guy like me, a guy trying to fit in. Shows you what seven years of self-abasement can do to a guy.

The more we dated, the more confused I was getting. I think I was falling in love, but I didn't really know what that meant. It sounds pretentious now for me to say that, yet it was real. Did loving someone mean that you would marry her? Did I have enough nerve to tell her how I felt? And what if she didn't feel the same way? Could I take the rejection?

Also, she took me once to see her father, a medical doctor who had a summer home in Blue Point, L.I. He seemed like a stuffy old guy who didn't like me. I told her about my thoughts regarding her dad. She just shrugged it off. "He's just like that."

Yet, my urges towards her were growing, and I didn't know what to do with that.

I had been cloistered for so long that I simply didn't know how to handle all of this, and was becoming anxious.

I just wanted to get away from my thoughts and feelings. I then did what I think is the dumbest, most stupid, callous, indifferent act of my life. We had a date one Saturday night, a happy date. I was never anything but happy when I was with her.

I will never understand what I did. I took her home to her apartment in Brooklyn, gave her a perfunctory kiss goodnight, backed off and said: "I will not be seeing you any more," She looked dazed, so I repeated it: "I will not be seeing you any more." As I turned to leave, I looked at her once more. She just stood there, a tear running down from her right eye, something I will never forget. My heart burns even years later.

I never saw Kathy again. As I grew in experience and personal development, it began to bother me greatly that I had done this, without any warning. In the brief few months we dated, we never had a cross word or a disagreement, so totally compatible were we. As time went by, I began to realize that my actions might have disillusioned her about people, might have fractured her trust in others, that they might not be what they seemed to be. I tried to express my feelings in one of the poems in my book called *A Quiet Conversation*:

Not in Time

I once told a woman *Goodbye*.
I won't be seeing you again.
As simple as that.

I died a little death that day
as I diminished her to a tear
that ran fast to her chin as I turned
and walked away.

I'd like to be that tear
with hands,
touching her gently as if
to say *I'm sorry*, and give her
a wild buttercup before
kissing her sweetly on the lips.

Years later, it still bothered me that I could have been that way,
though many years ago. I told my wife about the feelings I had had for
Kathy, and that I would be going to a reunion at St. John's University
to find her and ask for her forgiveness. Here's what happened (in
another of my books, called *Even Whispers Can Be Heard*):

Looking For You

I could not love you then
But then I could not love you now,
still unreachable in my mind.
Time has capped the bloom
of our spring, cooled the fever.
Yet I still feel the wisp of you,
brushed silk, light brown skin,
a soft hanging in my heart
I try to find in this snap of time.

But you are not here.

I think for most of us there are some things that we do in life that we cannot undo, as much as we want to. We might have no recourse or information. For example, the African-American boy I called *8-Ball* at the kiosk. I have no idea, never did, what his name is, or whether he is alive or dead after all these years.

So, it is with Kathy. I sometimes pray for her, that she is well and happy. It is all I can do, as I am stuck with the reminder when I think of her that I have the capacity to be a real jerk. Perhaps it was the beginning attempt to wash away the guilt I felt by taking long walks in the city during torrential downpours.

September finally came, and I started my new job at Memorial Junior High School in South Huntington, on Long Island. I continued to live with my parents for another two years, driving 120 miles round trip each day to work.

I belonged to a small group of friends from the old days in the area where I went to grammar school at Our Lady of Mt. Carmel. What I remember most about them is how wonderful they were to me when I first joined the secular world. They took me in, and tried to show me the ropes, so to speak, of this world new to me. They even introduced me to the world of politics.

But, mostly I hung out with teacher friends on Long Island, many times sleeping over on the weekends at John Nolan's home to which he gave me a key along with a standing and welcoming offer to sleep over when I wanted. His wife, Kathleen, is one of my heroes to this day, as I remember the mornings when she would welcome me, sleepy me, with bacon, eggs and coffee.

It was during this period that I began to feel lost. Looking back, I realize that I then started to drink excessively, especially on weekends when the Long Island crowd of teachers, a party-hearty group, drank. It was a time when I was getting the tiniest inkling that fear was running my life, though the realization was vague and fuzzy.

It was as if I didn't know that I didn't know that I was an alcoholic in the making, and that alcohol was my way to keep the fears at bay. I was, though, still years away from accepting this about myself. You see, as I might have already mentioned, my blood family drank alcohol the way that families not afflicted with the disease drank water and soda. I thought that drinking lots of alcohol was the normal thing to do, and I used that rationale for years to justify my drinking, and to keep the fears away, although now and then I would confront the fears.

For example, I began to fear being alone, especially when I moved out of my parents' apartment and rented a home at Huntington Beach with two other guys who were also once monks. They helped pay the rent, but they spent most nights at their girl friends, leaving me essentially alone in the house. I realized that I was afraid to be alone.

It was the beginning of self-knowledge. I confronted the fear by leaving the front door unlocked and open at night, an invitation in this neighborhood without lights to anyone who wanted to harm me. By doing this, I was beginning to access another part of myself, my courageous and loyal heart.

I also began to fear teaching, the very profession I wanted.

The next twenty years were years of enlightenment for me. I think it started the evening when I decided to move out of my parents' place. My mother had threatened me that afternoon: "I'm going to tell your father when he comes home tonight."

The threat was caused by my using a word that my parents thought was bad. The friction with my mother started when the phone rang and I picked it up and put it down kind of quickly. My mother shouted, "Who was that, Gerard?"

"I don't know, someone who said they'd call back."

And that was when the official parental breakup began. "Get this straight," she yelled, "I'm the only one who answers the phone in this house."

I answered, "What the hell kind of house are you running here?"

I had broken a bunch of rules. I answered the phone, answered her back, I raised my voice, I used a bad word, *hell*.

And thus she was going to tell the Enforcer, her husband, my father. The threat brought back to me a few realities that I thought had faded from the relationship I had had with my father long ago, a relationship ruled by a very heavy hand. I realized things hadn't changed much and that I didn't want to live in that context any more.

When he got home that night, I was sitting at a tiny desk in my bedroom. I could hear my mother telling him what a bad boy I had been. He came bounding down the hall and stormed into my room, standing over me in all his wrath.

He shouted at me, "I heard what you said to your mom!" He then raised his right hand, about to strike me across the face.

"Give it your best shot, Pop," I said back, "because it will be the last time you will ever see my face."

He began to cry! With that, our relationship changed forever to one of respect.

But, I didn't want to live there any more. I got in touch with Jack Ford and Tom Waldron to ask if they could use a third roommate in Huntington Beach. The answer was affirmative and two more years of heavy drinking began.

I dated a bit, and thought I fell in love once. When I told her that I loved her she laughed, almost hysterically. I took it hard, as I thought it a putdown, that it was very funny to her that she could ever love me, a mere school teacher. As I later found out, she had a long-distance boyfriend she never told me about. Perhaps that is what she found so funny about my declaration.

I was in a bowling league, and played a bit of softball. But my real interest was in drinking. I even began to fear women, and so I drank to go on dates. I drank hard whenever I thought I would have to do any public speaking, ironic now as I speak at venues all over the world, and without the aid of alcohol.

In the midst of all this, I began to think I was again falling in love, a problematic fall, or so I thought. She was a Protestant, and at the time Catholics were prohibited from marrying anyone not a Catholic. So, I broke it off. It was, though, one of the beginning doubts that I began to have about the strict teachings of the

Catholic Church. It seemed silly to me that I could not be allowed to fall in love with a woman because she wasn't a Catholic. There was something terrible self-serving with that, and I began to doubt that the Church was walking in the footsteps of Jesus.

I began to be a "serial lover," as I would often think I was in love when in fact I knew little about what it really means to love another. I "loved" Annie at the summer camp, Sue, Virginia, Vickie and her twin sister, Marie, and Lorraine. The list goes on.

I would always, though, find something wrong with each of them. One would have bad breath, the other a face that was not good enough, another was not fun enough.

For the first time in my life, I had to take care of my own dirty laundry. I was such a baby. I wore the same pair of pants every day for a year, and I didn't think that was odd. If my dirty socks and underwear passed the smell test, I'd get a few more days out of them before going to the laundry-mat in town.

I didn't pay much attention to my lesson plans for teaching, many times making them up on the run. One day, the principal of our school, Tom Calabrese, a most wonderful man, came unexpectedly into my class to observe. I was winging it:

"Let's talk today about the Seven Wonders of the World. Who wants to go first?"

They looked at me like I was a bit mad, as there was no context for exploring the Seven Wonders of the World. "Come on, guys, let's not be bashful. Who wants to answer?"

No one. Calabrese was taking notes. I couldn't even start the conversation, as I didn't have a clue about any of the Wonders, not even one of them.

I thought I could kill a few minutes by giving them a pep talk about personal initiative, the courage to speak up, and a few other bromides.

With that, Mr. Calabrese got up and left.

I thought that might be the end of a promising teaching career. So, I went to my faculty mailbox and there it was – a note from him requesting my presence in his office.

"Thank you for coming by," he said. "Please have a seat."

It seemed obvious, at least to me, that I was trying to teach with a nasty hangover.

Instead of telling me to clean out my desk and never come back, he simply said, "Thanks for coming in sick. Why don't you take the rest of the day off. I'll get someone to sub for you."

For some reason, probably trying to fake him off the truth that I was drunk, I told him that I would soldier on the rest of the day, as it would not be fair to another teacher to give up a free period for me, as that was the way contingencies were handled in those days.

Several years later, the faculty was informed that Tom was hospitalized and not expected to live. I later found out that he had been working while a fast-growing cancer was developing in his stomach. It was at this time that I was beginning to realize just how wonderful he had been to me that day of the Seven Wonders of the World. In truth, *he* was to me one of the wonders of the world. In a way that I find difficult to write about, he triggered something in my soul that began a life-long appreciation for the many people who had already been loving mentors to me, – Monsignor Kelaher, Br. Scanlan, Br. Carthage Ryan, Br. Eagan, John Nolan. I didn't know it then, but there would be more.

I wanted, for the first time in my life, to tell another man that I loved him. Yet, I didn't feel comfortable in saying it to Tom in person. At that time in my life, no one had ever spoken those words to me. So, I decided to sit at my typewriter and write a letter to him, a letter in which I expressed my gratitude to him for being an extraordinary leader in our school. And I told him that I loved him. I put the letter in the post office the next day. I never knew if he read it, as he died three days later. Another new lesson learned: don't wait 'til someone is dying to express your love. In fact, I hope I can get a little warning time before I die so I can tell all those I love in the fullest and most rich way my feelings about them. Our culture often conflates love with sex, and so it is not easy to express love, as the expression can easily be misunderstood, especially one man to another.

In all, I kind of wandered around in my tiny world. My drinking got worse, occasionally incapacitating me. It was only on the day that my room-mate, John, drove me to the school I taught at because I was so hung-over that I couldn't drive that I began to realize there was something wrong. That day remains memorable, also, because when I got out of the car I puked on the walkway in front of the main entrance. He drove me back to our little house on the beach.

I began to realize that I was addicted to alcohol. But, the realization didn't mean anything to me. Any time fears arose in me, I wanted to drink. But I still did not realize that drinking was but a symptom of my fears, not the cause of my fears. It took me almost twenty years to accept this reality and begin the work. I still had to have a few more shocking experiences to accept that I was getting out of control.

One of the needed experiences came on the night when I was taking a course towards a master's degree at St. John's when we convinced our prof to let us go to the school lounge to watch President Kennedy address the nation about the Russian missiles based in Cuba.

If it was fear that pushed me to drink, listening to the President made me crave for one, if not two, or three, or more. One of the problems with an addiction to alcohol is that there is *never* enough. Waiting for the next drink is like waiting for Godot who never comes fast enough. I phoned my parents the next day, and told them that I loved them, a breakthrough experience for me. In a small way, I was beginning to grow up.

Mainly, though, the first few years after I left the monks were wasted years. It was a time of getting used to a new kind of life, one in which I found it difficult to be responsible for myself. I think of it now as a time when I was a minimalist human being who was trying to find himself, as difficult to find sometimes as the proverbial needle in the hay stack.

CHAPTER 5

And Then

Jesus's tomb near Jerusalem

Komodo dragon in Indonesia

**Nose touching with Maiori
Indian in New Zealand**

On the Gobi Desert

On the Great Wall of China

Pryamids in Egypt

By THE TIME I was beginning my 4th year teaching at Memorial Junior High School, my life had leveled off into a hum-drum. Not just any kind of hum-drum, but a mediocre one at that. Literally, I was up to nothing. I think I was depressed and didn't know it.

Then one spring Friday afternoon I was invited to a party. Nothing special. Just a small get-together hosted by a teacher I knew. Sometimes, though, I think certain elements of our inner life connect in a special way with events, and the meeting makes a bigger meaning than it normally would.

I remember pulling up in my car to the party house. The sky met the roof of the house in a special way, as if it was greeting me. I could smell honeysuckle and the sounds of Miles Davis wafted out of the open windows. It gave me a moody sense of sounds and smells. As I entered the house, a woman came up to me. "Hi, my name is Angelica. Would you like a drink?" she asked. It wasn't that I was attracted to her, as she had on lots of lipstick and mascara. Yet, she gave me a feeling that I belonged. I don't know why. As I said, things sometimes connect. I had a feeling that this house on this afternoon was near the center of the sun, as it wrapped me in its warmth.

After Miles took a rest, a guy named Black Henry riffed loving justifications for jazz from a side room, and we listened because his music was good and the vibrations right. I could swear that the shafts of the late afternoon sunbeams entered my soul, lit me and lightened me. I left the party early, as I remember it. As I drove home to my little house near the beach, the long reach of depression was gone.

And then there was another party, a Halloween party. I immediately noticed a pretty young woman who seemed to be the life of the party. I asked my room-mate, Tom, about her. He didn't know her well, but he did know that she was a home economics teacher at John Glenn High School in Huntington, also on Long Island.

I called the school, got her on the phone, and asked if she remembered me from the party. She did. We dated for about a year when her name changed from Marcia Flynn to Marcia Brooker, the prelude to an "up again, down again" twenty years.

As I look back on those years, I realize that I was again trying to discover who I was. I remember that even on the second day of our marriage on our honeymoon on Cape Cod how full of myself I was. The sad part is that I didn't have a clue.

I wanted to go up to the top of the Pilgrim Monument in Provincetown. My new wife didn't want to go. "It's raining, thundering and lightning. I don't think we ought to go." I wouldn't listen to her. "Don't be a scaredy cat," I taunted her. We went, but all the while it was nagging at me that I wasn't putting her into the equation. Nor, later, the kids.

The *nagging* part was about as far as it went in moving me towards being responsible to others. The reality of it is that it took time while I slowly inched forward to some real maturity.

Our first child, Kevin, was born two years after we married. We took him to Salt Lake City where I was awarded a National Defense Education Act scholarship to study psycholinguistics at the University of Utah. A few years later, I was given another one to study writing at George Peabody College for Teachers in Nashville, Tennessee, which later was absorbed by Vanderbilt University.

Quite soon after that I was given a full scholarship to study for a doctorate at Peabody. It included an apartment, my books, a tax-free bi-monthly allotment for me, my wife, and two children that now included our second son, David.

I went into this opportunity with some excitement that I would have a college experience unlike my previous one when I had a vow of chastity that prohibited me from talking with women, except if the conversation was necessary. I even bought clothes that I thought were "cool" for a student.

The excitement quickly cooled. My khaki pants seemed pretentious to me, and I was placed in an advanced statistics class with 150 students. Whereas I had once been a big fish in a little pond, I was now a little fish in a big pond. Our professor seemed to talk more about himself than about the course. I didn't like him nor the course, and began to question its value to the Ph.D. I was pursuing in psychology.

I began to drink heavily in the mornings while I tried to study. I would then run a mile on the school track and take a hot shower before going to classes, thinking that this routine would sweat out the signs and smells of alcohol.

So, what did I do? I went to see the faculty member who was in charge of my scholarship to tell him that I wanted to change my doctoral studies to English literature or I would leave the school and go back to New York. He couldn't readily switch my grant from one major to another, and then put a sort of choke-hold on me. "If you leave now," he said in emphatic tones, "You must pay us back all of the money the government has so far given to you." I couldn't do that, as I was walking a financial tight rope.

He then let up a bit. "I'll tell you what. Finish out the semester here, and if you still want to leave, you can, no strings attached." I sent my family back to New York to live with my wife's mother, dropped the stat course, and finished the semester while living in a basement cellar.

I drove my car back to Long Island, putting in new oil every 70 miles or so.

The car was a symbol of how I felt at the time, broken down and in need of something to fill me up. I took a course in public speaking with Toast Masters International which gave me a boost, as I won a trophy for winning a competition with a speech called, "An Oak Tree From a Fallen Acorn," a reflection, I wish, on my life up to that point.

I soon was offered a job in the social studies department at a very large school called Northport High School where I was sort of dazzled by the professionalism of the staff. I learned much from them, and was offered a full time job as a teacher of English, the area in which I was certified.

That year did not go well for me, as I continued to drink heavily and did not pay much attention to my teaching. I was, though, trying to do some of what I thought to be "post-modern" teaching, which only got me into trouble. When one day the English chairman came to supervise my class, it was empty, except for me sitting at my desk reading.

"Where is everyone?" he asked. "I don't know specifically," I answered, "but I know they're out there somewhere."

He kind of laughed the knowing laugh of a father looking at his foolish child who didn't know what he was doing.

"What do you mean out there somewhere?"

"I gave them a writing assignment to interview someone on campus about a variety of topics."

"Well, let's go find them," he said, sort of taking me by the ear, or so I felt.

I was angry with him. We couldn't find any of my students. Lord knows where they went. Of course, I got a good "comeuppance" from him about what constitutes good teaching from bad.

I made it worse a few weeks later, much worse. As faculty moderator of the school newspaper, I allowed a front page story about the police checking student lockers for drugs. The school principal called me in a few minutes after the paper came out. I knew I was in trouble as the entire administrative staff was there.

"How dare you allow that story to be printed?' was the essence of his remarks.

I was naïve and liberal in my defense of the story which, quite frankly, I thought was very good.

Here's where the "much worse" comes in. When the chairman of the English Department complained about me to the principal, who I didn't know was his personal friend, I told the principal, "If you don't get rid of him, I'm going to resign." I was fired soon after.

I don't know how many times in my life that dross turned to gold for me.

Sometimes, I think of it in the context that I am being watched over by a Force I don't know. It sounds kind of arrogant to say this, as if I am someone special, yet it is what I believe, not as special but one of many, I am sure, who is taken by the hand and escorted to where they are destined to go.

My thoughts on this are still quite fuzzy as I struggle to find a transcendent being, perhaps God.

I was soon hired by the principal of John Glenn High School, the school where students of the little village of Elwood lived. We also lived in the same village and my wife was a teacher there. It was there that I began to find my teaching wings under the guidance of a wonderful and supportive chairman, Gene Auriensen. In fact, the word spread and I was named chairman of the English department at Kings Park H.S. the following year.

Those years before we moved to Connecticut were hectic, as well as years of growth. We soon had another child, Suzanne. I guess I just kept screwing up. I lasted for two years at Kings Park before I was fired. My relationship with the principal was edgy, really edgy. I tried to upgrade the English curriculum but, in retrospect, I went about it too fast, and didn't bring the members of the department along with me.

One day, too, he asked me to meet with him. "You've got a teacher in your department who's been acting like a whore," he said. I was astounded to hear this. "What do you mean?" I asked.

"I'm told that she has been bringing men into her apartment at night, right here in Kings Park."

I asked him why he was telling me this, as the person in question was a good teacher. I didn't see the connection. In fact, there was a part of me that thought, as long as she was doing a good job in the classroom, it was none of his business how she spent her private time.

"I want you to look into this," he said. I didn't know what he meant by my looking into it. "I want you to see if it is true what I have told you about her."

"And how do I do that?" I asked.

"I want you to go to her apartment at night and tell me what you find out. Just stay in your car, watch and let me know."

Immediately, I got angry. It is not a character defect to speak the truth, though it probably is one to speak the truth in harsh terms that might demean the other. I must admit that I did not have the skills during that time in my life to speak the anger I felt in ways that did not shred the fabric of a relationship.

"Why don't you just mind you own business!" I responded abruptly. I could see the anger in his eyes. I didn't care, as I still didn't have enough experience to realize that words can have grave consequences.

"I am not an FBI agent," I said to him. "I came here to be the chairman of the English department, nothing more. I am not going to be your spy." With that, I simply got up and walked out of his office.

Needless to say, I simply walked out of another job. He made everything difficult for me, including running the department. The new wing that was added to the old building included a suite for members of the English department. As it was a bit of a walk from their classrooms, the members of the department remained in their old offices.

I was directed to order them to occupy the new spaces. When they wouldn't, he blamed it on me. When they wouldn't cooperate in implementing the new courses, he blamed it on me. I guess I had three strikes: the "whore," the new office space, the new courses. The union offered to help me, but I was so arrogant that I refused help.

It is not necessarily a bad thing to get fired, as it offers a person a chance to examine his life. It was a crucial time in my life, and I did begin, perhaps for the first time, to really examine my life, especially my relationship with my wife and children.

The best way for me to explain these years is to say that I often was not on the same page as my family. I am not saying that anyone was wrong or bad. We were just not on the same page.

I remember asking my wife and the kids to spend the year between Christmases making creative presents for each other. I was tired of all the commercialism that surrounded the Christmas season. The theme seemed to be the wonders of capitalism rather than the wonder of the birth of Christ.

When pressed up against their resistance to my idea, I got tough and directed them to do it. For my part, I decided to write a daily one full page entry to my wife for her present. I wrote a letter to her each day, and actually put some real effort into writing it and putting each one, 365 of them, into a nice binder.

Nice, right? Not! I thought that the letters should tell my wife how she could be a better wife to me. So, in effect, I had a set of 365 complaints to give to her for a Christmas gift. As might be expected, it did not go over well, as I had not yet learned that assertive and non-diplomatic words were not the way to win over hearts and minds.

Joy to the world became glum to the Brookers that Christmas.

On and on, I was not on the same page with the kids or my wife. The sad part of it is that I didn't try to talk through my ways. I remember gathering them all together now and then. I called these meeting "A Family Gathering," as in "Tonight we're having a family gathering," which were really complaint sessions on my part. My children now, years later, have much fun when kidding me about those talks.

They have names for them, as "The Great Shit Talk," when I complained about how many times I cleaned up after the animals. Then there was the "Who Ate My Cheese?" talk. You see, when I was a child, my mother forced me to share candy bars I bought with my own earned money with my siblings. I did not like that, as I thought it was unfair and unjust, even immoral on a bad day. I vowed that when I had the upper hand in life, I would buy things for myself and not have to share them. My kids did not know this about me, and I never shared my thoughts about the cheese with them. So, when they thought the cheese in the frig was fair game, I felt the injustice of it all.

"Who Ate My Cheese?" lasted for a good fifteen minutes. There were more meetings, the re-enactments of which bring howls of laughter today.

I thought, too, that watching the T.V. too much was not a good thing. It bothered me, especially when I would come home from work to find them sitting on the floor watching the T.V. and not getting up to greet their dad. My rendition of *Father Knows Best* was not in their script.

So, I decided to put a few rules into place regarding the T.V. Here were the Rules: each one of them could watch it 5 hours a week, according to a schedule of their choice. But, no more than 5 hours. I would put their schedules on the refrigerator door.

Sports and news were exceptions, unlimited watching, because I thought these items were good for them. Needless to say, I was bucked at every turn. Besides, we had just the one T.V. set and so their schedules of choice were filled with conflicts. It did not work.

Again, not on the same page.

It was the same with my schedule for their study habits, two hours a night monitored by either their mom or me. Their mom would often let them go before the two hours were up, causing conflicts between us. Interestingly, I would have to *stop* my daughter, Suz, from studying after the two hours were up.

So it was that there was the tension of not being on the same page as a family.

We did, though, have out share of good times. We traveled lots in the car with the kids, even while I began my doctoral studies at St. John's University in Jamaica, Queens.

We took the kids out west to see friends in Utah. We camped, always a fun experience.

Marcia and I even had a bear walk over us as we slept outdoors on a hot summer night in Yosemite National Park. Fortunately for us, the bear was looking for non-human food.

I tried to be a good neighbor. Mostly, though, I buddied up with the neighbors who drank a lot. I think the condition of one who drinks a lot but is still functional is called *mocus,* a state of being sub-par yet not so bad as to prevent him from doing the rudiments of whatever job he had. I realize, looking back that I wasn't really fully present to my work, my colleagues, my family.

It began to bother me, probably because I always had a notion of who I wanted to be, and knew at some level that I wasn't being that person.

You see, I have this vision about each one of us. It goes something like this: There are 100 billion galaxies in the universe, and each galaxy has 100 billion stars.

Our galaxy is called "The Milky Way," and the star that each one of us was born on is 143 called Earth, the only star that science presently knows can sustain life as we know it.

The conditions, such as distance from the sun and various temperatures must be perfect for us to live on this planet, this star.

And how special each of us it is to have been born. Think about it: the male ejaculation releases about 200 million sperm, and only one of them makes it through the Amniotic Sea to join with the female egg. I made it, and I am not even a very competitive guy. And you, the reader, made it. And you and you. Winners all!

Given all of this, it is easy to see how each one of us is very special. And so I believed this back then, and I believe it now, about myself, too. I wanted to truly live the gift of me, to maximize my potential, which was difficult at that time because I rarely knew what my potential was.

I think, though, that we begin to discover our potential in small ways. At least, that was true of me. The war in Vietnam was beginning to bother me. And then it began to smolder in me, as one of my students, home from Vietnam, at Queensborough Community College, where I taught one class as an adjunct professor, began to tell me what was really going on there, the killings, the injustices and atrocities.

My feelings were growing intense about the war. And my actions began to alienate my family life. One Sunday, for example, at our Catholic Mass the priest asked, as was the custom in those days, if anyone would like the congregation to pray for anyone or anything. I yelled out, "I would like us to pray for all the Vietnamese children we are napalming." The hush of expectation fell over the congregation. How would the priest handle this?

After all, I had broken the code, the assumption that God is on the side of America.

"Let us pray," he said, "for all those who are dying in Vietnam." And then came the low roar of disbelief. Were we then expected to pray for the bad guys, too? When we got into the parking lot after the Mass, there was a flurry of conversation, mostly inquiries about who was the bad guy who asked us to pray for the Vietnamese.

As we drove away, my wife said to me, "If you ever do that again, I will never talk to you." She laid down the gauntlet as I began my potential to be a left-leaning liberal. I even went to Washington and sang with Ralph Abernathy at the Lincoln Memorial.

At about the same time, I was ordered by the government to go to the induction center at Whitehall Street in Manhattan. There was some small chance that I would be called to fight in the war. Actually, there was no chance, as I had several children.

So, there I was in the middle of a large crowded hall, in my birthday suit. The Gunny Sergeant gave us instructions: "Each of you has to pick a branch of the service and go to that branch now, Army over here, Navy there, Air Force there, Marines there," pointing all the time to guide us. I realized quickly that I was in the middle of the floor, alone. The sergeant yelled from the balcony, "And where do you want to go?"

I cupped my hands and yelled back, "I want to go home!" Everyone, including the sergeant, laughed. "You've got to go someplace," he replied. "OK, I'll be a Marine."

My response was curious, as one day, many years later, I would be made an Honorary Iwo Jima Marine.

We were each asked to go into about four offices for a series of interviews. I sat down in the first office. The doctor read my papers, looked at me and said, "I see you've got children. Go home and take care of them." I tell my Marine buddy, John, that I was once a Marine for 15 minutes.

One of my professors at the University of Utah, Dr. Kenneth Eble, wrote a book called "A Perfect Education" that had an enormous impact on me, probably a negative one at that. He encouraged his readers to not allow their children to get in the way of their ambitions in life. Unfortunately, I took this literally and as a rationale to be self-centered at every move I made, professional and personal. I moved the kids around from place to place in order to follow my dream, I turned down really good positions as an administrator, either because the school did not seem to my liking, or they did not offer me the money I wanted, usually a lot more than I had been making.

I even took a semester off until I realized that my savings were about gone, and I began to get nervous. I tried to lighten things up a bit. I did a "boys night out" with a neighbor who said I was too serious about life – the old rubber band theory. We went to bars, played darts and shuffle board, visited the firehouse where my friend volunteered. I realized fast that I wasn't a "boys night out" kind of guy.

I tried to do something creative for friends, something different for us all. I would create my own Bingo game in our house. I bought a bunch of bingo cards, and bought a lot of cheap presents at the local party for kids store. I rented chairs so everyone had a seat. I got beverages and snacks for the players, as well as a big transparent bowl to pick out the numbers.

I thought this would be great fun. Others didn't. About 5 invitees came, and my creative night was over. Forever. I felt disillusioned, as I thought the bingo game would be great fun, you know, friends, food, drinks, laughter.

A first awareness that I was driven by fear began during this time. It is difficult to acknowledge this even now as I write these memoirs. Everything in my childhood scoffed at fear, as if it didn't really exist. To acknowledge it was to be a "pussy," that vulgar word in Astoria that meant you were a girl who was scared. Fear was not to be acknowledged. It was to be covered by the mask of macho. To some extent that was true of me, even in the way I was a father, sort of "do it my way, always my way."

To a greater extent, though, my way to handle fear was to drown it with alcohol. A little bit of that reality broke through to me one day when my family and I went to an amusement park. I took a ride on which I sat in a chair, pulled a wooden bar to my waist before the ride began to go faster and faster until the centrifugal force of its speed moved me on a horizontal plane. It scared me, absolutely scared me so that I felt like screaming out to stop the ride.

I didn't scream, but I knew, really knew, fear. I finally acknowledged it. I made up my mind in thinking about the fear I experienced that I would never again allow this feeling to get in my way. I went back to the ride the next weekend and took it again, this time realizing, acknowledging, that I was afraid. It didn't seem so bad, and I realized that if I faced fear that I might be able to conquer it.

I then made a vow to myself: that I would identify all the ways that I allowed myself to stop my development because I was, literally, afraid of being afraid.

I knew that public speaking brought up fear in me, as it does to many people.

In fact, in many national polls it ranks higher than the fear of death. So I made up my mind that I would speak in public whenever I could. No matter what. Even if my heart began to beat faster, my mouth dry up, my knees shake, no matter what, I would speak in public.

I felt confident that with repetition, I would be comfortable.

Fear of heights had gotten in the way of travel. So, I decided to do everything I could to go up high. No more sitting up straight on the edge of my seat on airplanes where I felt if I sat back the plane would go down. I flew in WW II trainers, in heli–copters, in hot air balloons. I parachuted from 3,500 feet, even though I was so scared that it felt like an out-of-body experience. I did a free-fall from 12,500 feet with a trainer latched on to my back. It was a remarkable experience falling at 120 miles an hour, although it felt like I was not moving until our regular chute was opened.

I was in awe, so much so that I didn't feel my instructor tap hard on my shoulder, the signal for me to pull the rip cord. Of course, he did.

I remember as we came down to land, my instructor yelling in my ear to keep my legs up as we would land on our butts. We landed gracefully. "I'm alive, I did it," I yelled. And so I did.

All of this confrontation with fear took place over time. The missing piece of the equation of fear would only be put in place when I stopped drinking.

I still remember the time when I realized that I didn't have whatever it takes to really love another, that I was so self-centered that I couldn't reach beyond myself. The realization took place when I went to see the movie "Dr. Shivago," and realized deep in my soul that I didn't have the inner resources to fully love another. I knew that the movie was romantic and idealistic in the way it portrayed love, yet I knew, too, that it gave me something to work at, in the same way as I was working at my fears. I wanted, really wanted, to fulfill my ability to love. I have worked very hard at that, and continue to do so, as I believe the purpose of life is to love others. In fact, to love all living creatures in whom the Principle of Life has chosen to take up residence, even insects.

Whenever I am at my desk, and a creature so small I can hardly see it walks across the paper I am using, I reach for my magnifying glass to look at it. I am dazzled, awed, that something so small has within its microscopic body everything needed to sustain life.

I remember, too, coming back from seeing "Dr. Shivago" and taking my 8 mm. projector apart, with the help of a variety of screwdrivers and knives. I took it completely apart, a stupid thing to do as I tried to fix a defect. As I looked at the hundreds of parts on my desk, I realized that I didn't know how to put them back together. I had deconstructed a projector, my own Humpty Dumpty, that couldn't be put back together again.

I know it sounds wildly Freudian, yet I think I was trying that night to understand what was going on. I was getting a peek at my soul and how undernourished it was. I was trying to get to the heart of the matter of me or, saying it in another way, what was the matter with me.

So, the days became inwardly more intense with me. I had come from a strong Catholic background that said divorce was *verboten*. Yet, I knew that I was going in that direction.

For a long time, then, I tried to make a "go" of it. Many years later, we had another child, Jay, who embodies for me how affectionate a child can be to his father when his father is totally present to him. You see, I got sober around that time, so he didn't experience how self-centered I could be.

I remember one summer when I took my car's engine apart because the pistons or cylinders needed work. I knew nothing, really nothing, about cars, especially the engine.

Over time, I separated each part of the engine until I got to the pistons that needed to be re-lined.

As I disconnected each of the parts from the whole of the engine to get to the pistons, I wrote down the name and a rough drawing of the part before putting each of the parts on garage shelves in the order I took them out, so eventually it would be last out first in.

I did this to stay busy, to save money, and to impress my boys that their dad was good at something besides academics. When I got the parts back from the machine shop, after my de-construction of the engine, I began the job of putting it all back together again. I would periodically ask the boys to come look at what I was doing while trying to impress them with how difficult it was.

I had everything together after a few days. And now, it was the moment of truth.

I asked the boys to sit in the back seat, while I would make a big drama out of starting the engine. I had no idea what might happen when I turned over the ignition key. If I had botched the job, the engine might explode for all I knew.

I then created drama. "OK, boys, let's have a 10-9-8 . . . countdown before I turn the ignition key." We counted down together, I turned the key and, Viola! the car started. At the time, I thought it was near my greatest accomplishment ever.

And so, life continued as I tried to be a better father, and a man who would keep his religious training by staying married, even though we were fast becoming the definition of "irreconcilable differences." If I said *up*, she would say *down*. If she said *left*, I would counter *right*.

Yet, we kept on trying. I later tried politics, being elected to the Board of Education in Newtown, Connecticut, the town now widely known as the place where the Sandy Hook Elementary School massacre took place.

I find it remarkable now at how I did not have the skills then to be a contributing member of a group. In a way, I had what might be called negative skills. That is, I knew how to make the crooked beams straight. Or, perhaps, the straight beams crooked.

I thought that the superintendent of schools, for example, was not doing a good job, so I did everything at every turn to make him look bad. Finally, he was fired. Perhaps the beams were crooked only in my way of seeing things.

I was often the pariah to the other board members, the guy who would stick up for the community, a man of the people. It wasn't that there was anything wrong with being that way. It was the way that was wrong. I was becoming a cunning manipulator, and I didn't like it.

After I left Kings Park, I turned down job offers even as my saved money was beginning to run low. I got a call from an old friend, Mr. Sullivan, who was once my department chair at Memorial J.H.S., asking me if I would take a full-time job for the second semester at a middle school on Long Island where he was the chair. I jumped at the chance.

I taught 8th graders, not my cup of tea. I had no choice. Kids that age are much too lively for someone with my temperament. However, as the money was good and I was fast becoming broke,

I figured I better find a way to make this work for me. So, I began to season my teaching with fun. I really didn't know at that time how to have what I'll call organic fun. By that, I mean fun that was natural and real, amusement from the heart, so to speak. So, what did I do to make my classes fun? I stuffed a few of my old socks in the form of a baseball with sliced up newspaper, and I'd periodically have a "catch" between the sitting students and myself. A simple back and forth, nothing fast or too difficult to catch. They loved it, and I do think it helped my classroom discipline in that the spirit and tone of the throwing that I set seemed to permeate the mood of our teaching and learning.

However, I knew my method with the sock throwing was probably not inside the box of this quite serious school. I didn't clear it with my chairman, so I was always a bit afraid that he would walk in unannounced on one of our "throws" and I'd be in trouble again. I did at least have enough sense to ask him what the norms were regarding showing films in the classroom. "OK," he said, "just don't overdo it."

I had a great semester there, but I knew it was time to move on. I didn't like living on Long Island. It was too crowded for me, and Jericho Turnpike, which we often had to use, seemed like nightmare, one crowded with stores and honking cars. I knew, too, at some level, that living where we did was not in my best interests. Lots of drinking. You might think, *well, didn't that just suit you fine?* Not really, as that same inner urge to develop my self, no matter how soft and subtle it might have been at that time, was still talking to me.

I began to get the New York Times Want Ads to look for a job in education. I kept track: out of 139 letters of inquiry I wrote, I receive four invitations to interview.

One of them was in Westport, Connecticut, at Staples High School, an upper middle–class school that was one of the best schools anywhere. It was, too, where my wife's brother lived. I asked him about the community and the school, both of which were A+ in his opinion.

Even though I spilled my cup of coffee on the floor at the interview, I got the job as chairman of a very large English department. The entire set-up was classy and the salary was good. Things were working out, as my brother-in-law let me stay at his apartment during the week before I went back to Long Island for the weekends. That gave us the time to rent a nice house in Westport on the water of Long Island Sound.

I indicated to my wife that I'd stay there for 2-3 years, then use it as a jumping off experience on my resume to seek out more important and lucrative positions. Little did I know at that time that I would stay at Staples High School for the last 27 years of my career. Or that it would be the place that transformed my personal and professional life, the place where I finally found the core of who I am.

The learning curve at the school was quick and intense. My fellow chairmen met every Friday after school for several hours with the principal, who was also the assistant superintendent of schools. I had never before been in such an intellectually intense school environment, especially at the faculty and department meetings. Expectations were high, and I needed a dictionary.

The English staff had about 30 teachers in it. They were highly credentialed and very opinionated. In addition to teaching a class or two, my job was to supervise their teaching, monitor our curriculum offerings, develop our budget needs, and be the go–between them and the upper administration, give reports about various aspects of our departmental work and needs, sometimes at board of education meetings, structure our course assignments, rooms and teacher assignments, and whatever. The bulk of the work, as any department chair will tell you, was the "whatever." Keeping the tone of the communications was important, especially between the upper administration and the teachers. Whenever the upper administration gave me a directive regarding the department that I knew would not be welcomed, I would have to find the right time and the right words to pass on the directive. I would also have to know the reason for the directive and delicately make my case, even though boss types sometimes do not like to be questioned.

I ran the department collegially which helped a great deal in getting us through the bumps in the road. I was ordered once, for example, to give a quarterly report to the Board of Education on how many conferences each of the teachers had with students about their writing. You see, every teacher, except the English teachers, was assigned five classes. English teachers taught four, and in place of the 5th they were expected to conference with their students. At the same time, we had an item in our department budget called "The Lay Reader Program," volunteers with degrees from the community who were paid for marking some of the students' essays. In all, then, we had four, not five, classes to teach so that we could pay extra attention to our students' writing *and* we had extra outside help to edit students papers. It was a unique and generous set-up for the department. I tried to keep that in the forefront of their minds whenever they got disgruntled.

When things became a bit financially tight, I was directed to specifically account for the luxury of the "free" class. Some of the teachers did not like this, as they felt distrusted. It was my job to inform them of the directive as well as to point out that, given our unique position as a department, we needed to cooperate in order to preserve the *status quo*.

I then created a form that was to be filled out each quarter by each teacher.

Essentially, the form asked for the total number of extra-help sessions each teacher held with students that quarter. Now I had to do some delicate, and mostly private, conferences of my own with teachers, some of whom held 250 student sessions, while others held 50. I had to convince the "250" teachers to lower the number and the "50" teachers to raise it, that is, to do more. The "250" crowd was most agitated, as they felt I was lowering their standards of excellence.

We worked it out, and the *status quo* remained intact.

After a year or so, I rented a house in Newtown, about a half hour's drive to the high school and after a few years, we bought one in the same town. My life was moving along nicely professionally, yet badly in some ways privately. Running the department was taking lots of time and nervous energy which motivated me to drink more. And the more I drank, the more assertive I became in meeting my own needs instead of those of my loved ones. I was acting selfishly, yet didn't even know it.

It is sad to look back on those days and to realize now that I was almost unconscious about my preoccupation with myself. When I'd ask my family if they would like to go to the movies, I would pick the movie without ever thinking that they might not like it. I'd *tell* the boys that we were going to a minor league baseball game, and never *ask* them if they wanted to go. On and on. The point is that I was slowly pushing myself outside the core of their lives.

At the same time, I was organizing the students at school to do what we could about world hunger. I started a group called "YEH," Youth Ending Hunger, an up-beat slogan for a down-beat reality. Our motto was "Throw your pebble into the pond and watch it ripple out." We started by doing local projects such as taking a weekly assignment at the local soup kitchen, to cook and serve. As time went by, the group took on state, national and international projects which, of course, took more and more of my time.

My doctoral studies were time consuming *and* difficult. The course work was not as hard as was my relationship with the supervisor assigned to oversee my dissertation.

He was difficult to get along with while constantly being negative about my thesis. "This is not good," and "that could be better." It was all negative without a positive contibution. I was not thriving, and was afraid that years of course work, study, and time travelling to and from the university would be wasted.

Finally, I couldn't take it any more. I had strong feelings that my supervisor had compromised his integrity as a teacher by being so negative. Although I was still drinking, I was realizing its negative consequences, while at the same time being uplifted by the context of my job at Staples. I was beginning to touch my possibilities.

I decided to write him a letter, telling him that I was a person who needed reinforcement, and that I thrived with encouragement. I sent copies of the letter to all six members of the dissertation committee assigned to me. Perhaps I was committing doctoral suicide.

I received a phone call a few days later from one of the committee members who had guided me for several years. As I remember it, he said to me in explosive tones, "Are you nuts? Don't you know that Dr. McGlothlin is a senior member of the faculty? That he has a reputation for being tough? He has clout. Do you know that you have to get a 6-0 vote to pass the oral exam?" And "Why did you send copies to the other members? Don't you know that you have put him on the spot?"

Unknown to him or anyone, that is exactly what I was trying to do, put him on the spot. I kind of got the idea, over time talking with other students, that he was a sort of professorial bully that most everyone was afraid of. I think people like that fear being revealed, and I was revealing him. If I was wrong, I had Plan B. No way I was going to give up.

I listened carefully to the phone call, which ended this way: "Do not come around here until I tell you. I'm hoping that McGlothlin will cool down about you. I'll call." I had opened the bee's nest and felt as if I was about to be stung.

I went about my business, and the phone rang a few weeks later. "Ok, come on in.

He wants to see you."

"What does that mean?" I asked. "I think he's calm and wants to get to work with you on your dissertation. I think something good is happening."

His words calmed me. I felt optimistic. I made an appointment and went to see McGlothlin. I started off by wanting to speak about my letter. "I don't want to talk about that," he said quickly, "let's get on with the work."

And we did. His tone had completely changed. He was up-beat and suggested to me how I could make this and that part of the thesis better. I left that meeting feeling as if I was floating. Actually, I learned a great deal about teaching from the experience.

That a teacher has a choice to be understanding or not, and that the choice can be life–changing for the student. So, why not do the right thing and make the choice to be affirming. It was easy enough to do.

Things began to happen quickly. After a few more productive meetings with McGlothlin, I received a call telling me that my dissertation had been accepted, and that I should arrange a date for my oral defense of it. I arranged a date for me to be present at two defenses of others to see what was expected. I sat in the back of the room both times. Pertinent for me was that each person used 4x6 cards to periodically look at, and that each defense lasted about two hours. The use of the cards, as I will explain, became a bone of contention at my defense.

The defense was scheduled for February 8, 1978, my sister's birthday. I studied hard and prepared my 4x6 cards. Alas, an historic blizzard took place that day in New York and the new date was set for three weeks later.

I was nervous that day, driving in from Newtown to Jamaica, Queens. I remember waiting at the designated room for the committee to show up. They came in like a posse of wild west gunslingers, briefcases in place of gunbelts. I was told to sit at one end of an oval table, where three of the professors sat on either side of me.

And then the questions started. It was about when I turned over my 7th or 8th card that it began to go wrong. "I didn't come here," Dr. Mahdesian broke into the overall explanation of my thesis, "to hear someone read from cards."

"I've been to the last couple of defenses, and it was allowed," I explained. He didn't care. A time-out was called and they discussed the situation. He won the day, and I was told to put away the cards.

Mind you, I was still drinking heavily at this time, and I was angry. "OK, Gentlemen," I said, "if that's the way you want it, that's the way it will be." I scooped up the few cards I had used, put them on top of the full deck which I then clacked as hard and loud as I could on the table, wrapped a rubber band around the pack and tossed it onto the middle of the table.

I was so fueled by my anger that I got on a riff of my defense while feeling my confidence build. At one point going into the second hour one of the committee members asked me about the tables of statistics that were included. "How did you do this?" I was asked.

I was on fire. "The same way as you gentlemen do it for your academic articles. I paid someone to do it for me."

Not a whimper of protest. I finished my defense, and was asked to leave the room while they discussed my performance that day. A 6-0 vote was required in order to pass. It was part of the ritual for the body of university secretaries outside the room where the defenses were held to stop typing and just sit and wait as the student stood outside the door of the room where the six gunslingers would decide if he lived or died.

It seemed like a very long time as I waited, whereas it probably was about 3-4 minutes. *I failed, no I passed. I passed, no I failed.* On and on until the door opened. "Come on it, Dr. Brooker," the chairman said. They gave a polite clap when one of them told the group that he had a bottle of whiskey in his office, and that I might like a drink. Little did he know how I might like a drink! The idea was nixed when another of them thought they could get in trouble for drinking alcohol on the job. I was glad, as I just wanted to go home.

I thanked them, shook each of their hands to leave, when Dr. McGlothlin said to me that the margins on the title page were 1/8 of an inch off and I would have to fix that before turning in my final draft. Go figure!

At the same time as I received my doctorate in education, I passed the Mensa test that verified for me that I could handle the most difficult academic work. My confidence was growing and I was beginning to recognize more explicitly the ways that I wasn't being who I wanted to be. I wanted to be someone who made a difference.

I wanted to be someone who helped hungry children eat. I wanted to love my family in ways that meant more than bringing home a paycheck. And I began to get a sharp inkling that I drank too much, and that might be standing in my way. Yet, it would still be three years before I took action.

I was beginning to do things that were out of the mainstream. And I began questioning why people did what they did. I realize now that this passion to know *why* went way back to my childhood when my mother would beg me in the kitchen while she was cooking to "Stop asking me questions, Gerard!" When I wouldn't stop, she'd point at the clock on the wall and say, "You are not allowed to talk until the big hand (for example) gets on the 5." I would simply sit and watch the clock until the big hand struck 5 before I started asking again.

This need to question has helped me enormously as a writer. When I was a young boy, for example, I could not understand why anyone would drop an atomic bomb on anyone else. And I wondered why about the Holocaust. My questioning motivated me to develop an international peace conference in Hiroshima and to write three books about the Holocaust.

For a while there, as I said, I started to do things that were a bit weird. I wondered, for example, why picnics were only held in nice weather. Why not in a blizzard? Accordingly, I told my wife that I was going to have a picnic in the back yard whenever the next blizzard would come, and that she and the kids were invited. I explained that I needed to know in advance so as to prepare enough sandwiches, sodas, and condiments. They thought it was a joke and declined. I explained how it would be a delightful experience, that they wouldn't have to worry about ants or bees. To make a bad joke, my explanation did not cut the mustard, and no one came to the blizzard picnic. The only thing I remember about it was looking into the window of our kitchen and seeing how warm they looked as I flicked snowflakes off my eyebrows, and how the mustard froze in my sandwiches.

Sometimes, too, when a heavy rain came upon us, I would take off all my clothes, get a bar of soap and take a shower in the back yard. My wife told me that I could be arrested for indecency, but I didn't care.

There was more, but I guess you get the idea that I was drifting off, a bit unanchored.

In a crazy way, though, I loved my family. I remember one time when we travelled west on a vacation and stopped at a nice motel in a town in Illinois. It was a very hot day so the first thing we did was to get on our bathing suits and go to the pool.

I am not a very good swimmer. So, when I put David, about three years old at the time, on my shoulders and began to walk across the long pool unwittingly into the deep end, I began to drown. I came up once and screamed, "Help me!" I guess the people sitting and sunning around the pool thought it was a joke. No one responded.

I used all my might, weighed down by David, to come up once more and screamed again for help, hoping that someone, anyone, might realize it wasn't a joke.

Just as I was going down again, I saw this very big man dive into the water and pull me up and over to the side of the pool.

When I took David off of my shoulders, I realized that he was perfectly dry from his waist on up, that I had made sure that he wouldn't go under. In a strange and dramatic way I realized that I would willingly die for any one of my family. And then I began to wonder if it made more sense to think about how I could live for them.

I was beginning to pay attention. Paying attention was a sort of understood subtext to my job description, so I was getting lots of experience with it. I befriended an older man, in itself a big deal as I never allowed my self to know older people, thinking that they had little to offer. I know better now, as I know the wonder of their experiences and how much I can learn from them.

Anyway, this older man loved animals and liked to talk about how extraordinary they are, especially his own dogs. I, too, once loved a dog, my Kiki, so I would really listen to him. He taught me how animals are sensuous, and the ways that they are intelligent. That they could feel affection and identify in their own ways with their humans. I watch now as my wife comes home from work. Our cats, Annabel and her daughter Chloe wait at the top of the stairs for about a half hour, then greet her with belly rolls, rug-surfing, and flips. I see how curious they are. I see trust and spontaneity, expectancy and intention as they show her that they want to go outside by jumping as high up on the front door as possible. I see how aware they are, and I see their will as they choose to walk away from food not wanted.

I am grateful to this man, and I am grateful to Sheila, the animal whisperer, for asking me a long time ago, when I was unconscious about the extraordinary nature of animals, to explain to her why I nudged our cat at the time out of my path with my shoe.

"You know," she said, "she lives here, too, and has as much right as you to plop where she wants." I have such respect for her that I understood from that point on how extraordinary animals are. And I have grown to love and understand them as one of the greatest gifts in my life. They are mysterious and magical to me.

I was also paying more attention to my teaching. It was getting sharper and more relevant. I especially liked teaching a senior course called "Readings and Writings in Contemporary Issues," as I could combine the content with my own beginning travels around the world. I began to bring back artifacts from my trips to the classroom in order to make contemporary issues come to life.

When I went to Dachau, for example, I dug under the surface, while no one was looking, to find stones that might have been there during the Holocaust. I brought these back to my class and used them after we read Elie Wiesel's *Night*. I explained to my students the history and purpose of Dachau, and then passed the stones around, asking each student to hold one of them as tight as they could before letting go. I then asked them to write there in class about what these stones might have seen if they had eyes to see. The silence was deafening, the essays robust, and almost always without errors.

When we studied world hunger, I asked my students to do special projects so they might know a little about how it feels to be hungry. We tried boiling old leather shoes to take a tiny sip for the animal content in the leather, and we boiled their fathers' old belts for the same purpose. We even once boiled stones to have "stone soup," something ravenously hungry people have been known to do. That no one would try a taste made the point better than a taste might have.

I began to show my students the photos I took abroad, as I began to travel extensively. I showed them blistered roof tiles blown into the Ota River by the atomic bombing of Hiroshima. I began to collect rocks and an assortment of artifacts from historic places to show them in an attempt to go beyond the facts.

I began to want my students' imaginations to fly. I encouraged them to express their opinions, as it is a freedom they need in order to define what they think. I wanted them to understand with more than their intellect. I wanted them to know with all of their powers. I began to require them to create projects about the major issues of the day. I remember bringing in a head of lettuce, good, old-fashioned iceberg lettuce. Each student was required to take a leaf and then had to write about its growth, development, packaging, marketing and dissemination, and how all of this impacted the environment.

When we studied the impact of T.V. on us, students volunteered to stop watching it for one month. They were required to keep a daily diary, noting especially the times that they were tempted to back out of the experiment. They regularly read these to their classmates and, as time went by, the impact of the television set began to be evident.

I wanted to challenge my students with the most creative parts of myself so that they could attain knowledge, and develop new skills. At the same time, I was beginning to find myself by way of my teaching.

If I have achieved anything in my career, it is an abiding sense that I have challenged my students with the most creative parts of myself so that they can discover their unique talents. I have pushed them to see the remarkable results they can have when they work together with respect. It has always been rewarding to hear from them later in life, especially when they just want to say Hi and How are you.

My goals with them have been for each one to go beyond the "box" of circumstances in which they find themselves, and to show them, not just by words alone, but by deeds that they can soar high, identify with others, even those who are different from themselves. I wanted them to be involved in the world. I have urged them to be skilled and effective, engaged and committed. My hope has been that each one of them, in his/her own way, will try to know the joys and sorrows of being human as well as an appreciation for the wonderful gift of life.

And I always tried to involve parents. After all, they are my partners in the education of their children. In fact, several took my classes. I have them speak to my students. Some have lent support to my efforts to help ease hunger by serving as consultants, fundraisers, and participants in projects I've organized for their children.

Many have allowed me and my students to use their home kitchens to cook meals for the homeless. More than a few have joined me with their children in international conferences on hunger that I have organized. And I always considered it a blessing that they were my colleagues and partners.

And then came the winter vacation, the one I will always remember. I was on a ten-day vacation from school, and we were planning a family outing. Ironically, as I was growing closer to the heart of who I was trying to be as a teacher, I was growing farther apart from my family and the cause was becoming apparent: Alcohol!

As we were getting ready to leave, I think it was to an animal farm, my wife and children said they wanted to talk with me. "What's up?" I asked. They were blunt:

"We don't want you to go with us." I was dumfounded. I thought it was a joke at first. Then, when I realized they were serious, I felt like I had been hit in the forehead by a hammer. They went on to say that I wasn't any fun anymore.

More to the point was that I had come home the night before very late and drunk, and, led by my wife, they were being polite, saying I wasn't fun any more.

As they left for the outing without me, I just stood there, kind of in shock, that the patriarch had just been deposed. I began to pound my right hand into my left open palm, saying over and over and out loud, "Why am I doing this, why am I doing this?"

Now, what I am about to say might be hard to believe. Yet, it did happen. I heard a voice that said, "Because you drink too much," and then a white light about the length and shape of a long neon light bulb shone down from the ceiling onto the right side of my brain. Something was happening to me! I wasn't scared. I was open, finally open, to the obvious, that I was addicted to alcohol.

Little did I know at the time that I had had my last drink ever the night before, thirty seven years ago.

I called my friend, John, whom I knew socially. I knew, too, that he had been in the AA (Alcoholics Anonymous) program for seventeen years. I asked him if I could see him right away. He explained that he was at work and terribly busy. "Could you make it here at 2 o'clock tomorrow?" he asked.

I spent over two hours with him the next day, telling him about my life and how drinking was interfering with it. That at the same time as I was being successful professionally, I was failing personally. Complicating things, too, we had a great blessing come into our lives. Our son, Jay, was born. But not without drama. Marcia's doctor told us that there were complications. He would make an immediate "forced" delivery.

He told me to wait outside the delivery room, and if the amniotic sac spilled yellow liquid, little Jay was in trouble.

I remember waiting and praying, perhaps more intensely than I ever had. Finally, the doctor came out of the delivery room, and looked at me, about 20 feet away. I held my breath. He raised his right arm and stuck up his thumb in the iconic "Everything is OK" pose. I cried.

At the same time, I was beginning to see the edges fray on the professional side of my life. I started being unkempt, and doing stupid things like showing up late for meetings.

When I saw John the next afternoon, he asked a few questions and listened.

Finally, he said, "I think you have earned a seat in Alcoholics Anonymous. Are you willing to go to a meeting to see what it is all about?"

Of course, I was and told him so. I went to my first meeting the next night at a church meeting hall. I thought it would be filled with Bowery Street bums. Not so. They were middle class men and women, many in jobs of consequence. I quickly realized that alcohol is no respecter of gender or status.

I was still finding it hard to accept that I was addicted. Perhaps a little too much to drink at times? But not an addict. Until that night when I heard the first speaker ever at an AA meeting. I swear he looked like me, and since it was a Friday night and he probably was coming from work, he was dressed like me, suit and tie, one of the ways I tried to stay functional – shower each morning, clean shirt, tie, nice pants, good shoes. He had a professional job, he was convincing and told his story with a transparency that was convincing. I listened, and was moved. Yes, I allowed, I am addicted to alcohol.

As I began to sob, the woman next to me, a stranger, held my hand. A new life was beginning. I would never again have a drink of alcohol! Thirty-seven years now, as I write this.

In so many ways, I was beginning to be open to possibility. Ironically, in the aftermath of the death of one of my students I came to know more fully how I could be effective in the lives of my students. I had known Chuck for five years before he died.

A fine writer and aware person, he helped me write radio commercials for a campaign I had begun to help homeless children. The campaign was successful. Chuck graduated

And went off to the University of Missouri to study journalism.

Unfortunately, he developed cancer of the lungs and died during his sophomore year. It was with a very heavy heart that I went to his funeral. As I was offering my condolences to his family, Chuck's dad, a famous sports caster, asked me to step aside to have a private talk. He told me that two weeks before he died Chuck had gone through his own memorabilia in order to select a few for burial with him. His dad told me that he had selected five things, including as essay he had written in my class years before.

Along with the grade, I had written a note on it which I hoped would be empowering to Chuck as a writer. In it, I encouraged him to believe in himself and in his talents and to develop them to the fullest. He chose to take this note with him across the Great Divide.

I was moved, my spirit deeply touched that he chose to take my message with him into eternity. I began to realize that teachers not only impart skills and facts. As I listened to Chuck's dad, a new realization was born in me about the inspirational possibilities of the profession, and a new energy was given to my desire to be a teacher of excellence. From the experience, I renewed my commitment to work for the growth and development of children everywhere. Yes, everywhere! As time went by, I began to set my determination in motion, but not before two extraordinary events took place in my life.

My wife and I tried really hard to keep our marriage together. We received counseling and took workshops. We talked, always privately away from the ears of the children. By God, we tried. But the attempts failed.

I compensated by getting a bit more involved in politics, being elected to the Newtown Board of Education, singing on the steps of the Lincoln Memorial with Ralph Abernathy. But in the second year of sobriety, things caught up with me. That's a nice way of saying that at the same time as I was trying to patch up my marriage that I simply did not have enough band aids in my personal backpack to cover the wounds.

To top it off, I had a breakdown, a deep depression. It started one day after school was out. For a few days leading up to this, I was having strange things happen to me. I began to predict events that would happen at school. I could tell beforehand, for example, when a fight was to break out. I was kind of stunned by this, and it scared me. I didn't tell anyone, but I was scared. Around the same time my hands would periodically seem, at least in my mind, to blow up like small balloons, so I felt as if I would float upwards. That, too, scared me. A lot. Again, I didn't tell anyone.

And then came the day after school. I was standing in the hallways, talking with my friend, Paul, the chairman of the Social Studies department, when I suddenly fainted. When I came to, there were a few people hovering over me. I asked the assistant principal if he would drive me home.

I tried to go back to school the next morning, but I knew things were not right.

And here's where Ruth, a fellow teacher and one of the many great people who have come into my life, talked to me. "You appear to be suffering a depression, perhaps a clinical one," she said. "I suggest you go home and take some time off." And then she said something I shall always remember: "You can allow the depression to have you, or you can have it. If you are having a breakdown, you can use it to have a break-through to finding yourself. Remember, you are the executive agent of your life."

It was with this advice that I took five weeks off from my work to begin the healing process. I came under the care of three doctors. A medical doctor, a psychiatrist, and a psychologist.

The medical doctor quickly released me from his care, as there was nothing physically wrong with me. I stayed with the psychiatrist for a month or two. I remember just one thing about him, the rest seemed to me just babble. He asked me one day what I wanted most to do with my life. I was angry with his question. "That's about the most f–ing stupid question anyone has ever asked me," I replied, adding, "I want to feed every hungry child on the planet. Every one of them."

Most likely, he will never know how his answer impacted me. "Well, you probably can't feed all of them, but you *can* feed some of them." The "most stupid" question became the question that changed my life

I left his care after a few visits. Sadly, I don't even remember his name. I stayed with the psychologist for two years or so, sometimes along with my wife and kids, another way of trying to save our marriage. It didn't save our marriage. I told him that "I'm not winning here." He asked me what I meant by that. "You always take the side of my wife, and I don't seem to count." I really felt that, and so I quit.

The five weeks I took off from work were most extraordinary. The traumatic experiences of my early life that I had repressed bubbled up in me, memories came alive once again. I spent most days sleeping a lot and doing lots of exercise like chopping wood for our fireplace. And crying a lot as the memories came forth. I must have filled up buckets with my tears. I felt as if my psyche, my being, was being cleansed and I could put my fingers on my fears. I felt lighter. No more weird experiences.

I had written a note to my department when I took the time off, so I didn't anticipate that coming back would be difficult. It wasn't. They were exceptionally kind to me. As was the principal of the school, Dr. Marvin Jaffe. On my first day back I asked him if I could meet with him before I started my work day. He invited me to come in right away. And then he did a most wonderful thing. He picked up the telephone and directed his secretary to call each of the other department chairs to come immediately to his office. If they were teaching, they were to release their their classes right away and come to his office. Within ten minutes they were all there.

"I guess you're wondering why I asked you all here," he said, pausing to let his question sink in, and then simply said, "Jerry's back." I will always remember that, the loving simplicity of it – "Jerry's back."

I remember those days very well. It seems as if the word got around why I missed so many weeks of school. In the week or so after I returned, two of our students committed suicide. No one really knew why. It was decided to have an all-school assembly to address it. I was asked to speak last, after three or four speakers.

I welcomed the opportunity as I really knew what it felt like to be vulnerable. I knew, too, that I was a lucky boy to have family and friends who helped me to recover. I knew that a clinical depression could result in its victim hiding out or coming out, that we had a choice.

Never before had I spoken with such conviction. You see, I loved my students and my school. I asked them to try to be aware when they are starting to withdraw, to seek help from someone, a parent, a friend, a teacher, and not to isolate. I spoke about the passing nature of conflict and failure. I asked them to believe in themselves and in the gifts they had received. I ended with the slogan of that year: "May the Force be with you!"

Coupled with my involvement in the AA program, this cleansing and breakthrough of my spirit brought out a new me. I was not just changing. I felt as if I had been transformed to a new awareness, a clarity, about myself and others, as well as a worthwhile purpose, to do as much as I could to help the less fortunate, especially children who were hungry.

I probably came back too early, as my emotions were still a bit raw. I remember finishing a short story in my senior English class one day, a story about parents is all I can recall. I began to sob in front of the class. Really sob, shoulders heaving. Finally, a young man from the back of the class said, "Thank you, Dr. Brooker."

And then, one of the girls came up to me and gave me a big hug, right in front of the class. I composed myself and started to laugh. It broke the ice as they were all, I'm sure, glad to lighten up.

"I don't know what happened there," I said. As Staples High School was a kind of button-down place, our mission as teachers was to teach and not to cry. "Perhaps you can all keep what happened here right here. I don't think it would be appreciated."

I think we beat the Las Vegas slogan by about a decade.

As soon as the class ended, I went immediately to see my dear friend on the faculty, a great and beloved Latin teacher named Dan Sullivan. Fortunately, he had that period free.

"Do you mind if I close the door? I want to tell you about something in private."

He put down his work, and listened. I told him what happened, and that I felt humiliated, that I'd soon be the laughing stock of the school.

"Dan," I said sadly, "it was the worst class I have ever taught."

"My friend," he responded, "I got news for you. It was the *best* class you have ever taught." I was flabbergasted how easily he turned things around for me. It was as if he turned dross into gold. It was a new way of seeing things for me.

I asked him to explain. "You have taught them today that it's OK to be human. You have taught them that teachers are people, too."

Somehow, my being human with them had extraordinary results. They would come early to my classes, and their essays were written with a rare authenticity. I understood them, and they understood me. I remember saying good-bye to them at the year's end. I thought I would cry again, but I didn't.

As my teaching grew stronger, I was voted by the senior class to give the graduation address in 1987. I was deeply honored and, I'm afraid, long-winded, as Dr. Jaffe told me later that I could have cut it in half. I had a lot to say about the graduates being aware of what might be, to try to live their lives as possibility. I wanted them to always see opportunity in whatever might happen, perhaps even the opportunity to grow in spirit even as misfortune might rear its ugly head.

While I was being inducted into the National Teachers Hall of Fame, one of five teachers nationally, I was losing my job! Our school enrollment was going down, and so teachers had to be let go. The working principle for reduction in force was "Last in, First out." As I was a member of the teachers union and not the administrative union, this principle was operational for me. Though I was the chairman of the English department, I was the junior member in time of service.

As soon as I was given the bad news, I began to apply for other jobs. Fairly fast, I had an offer that I was about to take in a system that wanted to up-grade the curriculum of the English department.

But, then, the student body got hold of the information that I and a popular math teacher would be losing our jobs. They began their protest by periodically marching around the school hallways banging pots against the hallway lockers.

This soon escalated. Three hundred students sat in the hallway of the school superintendent's office, banging pots and pans, the newspapers said.

As it goes, some of the students used this interruption by venting every grievance they felt, from school lunches to a later start in the school day. It was getting a bit out of hand, so Dr. Jaffe held an open school meeting in the auditorium every day for about five days to hear their grievances.

I asked him if he would like me to address the students in an effort to calm things down. "No," he said. "On the contrary, I want you to lay low, teach your class and stay in your office." I didn't understand his logic, but I did what he asked.

I will always be grateful for the president of the WEA, the Westport Education Association, Dick Leonard, for the work he did in resolving the crisis. To save my job, he asked one of the middle school English teachers who had planned to retire in one year, if she would retire at the end of the current school year instead. In a *quid pro quo*, he had permission to offer her a full year's health insurance that would be paid for by the school system.

She agreed. Leaving early allowed the superintendent to assign one of the high school English teachers to take her place, effectively leaving my opening intact.

However, the deal soon became complicated, as the eight or nine other teachers who were planning to retire got wind of it. They demanded also to have their health insurance paid for a year. Somehow, it was all agreed to and my job was saved.

Needless to say, I was ecstatic as I loved working in Westport.

Again, though, as the arc of my professional life was growing, my personal life was on the rocks. As I said before, her *up* was my *down*. Her *left* was my *right*.

At the same time as this was going on, I was very busy implementing new courses such as African-American Literature, collaboratives with the history department, as well as infusing Indian, Hispanic, and Asian literature into our curriculum. I was helping, too, to have our department move from a teacher-centered to a student-centered learning approach. I was helping, too, during this period to urge alternative assessment practices as we were learning the different ways that students learn.

I was in fact achieving a way of life that I loved. Teaching was becoming a way of being for me. I was beginning to discover the mystery of who my students were. I was letting a poem by William Butler Yeats, called "There," be an inspiration for my teaching life. "There" is a place where all the images in the poem are actualized, and so they are frozen, static and dead. As a teacher, I began to try hard to not ever allow myself or my students to be "There." I wanted us to be always getting there, always learning, forever discovering. I remembered my third grade teacher who compared me to the beautiful green, orange and blue butterfly that flew as if by magic out of her desk drawer. She opened the world for me, a very shy kid. I was now dedicated to opening the world for each of my students. I began a practice each morning as I walked the twenty yards or so from my car to the entrance of our school. That I would be committed to be all that I could be that day to my students, my colleagues, my superiors. That I would put everything else aside for the time I would be there, that I would not let any problems I might have, personal or otherwise, to interfere with that commitment.

I always thought that knowledge without action is not worthy of us. I think, for example, that the Mensa high I.Q. organization (I am a member) is not entirely worthy of its existence because it is to a great extent self-reflective. I began more than ever to ask my students to use their skills with me in the real world because it is in the doing that positive change and the evolution of the human spirit occur. I took as my credo a saying I learned at my alma mater, Iona College: *To Teach and to Do.* I think that young people are a sign of hope to the world, and we should project their sign as brightly as we possible can.

Winston Churchill's definition of success was not giving up after failure. I believe in that, not only as a mantra, but in an existential reality that we can choose. It is a good one, as we all fail a lot. Even the greatest major league batters fail seven out of ten times!

Sometimes I think that today's generation of students is emotionally abandoned by our culture which seems to be indifferent to their welfare. Whatever sells is offered to them: sex, attitude, questionable heroes, drugs, rockers and rappers whose artificial lamentations express an angst hardly earned. Our children are not stupid. They are looking for something with substance. They will listen and learn from teachers who are authentic, that is, who will tell them, within appropriate boundaries, the truth of who they are.

With the backing and assistance of two of my principals, the aforementioned Dr. Jaffe and then Dr. Gloria Rakovic, I began to do what I could about this time to bring students together from different nations and cultures to understand each other and to do what we could to raise awareness about hungry children everywhere. We also developed many projects to raise money to feed children. It would be a decades long adventure for me. I would meet extraordinary people and, most memorably, exceptional teenagers who helped me over the years raise a million dollars to alleviate hunger.

With the backing of the Westport Schools, I was allowed to bring students to other countries, including the USSR, Japan, China, and Vietnam to give talks about hunger and development, and to create new friends in places that have had an edgy relationship with the U.S.A. I wanted children whose parents or grandparents might have once been enemies to discover the essential goodness in others.

Paul Newman, the legendary actor, financed three of these adventures through Newman's Own. His support brings to mind what a "lucky boy" I have been over the years to have had so many exceptional people who supported me in my quest to fill babies' bellies. Elie Wiesel, as I have mentioned, brought the eminence of his Nobel Peace Prize to support me. I've had university presidents, senators, and congressmen support the work that my students and I did around the world.

When it was next to impossible to work through the difficulties of creating a peace and development conference in Hanoi, the Vietnamese ambassador to the U.S. intervened to make it happen. My alma mater, Iona College, has been instrumental, as has been St. John's University, without whose help I could not have developed the peace conference in Viet Nam.

We helped locally (yes, there are hungry people in Westport, too), state-wide by starting The Week to End Hunger in Connecticut for several years with over 195 schools participating in their own communities by raising clothing and food-stuffs. At Christmas time, we visited the elderly in nursing homes and brought them small gifts that we solicited from local businesses.

Nationally, too, with a project for migrant children. We raised so much money with this one that I asked the receiving organization to have one of its lawyers meet with me to sign a document assuring the Youth Ending Hunger group that the money would go exclusively for food for the children of migrant workers in the south.

We were, too, instrumental in developing "The Balloon Launch to End Hunger" in America. And, too, internationally, we sent thousands of oral rehydration packets to children in Africa, as well as solar heaters for cooking. We opened a small children's park with swings in Hanoi, and collected teddy bears for institutionalized children in Moscow, as well as winter coats for the elderly in the same city. And a water well in Sanda Wadjiri, Cameroon, Africa, with the help of Tim Hartman who was in the Peace Corps there. Tim was in my first "Youth Ending Hunger" group, and is now the head of the Peace Corps in Botswana, Africa. I am so proud of him that my heart swells.

I stopped smoking, an 18 year habit, during that period. I could now say to begin talks that I was making around the world: "I don't drink, I don't smoke, I don't take drugs. So you are now listening to one of the world's most boring men."

Most recently, I have given talks on a variety of topics, including "Living a Balanced Personal and Professional Life" at the new military academy in Pristina, Kosovo, and "The Journey From Ordinary to Extraordinary" and "Bedside Manners From a Patient's Point of View" in Amman and Irbid, Jordan where I also clowned at Syrian refugee camps with Patch Adams. There is a wonderful new group of young doctors in Jordan that has started an organization called "The Human Doctor Project," whose goal is to upgrade the treatment of patients so that the art of being human plays as big a part in the treatment of patients as the science of medicine. They are some of the most extraordinary people, mostly Muslim, that I have ever known. We continue to connect daily on FaceBook.

In all, I've had the good fortune to speak at many places in America, as well as at peace, education, and development forums in the U.S.S.R., Guatemala, Japan, China, Ukraine, Vietnam, Iran, Cuba, Haiti, Jordan, Kosovo, North Korea, and Canada.

I have always been influenced by a passage in the Book of Hasidem that talks about what makes meaning for us. For me, it was the impulse I first felt in high school to be a teacher, and then the good luck to have great teachers along with great educational opportunities, having five earned degrees, including a doctorate in education.

In the Book, it says that in the end we will not be asked "Why were you not Moses, the Savior?" Rather, we each might be asked why we were not ourselves. In my case, I might be asked, "Why were you not Gerard Brooker, the teacher?" I feel certain that I have tried to lead my life so that I can answer, "I was."

Now came the really tough part of my life. While I was making progress working at feeding the hungry, one mouth at a time, so to speak, I was slowly coming to the low point of my life, one day at a time: my divorce.

As much as Marcia and I tried, we failed. I think in the old days what was going on with us was called "irreconcilable differences," a catch-all phrase that accurately described our lives.

I moved out early that fall, taking a tiny one bedroom apartment about five miles away from where we lived in Newtown. We called it a *separation*, but I knew it was the *end*. We had done all the trying that we could.

I asked each of the children to meet with me separately before I moved out.

I wanted them to know that they were not at fault, and that I would continue to love them, and would continue to see them, that I wasn't far away.

As I talked with each one of them, I thought my heart would break. "What have I done to them?" I kept asking myself. I felt like a complete failure. I walked around as if I was numb, empty of meaning and motive. I slept on the floor in my new bedroom, and used a sheet to cover the window in the bedroom. I couldn't bear going to that apartment after school, so I often bought the New York Times, only because it was big and would take time to read. I would go to a nearby MacDonald's, buy some crappy food, find a booth and read, every page of it, 'til it got dark before going back to the empty apartment which was truly empty, empty of furniture and the trappings of life, as well as being empty in spirit.

I was so empty and ridden with guilt that I sometimes would teach while grasping an AA medallion in my hand. There is a saying etched on the medallion: *God, grant me the serenity to accept the things I cannot change, the courage to change the things I can, and the wisdom to know the difference.* I would grasp the medal so hard in the palm of my hand that I think the words could be read on my skin.

Those first few months of not living with my family were the hardest of my life.

I missed them all. Kevin, David, Suz, Jay. Often times when I would think of them I changed the formula for taking life a day at a time. I would take it an hour at a time, sometimes a minute at a time, often a second at a time. I found that when I took it a second at a time, I would be in what is called "now," and when I did that the angst would mostly go away. I guess it's what is called being in the now.

A consolation during that time was when I would pick up little Jay, about six years old, every second weekend to stay with me. By that time, I was sober and before that he was too young to connect with my odd drinking behaviors. It was the one thing for a good while that even excited me, looking forward to that every other weekend that he was with me. On the other side of that coin was the heartbreak I would feel when I took him home. Each time, it would take me three days to feel normal again. I'd miss playing games with him, teaching him how to play baseball, going to movies, eating junk for dinners, wrestling.

I remember so well the day when we were waiting on line at the supermarket. He tugged at my pants leg. "What's up, Buddy?" I asked. "I love you, Daddy," he answered.

As simple as that, "I love you, Daddy." Simple words, true. Yet at that time when I was feeling so down on myself they meant all the world to me.

As time went by, my relationship with Jay was always a great consolation to me.

We liked to wrestle, until the day when he put one of my front teeth through my lip. It bled quite a bit. Poor Jay! He was shaken. I knew our wrestling days were over, as was my catching his pitching on the local ball field. I was a pretty good catcher in college, but he was getting stronger, his dad older and his fast ball faster. "Jay," I told him, "you're gonna have to get another catcher."

As he grew older, he began to have his own friends and, as is natural, he didn't come to live with me every two weeks, yet I still saw more of him than the rest of my children. My daughter, Suzanne, was older when her mom and I divorced, so she did not come regularly to my apartment, yet I saw more of her than I did the boys who, I am quite sure, blamed the divorce on me. I always knew that it takes two to tango, but it takes a certain maturity to accept that.

I was learning a lot about myself during this time of my life, mostly what it takes to love others. It was a slow process for me, as I was still emotionally not up to par. There was the New York City kid still in me, too much macho, too many guarded poses to keep from getting hurt. I was learning that it takes commitment to love another, to accept what is human in others, the virtues and the warts.

In time, I began to date some, yet none ever lasted more than a date or two. I never dated for the sake of dating. Once the initial attraction wore off, mostly after a single date or two, I would say my good byes and move on. I don't know if it's a good thing or not, but I always set the bar high for a relationship. Too, I think as I've said, that I was born with the template in my genes of the perfect woman. If I was lucky enough to come across her path, I would be blessed just to know her. If I was *especially* blessed, she would be attracted to me also.

I have been blessed three times in my life to meet the template. One of them is my wife, Sheila, whom I knew years before when she was a student in my creative writing class at Kings Park High School. I didn't connect with her then, she was just another student, a talented one, though. Her writing was honest and thoughtful.

It was about ten years after her graduation when I was invited to a class reunion. She was there. I remember that when she came to chat with her friend, with whom I was talking, I was awed by her presence, dressed in bangles and beads.

She was a flower girl who was involved in a protest. Put this into the equation: I was a kind of "square," a guy with a crew-cut and long side-burns, kinda conservative at the time, and here she was all dressed up in the garb that meant "freedom, here I am." I might have said Hi, and she was gone, and I never thought of her again.

Until three years later when I had my own reunion with that class. You see, I had taught them George Orwell's book "1984" and thought it would be a good idea if each of the students wrote their predictions about what they thought life would be like in the U.S. in 1984, thirteen years later. I got a magnum-sized bottle, had the predictions put inside the bottle in which the chair of the science department created a vacuum before sealing the opening. The father of one of the students was an engineer and he drew a map to guide us to the location of the bottle which we buried under the school football field. In the spring of 1984 I called up one of the students named Dominic to ask him to get the map from the school safe, and to call each of the students listed from the class of 1971, telling them the date and time for the reunion at Sunken Meadow State Park near the water in Kings Park. They were asked to bring their spouses and children, food and drinks. I asked Dominic, too, to get permission from the high school authorities to dig up the magnum bottle from under the football field. They were most gracious.

The turnout was huge. What I remember most from the day was that when Sheila walked into the picnic, I gave her a kiss on the cheek, which I didn't do to the others, and said, "Hi, Sheila Moore." I remembered her name and spoke three words to her, more, I think than I had during the entire time she was in my class.

I asked the students to sit in a circle. Using a microphone, I told each one of them the wonderful things I remembered from our days together. I did not speak one negative word.

The day went fast, too fast. As it got dark, I realized that Sheila and I were talking together, the only ones left! I asked her if she'd like to go to a diner with me, last of the big spenders, to have dinner. We had a wonderful evening. Our conversation was filled with aliveness. She was smart, had a great sense of humor, a pretty face, a wondrous smile. I knew right away that this would not be a one or two dates before *adios, amiga*.

That is, unless she didn't feel the same way.

I held my breath and called her the following Monday morning. "Hey, I've been thinking about you," I said. "I've been thinking about you," she answered. "How about if I drive out there Saturday night unless, of course, you have something else going on?"

"Sure, come on," she answered, enthusiastically.

It was 230 mile round-trip to her apartment, longer than I had ever gone to date someone. I would make it many times before we got married. She set a strange mood when I got there for our first date. I realized that she was interrogating me, making sure I wasn't some guy messing with her head about getting a divorce. I admired her, but not at that moment. It was frustrating to be questioned.

My first reaction was, *I've got to get out of here.* So, I thought I would change the focus of the conversation. "You know, I think I'm in a serious mood, and you might need a few laughs. I think it was a mistake for me to come here tonight. I'm probably not the kind of guy you'd want to date. I'm really too serious."

I will always remember her answer. "If I wanted a few laughs tonight, I'd have gone to a comedy club." A perfect answer, I thought. So, we kept our date. I don't remember what we did, but I do remember that we talked a lot.

Just about every Friday I would drive to her place and stay over the weekend. We had a favorite Chinese restaurant which burned down a few months later, one of three "favorite" restaurants of ours that burned down. We figured that we were a jinx on restaurants, so we never again thought of any as our "favorite."

When my divorce came through, we moved in together in a condo apartment in Brookfield, a few miles north of Danbury. Sheila's daughter, Jessica, by a previous marriage, was thirteen at the time and, of course, lived with us. She and I had a rocky beginning, but we learned over time not only to accept each other, but to love each other.

She is married now, to Jamie, one of the best and funniest men I have ever known.

It took me almost three years to ask Sheila to marry me. I was always certain that I loved her, but I was scared to marry again. It was always difficult for me to understand why my marriage to Marcia didn't work. We were both good people who wanted the best for our children. I think it was that my best for them was not her best, and hers not mine.

One of the marriage counselors we saw said it the best, I think: "If the children lived with either one of you only, there would have been little trouble in the marriage." As it was, they were getting mixed signals about many aspects of their behavior.

It wasn't as if I turned into a wise man when I met Sheila. Of course we have differences of opinion about this and that, but we know how to handle these differences.

I remember one day sitting on the stairs, head down, inside our apartment about three weeks before our marriage. "Whatcha thinking about?" she asked.

"I am so scared to get married again. I was a failure once, and I'm scared that I might fail again." She told me that she was scared, too.

"I've got an idea," I said. "Suppose that every time something is bothering one of us about the other, the one bothered says, 'We need to talk'".

She thought it a good idea. I remember the first time she said the magic words.

I kind of dreaded hearing them. I sat down to listen. "What's up?" I asked.

"Do you know that you are a very talkative person in the mornings and I am not.

"You follow me around yacking away about this 'n that while I am trying to get ready for work." I was a bit sad to hear this, as the news was stunning to me. I've always thought of myself as a private person who only talked when I had something relevant to say.

Not so with her. I began to realize that I liked spinning ideas off of her to see what she thought. And that I was making a surrogate mom in the kitchen out of her, asking many questions, something I've always liked to do.

You see, I think it is the unspoken word that causes marital problems. If one of the spouses has a problem with the other and doesn't express it, it then builds up. It is more than a scientific principal that a buildup will seek an exit, or maybe explode.

Same thing with humans. The problem or problems unexpressed will build up. The outlet will more than likely be about something or another that has little or nothing to do with the original problem. If this is continued and compounded over time, and problems are not expressed, the loving atmosphere that attracted the couple can gradually disappear. Viola! A divorce.

I have a poem in one of my books that expresses both my joy and my fear of falling in love with Sheila. We were at a beach on Long Island waiting for a concert to begin a few miles away. She seemed so happy that she began to dance in the sand by herself. Oh, I was so in love with her. I called the poem,

Falling in Love

She dances in a dress worn
out from looking good.
Spins in a slow-motion softness
on the beach aware only of the
stolen looks I take that today
have me puffed out feeling good

as a giddy kid.

She has just told me that she
loves me. My spirit is a wiggling
top that spins endlessly
as I watch in awe
feeling the joy
dreading the pain.

I used to keep a note book in which I would put the names of anyone I thought loved me. At one point, I had two names in the book, my son Jay and my daughter Suzanne. After Sheila told me that she loved me, I had three. I could hardly believe that someone so extraordinary could love me. I asked her one night to give me 10 reasons why she loved me. I think she said, "You are kind, generous, reliable . . . ." Then she stopped. "Can't think of any more right now, but I know there are more reasons." I was OK with that, but I didn't know how much I was annoying her with the question until I asked her again. "Look," she said, "I'm not playing your game. I'm not giving reasons. I just know I love you. Period."

Her answer gave me an extraordinary insight into myself, into loving and being loved by another. I wanted her to tell me about myself, how wonderful I was, that I had achieved, that I was becoming a man of consequence. As if being loved was some kind of reward for a good resume. She taught me that being loved by someone was not receiving a notarized affidavit that I was worthy. That somehow the essence of why anyone loves another is that he or she is simply loveable, that the mystery of him or her has been discovered and is found desirable. I no longer question it.

I cannot help that I analyze. I know that I have discovered the wonder of her. I know, too, that I tend to count the ways that she is pretty, generous, helpful, smart, independent and strong.

It seems as if every day of my life with her I learn something. She is independent, a trait I find most admirable, as I do not like to be unduly pressed upon. We are not joined at the hip, and she trusts me to take trips around the world, sometimes alone, sometimes with groups, sometimes with my Marine buddy, John Collier, sometimes creating conferences or speaking at venues half-way across the world. We even agreed to incorporate my desire to help the helpless into our wedding ceremony.

I find it annoying when I travel alone that people ask me, "Where is your wife?" as if it is obligatory for me to be accompanied. I remember when I was getting ready to go on a trip to the Arctic aboard a former Russian research vessel renamed The Peregrine.

Before I left I told Sheila how annoying it was to be asked this question. "I'm going to say something outrageous to the next person who asks me."

My chance came halfway through the Arctic itinerary at dinner. There were six of us seated at a table when the woman to my left asked me The Question. A silence came over the group, I guess because others were interested in my answer. I paused to maximize the thrust of my answer. "She's a drunken bitch," I said, "who embarrasses me when I travel with her."

A silence came over the group, as I think they believed me. I was now embarrassed. I humorously slapped myself on the cheek, explaining that it was just a joke. No one laughed. As I sometimes go over the line trying to be the funny man,

I added, "She works. Some one has to pay for my trips." Again, not a titter of laughter.

When I later told this story to Sheila, she told me that I ought to keep my day job!

She does in fact join me on many of my trips. We've been to thirteen islands in the Caribbean over the years, and to many places in western Europe, as well as to the Galapagos and Africa.

My first international trip came soon after we were married on April 11, 1987. I had gotten involved with an anti-hunger group called The Hunger Project, and wanted to do something specific to help a bit to end hunger. I wrote a letter to the USSR-USA Society in Moscow, asking them if I could meet with them in Moscow to discuss a joint project between Soviet and American students to raise money for hungry children. I received a letter from Valery Chibisenkov, the Secretary General of the USSR-USA Society telling me that he would be delighted.

I was extremely excited, nervous and scared that my first big trip was into the lion's den. Remember, 1987 was still at the height of the Cold War. And I must tell you that I drank the cool aide about Russia, the Evil Empire. However, what I found was the same thing I have found in all my subsequent trips: good people who wanted most in life to be left without fear for their children. How loving they were of their children. They were not living their lives so they could seize the moment to A-bomb the U.S. In fact, the students at a high school in Moscow told me that they feared going to bed because they had been told by *their* government that the Americans would A-bomb them while they were sleeping.

Sheila has always encouraged me to realize my dreams. She has always empowered me by giving me the space to feed hungry children, whether it was somewhere in America or places around the globe.

And so we did a project with Russia. The Russians put on a music concert with celebrities, and we did "The Balloon Launch to End Hunger," with bio-degradable balloons in 16 states. Together we raised thousands of dollars. We gave our money to buy oral rehydration packets for children in Ecuador, and the Russians gave theirs to the International Red Cross to use in Ethiopia.

I went back a second time to the Soviet Union a year later, this time bringing students from age 10 to 20 to give talks about world hunger. We carefully distributed among us the informational handouts we brought with us, as we were a bit scared that the authorities at the Moscow airport would confiscate the material. The USSR was known at the time to be secretive, especially not inclined to give out information that put them in a poor light, as some of the information did. In fact, they didn't even search us and never seemed to be bothered by the facts.

It is somewhat difficult to give talks about peace, especially for teen-agers.

Hunger was an easier entry to peace than peace per se. Our journey was a huge success, as we were graciously received everywhere. I've always thought that young people were better spokespeople than older folks. Perhaps audiences find them more believable, more authentic than their elders who might have many agendas.

Here is an introductory speech I gave to Soviet teens on that trip:

"Thank you for inviting us here today. We come with a sincere desire that Soviet and American students will work together for peace by helping to solve world hunger.

"When I was in Moscow last year and spoke with Mr. Valery Chibisenkov of the Friendship Society and he in turn talked with your principal, Mrs. Kudryavtseva, about the possibility of your putting on a concert for world hunger, he asked me what American students thought about the future. I told him that I thought they were pessimistic. He said to me "Doomsday, Doomsday!" I still remember his words. I want to thank everyone here today for not sitting in resignation about the possibilities for the future. Too many young people are resigned to thinking that the future will be terrible. We are not resigned. I congratulate you and I acknowledge you for hearing us asking you to be our partners so that together we can help bring peace to the world.

And together we can help put an end to the 26,000 children under the age of five who die each day on this planet. Together we are a powerful force."

I ended by using a few Russian words I had learned. "On behalf of all Americans who would want to say this to you: *ya lyublyu vas*" (I love you).

Over the years, I would take three more trips to Russia after the breakup of the USSR. But more about that later.

At this time, I began to take many seminars with a company called Landmark Education. Each of them lasted for 10 weeks, 3 hours each week. They focused on the many aspects of each of our lives: health, personal appearance, the use of money, our romantic and sex lives, etc. They were extremely enlightening to me, and many of its principles remain as a part of my life. I keep it close, for example, that I am responsible for almost everything in my life excluding, of course, what are called acts of God. In this way, I am accountable and do not blame others for my behavior.

I wanted so much to learn about myself in so many ways. Q: Why was I so careless with words? A: Probably because that was the way I was brought up – New York feisty. Q: Why did I wear my hair so long that you could hardly see my face?

A: Because I didn't want anyone to really know me and I was shy about my appearance.

Q: Why was I broke a lot? A: Because I had no training in how to handle money. Etc.

All of these seminars helped me in many way. Just to give a few examples, let me tell you how I measure my words now so well that I can even express my anger, something I could never do in the past when I would either blow up with anger or suck it up, to blow later at some lesser matter.

I wear my hair now in a pony tail, so everyone can see my face. I handle money well now. I own our home and I have enough money to spare so that I can buy presents for my loved ones without having to look at my checkbook to see if I have enough in it.

In fact, I have sometimes helped students financially go to school here in the U.S., in addition to, of course, my own children and grandchildren, as well as a couple of foreign students in China and Vietnam. Do you know that it costs less than two thousand U.S. dollars per year for room, board and tuition in both China and Vietnam?

It took me a long while to realize that it is a good thing to have money. As I come from poverty, I had to learn to not be ashamed when I had money. In some weird way I thought having money compromised my past, something I do not ever want to do. It is *my* past, and *my* parents who did the best they could in spite of daunting obstacles.

I might have said this before that my dad had to quit school in the 3rd grade to help support his parents, that he had back-breaking jobs for menial money. Sure, he had his faults. He drank too much and he smoked too much, three packs a day! He wielded a heavy hand, yet we were never without food, and sometimes treats, as when he would bring home a dozen steaks for Rit, my mom, to cook to specifications. And he would work several jobs at Christmas times so we each had gifts under the tree on Christmas morning. Now, there's a man!

As for mom, she quit school after 6th grade. I never knew why. Quite frankly, I'm not even sure if she ever learned to read. Yet, she did her job. She always cooked a very nice dinner for us all, kept a clean house, and got us shoes and clothing, albeit not always the best clothing nor the most appropriate. She kept after us to do our school–work, and made sure we didn't miss a day of school. Although I never liked it, she gave us responsibilities around the house, and arranged a visit from a doctor who in those days would come to your home, carrying the typical black bag, to diagnose and prescribe. I remember how the insurance man would come to receive weekly payments, I think a quarter, on a policy to cover funerals. He had a little black book in which he would check off the payments.

I loved when I got sick. She kept me home and in bed, fed me soup, got me The New York Daily News to read, and coloring books with crayons to keep me occupied. She was always at her best and most caring when I was sick.

One of the things that money has enabled me to do in my marriage to Sheila is to seek what I guess are called discretionary experiences. I have always wondered, for example, if each of us has lived a different lifetime or many lifetimes. So, I decided to do what is called *past life regressions*. I took six hours of this, three one day, three the next week, under the guidance of a licensed psychologist at his office in upstate Connecticut.

The experience is kind of strange. I was asked to take off my shoes and sit in a plush chair. He asked me if I was comfortable. "No," I said, "my feet are cold."

He got me a blanket to cover my feet and we began the journey that would last for the next three hours.

I always thought that I am so strong-willed that I could never be hypnotized by anyone. Well, under the guidance of the past life regressionist, I hypnotized myself!

Would you believe it – I hypnotized myself. I knew it had happened when I couldn't open my eyes which felt as if they were glued closed.

Let me simply tell you how this all went down. Some of it seems strange, some almost beyond belief. I don't know if I even believe in it myself. But, in all, it was entertaining and highly imaginative, which tinkled my fanciful imagination. You be the judge for yourself.

I took myself to what the psychologist called the 3rd level of reality where I was asked to create and describe a perfect setting for myself, a kind of heaven on earth, so to speak. My house, as I remember, was kind of a ginger-bread small cape-codish type, set in a lush, yet friendly, woods. It was from this spot that I discovered my past lives.

The first one that I remember took place about two hundred years ago, on a tropical island, as in French Polynesia which is probably the closest place on earth to a mythical Paradise. I was being groomed on this island to become the king when my old father would die. Yet, each day, I would paddle a canoe across the lagoon to a small island to see the woman I loved. I would always set the canoe in the sand about a hundred yards away from where she would be waiting for me. I loved her dearly and was always in a state of infatuation with her – her kindness, her joy at being alive and engaged with her life. She was always interested in me and what I was doing with my life. She would ask me many questions about life on my island, a much bigger and populated place.

Our meetings were always very romantic. In the dream sequence I would get out of the little bark canoe and run to her in slow motion, as if in a movie, while she stood waiting for me. As I got closer and closer to her, I would begin to see her beautiful face and lovely body. I sometimes would embarrass her when I could not stop staring at her face. "Why are you staring at me?" she would say, or "Stop looking at me!" Her face was not the classic magazine cover face which, in real life, I never liked as each one seems like the next without individuality. My dream girl's face had character and the parts so complemented each other that I could hardly take it all in. Looking at her was as if trying to look at the sun.

As I ran to her, I always got excited both in mind and body and then, as I would hug her tenderly and she would kiss me passionately as we stood on the white sand of this desolate beach, she let me pull the two strands at the neck of the soft garment she wore so that when the knot opened the light cloth would slowly fall from her shoulders and drop onto the sand, revealing her naked body to me. We coupled on the garment, often several times, before letting the heat of the sun bring us back to the reality in the dream. We held each other and talked, but I could never bring myself to tell her that I was being groomed to be the king, and it was in the tradition of the island for the elders to choose my bride from the village.

The story went on. We continued these liaisons for several years until my father died and I was anointed king. I snuck away a few times after that to see my true love, but when I married the choice of the elders I would never be allowed see her again. When it was discovered that I was still visiting her, they took away my canoe. I never had a chance to say goodbye.

I was a good king and a good husband. My bride delivered many children to her people, I think nineteen. I lived for many years. A day never went by, though, that I didn't think about my true love on the beach. Her name was Sheila!

I remember, too, the past life I lived as Laka, a Lakota Indian that was a part of the Sioux in the Dakotas. I was a young buck doing the normal things a young buck does, you know, hunting, fishing, making war, when the tribal council, which included two women, told me that I was no longer to do these things, but to take a year to find out about the legacy of the tribe and to then to pass it on to the children. I was to become a teacher!

I was happy with this as I did not like killing people or animals. So, I spent a year asking lots of questions, mostly to the older men and women, to discover our history. I also spent time with the wives of the children, and that was to become my downfall, a fatal one as it turned out. Over time I began to be bored in my role as teacher. When the men were off on hunting or in war parties, I began to spend my time making love to the wives left behind.

Soon enough, word of this got around and one of the jealous husbands speared me through my lower left shoulder. I lingered for three day before I died. The buck who killed me was put on trial and was found guilty, and executed. I don't know if I really believed any of this, but one thing about the experience resonated. After each session, the psychologist would telephone me to debrief me, so to speak, to compare my recollections with his taping my vocal responses during each of the sessions. He asked me after the "Laka" one if I have any marks on my left shoulder. I do have one, a kind of dark brown birth mark. He asked me if I ever have any pain there. "Yes, I do periodically, a sort of swift stinging pain." Could it be the remnant of the stabbing?

I used to think, also, that Indian women were not allowed to be on the tribal councils, yet I discovered in my research after the experience that women are on the Lakota councils!

Another of the memorable past lives I discovered took place in the 15th century.

My name was Gesu Maria, a young man ordered by the Medici to be the Pope's banker.

I did not like this work because I was convinced that the Pope was a thief, that much of his wealth was ill-gotten and I had no respect for his hypocrisy, a bad man putting up a good moral face. I despised his hypocrisy and told my superiors that I did not want to serve as his banker.

I was told to do it or else I would be shunned from the life of wealth to which I had become accustomed. I caved and kept on serving the Pope's acquisitive ways. For the rest of that life-time I felt the guilt and shame of turning my back on what I knew was wrong. I was a coward.

Several years after these sessions, my wife and I took a trip to Italy. As we were walking about in Rome one day, we came across a medium sized church that had a special large room where many members of the Medici are buried under horizontal grave stones. It was with a gasp that we saw a stone marked *GESU MARIA!*

Several of the other past lives were explored, but briefly. One was back in Italy where I was attacked by wild dogs in an alleyway while bystanders stood by and cheered while the dogs killed me. I remember the experience left me feeling in my contemporary life very sad and disappointed that others would not only watch another human get mauled to death but would clap for the animals that did the killing.

Apparently, I got my revenge in the woods of Belgium. I don't remember the exact time period but it must have been a long time ago. I say this because I was dressed in rags around my waist with no other clothing. My only means of defense was a sharp, dagger-like piece of wood I always had tucked in the rags. Wherever it was, the climate must have been warm. I was always alone and the only other living creatures were, you guessed it, wild dogs. But, I had an understanding with them: as long as they would not bother me, I would never bother them.

As I walked through the woods on one summer day, one of the dogs attacked me.

The dog was quite large with ferocious looking teeth. As he leaped for my head, I quickly grabbed him by the throat with both hands. He continued to scratch me with his paws as I squeezed his throat harder and harder. I was more angry and strong at this betrayal than I have ever been, whether in a regression or in real time. His eyes began to pop out of his head and then he went limp as I stuck my wooden dagger through his throat. All I remember is what I said to the dead dog: "I told you guys never to fuck with me."

The last of these regressions took place in pre-historic times. I was about thirteen years old and lived with my mother in a cave. She would leave my alone in the cave every day when she left to hunt for food for the two of us. It was dangerous outside the cave and she never allowed me to leave it except now and then when we might step outside together, I guess to get some sunshine.

Needless to say, I loved her. She was the only human I ever knew. She was my life-line. There was never anything for me to do when she left to hunt. Imagine a world without friends, without TV, telephones, books, or any means of communication with others. There were no others, only my mom and me. So I slept a lot.

One day she did not return home. I waited and waited and waited. For many days.

As time passed and she did not come back to me, I figured she had been killed, perhaps by some wild beast, perhaps by another human. I never saw another, but she had told me about them.

As I did not want to live without her, I decided to lie down with my head on a rock as a pillow and go to sleep. There was no food to be had, so I decided to die there on the rock. No food, no water. No mom! And so the regression ended with my committing a slow form of suicide.

As you can see, these past lives, if they are true, are not very uplifting stories.

Perhaps it is why I have always had a sort of depressed psyche. It is a rare event that my inner being overtly dances with joy. My usual dance is informed by a certain seriousness of mind. It is not that I don't experience joy, as many parts of my life lend a buoyancy to my soul, especially the love of my dear ones, sitting down to a good meal with someone I love to be with, sharing their triumphs and losses. Sometimes my professional accomplishments give me joy, yet usually for a short time only.

Sheila and I lived in a condo for about eleven years. We are both private people, and it became increasingly difficult for us to stay there. We had a neighbor to the left that Shiela left a note. In a funny turn of events, the guy moved out about a week later. To this day, I don't know exactly what she said in that note!

Another neighbor across from us had a cat. The cat, whom we later named Oreo, began to stay at our apartment where Sheila regularly fed him. When we decided to move, Sheila told me that she was having a moral debate going on: should we take Oreo with us when we left the condo, or leave him behind? Did we have any right to take him away? Or was that stealing?

She wanted to know what I thought. "Let's take him," I said without hesitation.

"He is better off with us. We treat him with affection, you brush and feed him. You love him. It's a simple matter, no conflict. Let's take him."

And we did. He was a great and loyal cat to us. He is the only cat I ever saw "swim" on the top of snow after a blizzard as he came home to eat. He was an unusual combination of indoor-outdoor cat. Even in the cold of winter, he liked to sleep on the front porch of our home in a box-nest that Sheila lined with covers to keep him warm.

Sometimes at night he would get in the box and wait for her to wrap the blankets around his tiny body to keep him snuggy-warm for the night. In the morning, she'd open the door for him to come in the house and eat.

He would sometimes stay away for a few days before coming home again for good food and affection. Sometimes, his fur would be covered with goo, probably from hanging out with horses, we think, that would lick him. At other times he would be wet with rain or some kind of rusty water. He would be filled with delight as Sheila would wipe him clean and dry with paper towels.

One day he staggered home and collapsed. Sheila held him in her arms for several hours before he died. I made a small coffin for him. Several relatives and friends came to take a look at this great cat Oreo before we buried him in the back yard.

Over time, we repaired or renewed every defect in our home in Bethel – new doors, new windows, new roof, new rugs, and more. We did this by handling one major project each year, so that, finally, it was and is the way we want.

It has been thirty-five years now since I had my last drink. I continue to go to AA meetings, not because I am tempted to drink. I am lucky that way. I go because I have seen that when other men go out and drink again it is usually because they have stopped going to meetings. In fact, alcohol *to me* is like an enemy who is constantly lifting weights, doing pushups, as they say, waiting to do me in at the first chance it gets. I know that if I even think that I can have just one drink, that the one drink will turn quickly to two, and then three, on and on. That for an alcoholic there is never enough. Never. I am convinced that I simply must stay away from all the circumstances that might lead me to drink or trick me into having a drink. I know that alcohol appeals to both my weaknesses and to the strengths of my mind. I will always remember going to a party when I was about one year sober. A friend yelled, "What can I get you to drink?" I answered, "Just get me a coke, no ice."

He yelled back, "Come on now, you only live once!" That made so much sense to me because it appealed to my intellect. It is true: we each live only once (except if you really believe in past lives). So, I thought about the truth of it and a little voice said, "He's right, have a drink, you only live once so what the hell!"

I quickly demanded my coke once again, and that was the end of the temptation. I learned much about alcohol from that experience. How easy it would be to start the journey from sobriety to active alcoholism, how quickly my life would go down the toilet bowl.

I have learned to relate to my alcoholism by keeping six degrees of separation from it. If I see a photo of a martini, for example, in a slick magazine, I immediately turn the page; if I am watching a movie on TV that has its actors enjoying drinks together, I change the channel; if friends who drink alcohol are coming over to the house, let's say for dinner, I ask them to bring their own bottle of booze and take home with them whatever might be left over. As I mentioned before, I am lucky that it does not bother me to see others drink. Even with that luck, though, I am careful when I am around alcohol, especially when it is free-flowing at weddings. I tie a red rubber band around my drink, and sometimes even ask Sheila to take a sip before I swig.

She is an integral part of my support system. Although she is not an alcoholic, she does not drink in our home. The only time I have seen her drink is at weddings, and then not always. I am deeply grateful that she shows respect for me and my vulnerability with alcohol.

My 25 years as chairman of the English department were sometimes rocky, sometimes smooth. There were as many as 28 people in the department, each of them highly credentialed, articulate and opinionated. Sometimes I think that I lasted for so long was because I was more credentialed, just as articulate, and with as many opinions as they had. In a word, I could keep up with them, and I had an ability to negotiate the space between them and my superiors. Sometimes, the five principals to whom I answered over the years thought the ways I collegially ran the department worked well for them as principal and their greater responsibilities.

We always took care of our side of the street. That is, we took care of our internal business with an extraordinary integrity by lightly monitoring each other, not in an intrusive way but in a way that assured each other that we were a first-rate department.

We shared responsibility by coordinating our efforts to keep our courses refreshed, by introducing new courses that would keep our students up with the times. For example, we realized at some point that most of our literature courses featured the works of dead white men. And so we studied the matter as a department, pondered our own recommendations, made decisions, introduced new courses while refreshing the tried and true standard ones with other racial and ethnic writers. This is one example of how we always kept moving forward. Various department members regularly gave formal presentations to their own colleagues. We had Christmas parties and end of the year parties. Oh, we had our disputes and we had our disagreements. But we were consummate professionals. I would sometimes begin department meetings by asking, "How is the best English department in the United States today?" They would not respond as that would not be cool. But, I could tell that they appreciated the question.

I am enormously grateful to the Westport Schools and community for having allowed me to lead the department for so many years. And I am grateful to the many teachers of excellence for appreciating my collegial ways. I know that sometimes they wanted me to be more commanding, yet withal they allowed me to be myself. We remained steady through many principals and many different boards of education and superintendents. Of them all, Claire Gold was my favorite superintendent because she was fair and mostly left me alone, something I always appreciated. Dr. Marvin Jaffe was my favorite principal because he acknowledged my skills and was a down-to-earth, a no frills kind of guy, a street-smart kind of guy who reminded me of the rough and tumble of my boyhood. He, too, respected my ways.

Except for the one year when I was appointed interim curriculum headmaster, I taught classes, mostly Readings and Writings in Contemporary Literature; a research paper course; and Shakseapeare (I never liked the medieval language and the themes were nearly always beyond teen-age understanding, and depressing). I sometimes taught a speech course. Ironic, wouldn't you say, for a guy who stuttered in high school?

I loved teaching the Staples H.S. kids, as they were motivated students. In fact, we regularly sent 98% of our students to some form or another of higher education, numbers that would make any private school proud.

During this period, I started a club called Youth Ending Hunger at school. It literally changed my life. It's mission to feed the hungry, the students who made it work and the constant support of the administration gave me a sense of involvement with a reality bigger than anything I had ever been involved with. The energy of YEH's student members allowed us to help hungry kids in our own town (Yes, Westport has a soup kitchen), kids across Connecticut, the U.S., and hungry babies in many foreign countries.

Perhaps I shouldn't be saying this aloud, but there were times when I was allowed to take time off with pay to run a mission in a far-off land such as the U.S.S.R., China, and Japan, e.g., and to bring students with me.

I remember Dr. Jaffe telling me a story about a buddy from Pennsylvania who was also a high school principal watching him sign off papers to allow me to go to Guatemala to help open a home for abandoned baby girls. The friend couldn't believe what he was seeing. "My school wouldn't allow me to do that in a million years," he said.

It was a time, almost two decades, of growth and maturity for me. I sometimes would look at me back in the day, and ask myself "Who was that guy?" I was growing as a husband who was no longer being so interested in being right about things. I was truly learning how to really love others. That is not to say that I no longer had faults or character defects. It was just that I knew spiritual growth was taking place. I was growing as a grandfather and doing the work of friendship. I was even starting "project Uncle–dom," my way of saying that I began to take an interest in being an uncle. It amazes me now that these things took me so long to actualize.

Indeed, I am a lucky boy in so many ways. I have wonderful friends. For the past four or five years I have lunch each Tuesday with a group of men. I call them the Knights Of The Oval Table, as they are royalty to me. They are men of consequence, cartoonists for the New Yorker and Playboy, a Sunday newspaper cartoonist, professors, an engineer who helped put up the Hubbel Spacecraft, and several novelists. They are mostly older than I and they are still making contributions. I find their conversations uplifting.

I play in an Over 50 basketball group twice a week. It is a game that I have always loved. I am only adequate at it, but I still love it, and I enjoy the camaraderie.

I have been playing it less lately, as a bad back will not allow me to go "all-out." And for many years I played 3rd base in an Over 40 men's softball league. It was only when a ball I once gobbled up at 3rd went under my glove that I began to realize that my reflexes were not what they once were. A friend of mine moved with his wife to a community in New Jersey that has an over 60 softball league. They play about 40 games each summer, sometimes travelling by bus. I loved the game, but not that much!

Indeed, I was learning how to take care of myself and to love others, so that now I think loving others is our highest calling, the essence of what it means to be a fulfilled human being. All the honors and recognition mean little when compared to the greatest achievement of all, the ability to honor and respect others, all others. Indeed, the ability to love I stayed at Staples for 27 years. It was a good place for me, a place where I learned a lot about excellence and what it means to be a professional. I think we all want to sign our signature in life. By that I mean we want that others know that we were here, and would like to have that acknowledged, if only in a small way. It is why we like birthday parties. It is why I love Staples High School.

What I will always remember about my time teaching and administrating in Westport are the students I taught, some of whom I still hear from today, and the opportunities the system gave to me to do what I could for kids, especially hungry ones, and in pursuing these opportunities the chance to travel the world.

CHAPTER 6

My Travels

Sand dunes of Mongolia

She came out of the jungle in Peru to drink my coffee

**Talking with young medical
doctors in Jordan**

Teaching in Haiti

**With a koala bear
in Australia**

**With officer corps
in Kosovo**

WHEN I WAS a child living in Astoria, Queens, I would often look out the window of our apartment onto the hustle and bustle of the streets below. I remember most the movement. It was as if everyone had somewhere to go. And where did I have to go? Nowhere, I thought.

I always liked it when it rained, as the wetness of it all, in my mind, leveled the playing field, so that even the ones who were going somewhere might not be able to get there. I do remember when I was about thirteen years old and had only once gone anywhere (to New Jersey with my dad) outside my little box that I declared to myself, "Someday I am going to see the world."

And I have! I did, though, have a problem getting started, as I was afraid of heights. I bet the first dozen or so times I flew I was so filled with fear that I always sat straight up in my seat, thinking that if I relaxed the plane would spin and go straight down to crash and explode into a million pieces.

It was at this point that I made a decision that would affect the rest of my life by helping me to mature in the ways that I wanted: I would confront my fears, every one of them, in planes and out of planes, that is, in every area of my life.

There was a lot to confront, both inside my psyche and outside in the world. It is well known in the psycho-emotional studies about alcoholics that one of the main, if not *the* main, driving forces motivating those afflicted with this addiction is fear. Raw, naked fear. Alcohol can relax the fear(s) for a awhile so that one feels what is presumed to be normal. Being under the influence, for example, can allow a guy to feel at ease around women, socializing, making love, making a speech, mingling at a party, going up in an airplane!

One of the ways I confronted my fear of heights was to bail out of airplanes.

I did this twice. The first time I did a static line jump from about 4000 feet. I was so afraid that the jump became an out-of-body experience I did by sheer will power! I was directed to step out of the plane and stand on a piece of metal about two feet long, while holding on to the side of the plane's door. I was to look straight up at a dot the the size and color of a clown nose, then fall over backwards into the void! The static line worked immediately, my chute opened and I was on my way towards conquering the fear of planes.

At least I thought so until several years later I began (see, "overly pensive") to wonder if I could do it again, though on a grander scale. So I decided on a trip to California to see my friend John Collier, who is a sky-jumper, to do a tandem skydive from 12,500 feet. As you can tell, I survived again. After we landed, I kept on yelling,

"I did it, I did it, I did it," and the jump-master kept yelling, "Get off me, get off me, get off me."

Now that I know I can do it, I no longer have the need to prove it to myself again.

As of this minute as I write, I have flown over 900,000 miles, visited over 100 counties and every continent.

Those who study the addiction to alcohol conclude that its cause is genetic or by temperament. I believe that my etiology is both. My parents were alcoholics, so it's probably in my genetic makeup. Of all my brothers and sisters only one, Eileen, by my reckoning, has been blessed with a natural sobriety.

My temperament is edgy, overly pensive, overly sensitive to touch and sound, and bears the marks, as I have said, of beatings and sadistic treatment in my formative years. As I look back on my life, I see that I drank to stem the tsunamis of fear that often washed over my psyche.

By facing my many fears, I have grown and developed in different areas of my life. I was once a young man who stuttered. Now I give talks in the mid-east to young doctors in Jordan and to literature professors and new cadets in the Balkans in Kosovo. I have given eulogies, and inspirational talks here and there in the United States. I have been on regional, national and international television. I give book talks. I've given speeches in the USSR,

Japan, China, Vietnam, Cuba, Guatemala, Ukraine, Iran, Haiti, Russia, Jordan, Kosovo and Canada.

I was once a man who was afraid of being around people I considered to be above my social class. Facing my fears about this, I now talk with ayatollahs, mayors, academy award and Nobel Prize winners, and university presidents. In a word, doctors, lawyers and Indian chiefs!

From a guy who wasn't sure if he had what it takes to get ahead academically, I have five earned degrees, including a doctorate in education from a leading university.

This, too, by facing my fears head on. It only seemed natural to be involved in the world. So I decided to speak in public, even though it frightened me. I was committed to that. Even if my legs wobbled, my voice crackled, my mouth dried up I was going to speak in public!

I am spelling this out in some detail for several reasons. I hope one of them is not to show off, although I think there probably is a measure of that here. Mostly, though, I want to acknowledge the mystery of it all, the mystery of our lives. Why was I lucky to be born with a good brain? I did not earn it. I did nothing to claim it. Yet, it is mine to respect, to develop. Why have I always, to this minute, been so intense in my attempts to enhance it? Why do I love being in the world so much that I want to see it all? To write about it? I don't know, and I no longer look for the answers.

My commitment to see it all began the year Sheila and I got married. I had gotten very involved with an organization called *Est*. There were some things I didn't like about it. I thought they were too harsh, prescriptive, and unrelenting in the ways they tried to take their clients to human fulfillment. I profited, though, from some of the ways they inculcated self-discipline and personal vision as ways to break through an ordinary life to an extraordinary one, or from change to transformation. I now give presentations on these topics.

The *Est* teachings began to spark in me a desire I had for many years to feed the hungry, especially children. It would grieve me to tears when I would see them being hungry. Before I got involved with *Est*, I thought it was out of my reach to do anything about it except to give money now and then to charities that purportedly used the money for that purpose. I thought it would take more talent than I had and more will than I had to do anything directly about it. But, after the awakening of my deep depression in 1984, along with marrying Sheila and taking the *Est* training, I was ready to step over the line and try to initiate something myself. So I wrote to the Secretary General of he USSR- USA Society, as I have explained earlier, to see if together we could get school children in our two countries to raise funds for the hungry. I told him that I would be willing to fly to Moscow to see him.

He agreed, and so I flew to Moscow in the winter of 1987, quite soon after I came back from my very first trip abroad, to Guatemala. I was very nervous and frightened about going so far in an airplane, and into the Cold War enemy. I remember waiting on line at JFK to board the plane. I was cold and alone and feeling out of sorts that I left my bride home alone. She seemed troubled that I would be going to one of the Evil Empires to negotiate a deal which at the time might have been Pollyannaish.

I looked for a nice face, as I often do when I am abroad and need of help, mostly about public transportation, and found two! A young couple recently married. They were gracious and entered into a conversation with me. Suddenly, I no longer felt alone.

I was lucky that the group I was with had a great guide, a Russian woman whose name I no longer remember. I immediately told her that I was trying to set up a meeting with Chibisenkov, asked her to call him for me and gave his telephone number to her.

For three days she told me each morning that she could not contact him. Suddenly, on the fourth morning at breakfast she told me that he wanted to see me at his office in one hour.

There I was, unshaven, in soiled dungarees, and his office was about 45 minutes away! She gave me his address in Russian Cyrillic, told me that getting cab at this time of morning, rush hour, would be difficult. "Go into the road, hold up a pack of

American cigarettes, and you will get a cab right away. The people will yell at you. Just get in fast, give the driver the address and tell him to go. It will cost you about 25 rubles each way."

I did what she told me, held up the cigarettes and voila! (vualya) I was in a cab.

I really couldn't believe what was happening to me. I was in Moscow watching the way the working class was busy getting to their jobs, seeing the loving ways of the grandmas on the streets with their grandchildren, people cleaning the snow off the streets. And I was on my way to meet a Russian big shot. I suddenly realized that I had drunk the cool–aide about the Russians. They weren't spending their days trying to figure out ways to defeat America. They were simply going about their business as human beings, just like the ordinary folks back home. It was the moment that I first began to question propaganda, both ours and others.

Then an unexpected thing happened. The taxi driver wanted 125 rubles for the ride. Perhaps it is growing up in New York that I can never abide by being treated unjustly. It seems to bring out the macho in me. "I've been told by my Russian guide that it should be about 25 rubles, not 125." I was sure he knew what I was saying to him, as my arms and body language was saying *NO*. He insisted on the 125. I saw a policeman standing about 15 feet from us. "Do you see that policeman over there? If you insist on charging me 125 rubles, I will get out of this cab and tell him that you are cheating me, and you will have to deal with him. He will put you in jail!"

To be sure, he knew what I was saying. He smiled and took 25 rubles. I gave him a one kopek (about a penny) tip, my way of telling him how pissed off I was.

I arrived on time for my meeting with Chibisenkov who was a Fancy Dan, and his translator. I immediately thought that this was not going to go well, as he was dressed with expensive suit and tie, while I was unshaved, with back yard clothing. I was never so wrong in my life. He was warm and gracious to me as I explained my vision to him about having Russian and American school children do a joint project to feed the hungry. It was a good time to make this kind of proposal as things were thawing between the U.S. and the U.S.S.R. He wanted to know what American students thought about the world. I told him that they were afraid that the U.S. and the U.S.S.R. might go to war.

I remember how grim he was when he responded, "Doomsday, Doomsday." I was beginning to realize that our lives were not about a doomsday waiting to happen. We could do something about that way of thinking He seemed anxious and most pleased to enter the partnership. He gave the relevant contact information to me, a Nina Kudreavstava, the principal of School No. 23 in Moscow, who would then become my partner. The only part of my overture to him that he did not agree on was my suggestion to give whatever monies raised on both sides to the American Red Cross to send oral rehydration packets, which replace the water, salt and potassium lost by the body through diarrhea, to Ecuador. He wanted Russian money to be sent to Ethiopia for similar use. That was fine with me.

He told me that the request would have to go through channels, but that it would have his strong personal backing. I felt really good about that, and I also felt that I could trust his word. I remember walking down the street after I left him. It was snowing, and I just wanted to walk in it, something I have always loved doing.

I passed some kind of boundary that day walking in the snow. Snow and rain have always been the great emotional equalizer for me, since my earliest years. No one was immune. I seemed to have crossed a boundary, my own little boundary, that separated the Russians and Americans in the Cold War. I was re-shaping my image of the Soviet Union, and of the possibilities for peace. For the first time, I realized that each of us could make a difference. I had actually thrown my little pebble into the big pond. I felt as if I was not walking. I was floating. I could really help hungry kids!

I found out later that a musical group from Ethiopia came to Moscow School No. 23, to thank the Russians for putting on, not one, but two concerts to raise money for the children of Ethiopia.

I found out because the concert was on Radio Moscow which sent a copy to me.

Eventually, Mrs. Kudreavstava and I became partners in fighting hunger. She would organize a concert at her school, and I arranged with Dr. Jaffe to allow the Staples student body to participate in The Balloon Launch to End Hunger, along with about 18 other schools in Connecticut. We did it on the last period on a Friday. Our school band played, those who bought balloons at $2 each sat with the rest of the students on a hill, a few notables in town made speeches, and on a 10-9 . . . . 0 countdown the balloons were released. It was a joyful moment watching the bio-degradable red balloons, about 400 of them, float across the sky!

The next year, I took 15 students from around Connecticut with me to Moscow to give talks about world hunger and give out materials, translated into Cyrillic (Russian).

We were concerned that the materials, not being kind to members of the Soviet Union, now breaking up, might be confiscated, so we divided them up evenly in each of our bags. It was a false alarm on our part, as they allowed us to give out materials and students to sign up to join an American organization, The Hunger Project, geared up to end world hunger.

The talks went well, but the behavior of our students was embarrassing. I had spent considerable time organizing home stays with Soviet families in Moscow. I found out that the mothers in the home-stays were disappointed that our students were regularly going to McDonalds to eat. Russian moms love to cook and they are very good at it, so it was a sort of slap in the face for our students to skip their dinners. Keep in mind that the McDonalds in Moscow was the first one in the Soviet Union. The lines were long and it was the place to be. One of the young Russian girls said it was her life-time ambition to eat at McDonalds!

It was annoying enough to me that our students were being rude. But that was not the worst of their behavior. Near the end of our trip, I organized a dinner for our students to take their host students to a dinner at a nice restaurant. In the middle of the entrée, a food fight broke out! I stood up and yelled, "Stop it, Stop it!" I was totally embarrassed.

Here we were doing a tour to speak with Soviet students about world hunger and they were throwing food at each other! It was the ultimate in disrespect for our mission.

About a year later I arranged for 14 Russian students, 2 teachers and Nina Kudreavsteva to come to Westport to live in our town with host families. Although it was "sold" to the town on my part as a way for our respective students to talk about world hunger and what might be done about it, that aspect of the exchange drew second place to visits to New York City and shopping for clothing and cosmetics that were not available in Moscow.

I remember, too, the day that we took the Russians to the local supermarket.

Having been to Moscow several times and knowing how scarce food was, I asked them to gather together to let us Americans know what they thought of the experience. The boys were especially expressive. One of them had a hard time holding back tears as he spoke quite articulately about the abundance of food available. "It is overwhelming," he said. Another boy was angry that the store was so big and had so many products for it customers. "It is disgraceful," he said. In some ways, I regret having taken them to the store. Perhaps we were showing off, and it became a political matter with them.

It was a very hard time for the young Russians. A few were willing to express their fears about their homeland. The Soviet Union was breaking up, Gorbachev was resigning, Yeltsin was gaining power and they did not know what to expect for themselves and their families. Uncertainty was in the air for them, worse than it was here after the elections of 2016. A few of them admitted that they had ambivalent feelings about leaving America.

I went back to Russian in March of 1990 with a group of 24 high school students and teachers to deliver food and clothing to the elderly poor of Moscow, and teddy bears to children in a home for what was then called "retarded" children. It was one of the most memorable experiences of my life.

You see, our school was, in addition to being one of the top schools in the U.S., a regional special education center, a place where students from around the area could come to have their special education needs met. Some of them were placed in classes with the regular school population. When I taught, they were often placed in my class up to, I think, seven students only because they each had an "IEP" (Independent Education Program) which the teacher had to fulfill in edition to teaching the regular students. I liked teaching them and always had a special place in my heart for them.

Now and then, too, when I needed a break from my desk I would walk to the Special Ed section of the school to mingle with the kids and their wonderful teachers.

I had an idea that I ran by these teachers: would their students be interested in buying teddy bears from the stores in Westport so that I could bring them to Moscow with me and give them to their counterparts? They got back to me, and told me that their students were very excited to be a part of this. I told them that I would tape the giving of the gifts for them to see the good thing thy had done.

Well, it turned out that they bought every teddy bear in every store in Westport!

I managed to get their gifts and the many boxes of clothing for the elderly to Sheremetyevo International Airport in Moscow by way of Bob Mccauley, the founder and chief executive of AmeriCares. At the time, he asked me not to tell anyone of his generosity because many companies were asking him to do similar shipments and he was turning them down. He is dead now, so I guess it's okay to acknowledge him, a great man. His motto, "Make Things Happen," resonated.

The big boxes of teddy bears arrived on time, although the clothing did not until weeks after we came home. I set up a meeting, though, with the home for the Russian children so that our students could present the bears to their kids.

We had to first decide with the Russian teachers how to give out the teddy bears. It might be problematical because some of the bears were tiny and some huge.

We anticipated that the big ones would be the prizes and might create some bad feelings with the kids who got the small bears. We decided to direct the kids to put their hand into the boxes while closing their eyes. Whatever they grasped they were to pull it up, no second chances, that was it.

Well, we were wrong. There was no fussing. Each of they children did as they were asked. Indeed, they got different sized bears, yet their reaction to what they received was the same in all cases. Imagine a six-year old closing her eyes, reaching her hand into a box and pulling out a teddy bear, big or small. And now the magic. The goodness, the graciousness, the surprise, the fragility as she took the teddy bear in her arms, closed her eyes and rocked the bear back and forth as if it was her baby!

That is what each of the children did. Sometimes the phrase *there wasn't a dry eye in the house* is accurate. That afternoon in Moscow it was.

I remember that day. Yes, indeed. You see, although I had worked for over two decades to raise money to feed hungry children, I never saw them sitting down to a meal and eating the food. It was always a matter of trusting the organizations we gave the money to that they would feed the children. That day in Moscow I saw with my own eyes the efficacy of the work the Staples members of YEH, Youth Ending Hunger, had committed themselves to. I was certain that we had given joy to children, had shown their world to be a little brighter that day than usual. We saw the smiles, the joy, as they rocked the bears back and forth. It touches me deeply that perhaps some of these children, now grown-ups, rock themselves to sleep with the same teddy bears.

I was happy, too, that our own special education students felt the joy of giving, even if the children they gave to were half-way around the world. I imagine that their parents, too, were proud of their children for what they had done.

After we got back, we had a celebratory party with the kids who had bought the bears. We had soda and cookies, laughter and tears as I played the video twice of the day we gave the bears. I could see the satisfaction and excitement on the faces of these lovely and generous kids. These are images that will stay with me forever.

I believe that every person is a leavening agent, if they choose to be one. Just a little leaven in a loaf of bread eventually turns the loaf into more than itself. I think each of us can be a stand for possibility. Once possible, then do-able. On the day that do-able turns to done – Ah, that is the day!

I spent a little time on this trip trying to find a church that would cooperate with a local American organization that was selling guardian angel pins to raise money to buy bibles for Russians who had been denied access to the Scripture. In time, I found one that was willing to receive Russian language Bibles bought from these angel pin funds. It was a bit of a small risk to set this up, but I never felt endangered. Openness (Glasnost) was setting in and I think they just looked the other way.

Again, in 1992, I took Staples students, most of them members of my Youth Ending Hunger club, back to Moscow. These were great times to be there, watching the political, economic, social and cultural changes taking place before their very eyes. When their own children come home from school one day telling them that they had studied the breakup of the Soviet Union in class, they could say, "I know, I was there."

Our kids went to English speaking classes every day at School No. 23. I taught classes to English speaking Russian students in American literature, specifically popular short stories. Our dean was a technical adviser for a play that the Russian kids put on in English, and one of our social studies staff taught economics classes. A famous lawyer for the American Civil Liberties Union, Emanuel Margolis, asked if he could come with us, as he was fascinated with the breakup of the Soviet Union. He volunteered to teach invaluable classes to the Russians and Americans about the developing beginnings of a democracy. Our Staples students, too, gave classes to their counterparts about American life and culture, teen-age life, television and sports in America. I am so proud of them all.

I remember, too, the Bolshoi Ballet and the Moscow circus that was far more creative than any American circus I had ever seen. We went to St. Petersburg on the Red Star Express, sitting up in our wooden seats for the 8 hours overnight trip. We visited the Leningrad cemetery where 900,000 Russians who died during the siege of the city, now St. Petersburg, surrounded by the Germans, are buried, sometimes in groups of 20,000. The somber music coming from loudspeakers in the cemetery trees made a deep impression on us all. To top it off, we spent time at the Hermitage museum, huge and extraordinary, where in 1917 the Bolsheviks stormed the Czar's palace to start the Russian Revolution.

I was asked while on one of these trips to speak with the Education Committee of The Moscow City Council. I told them that we were pleased that they were developing laws which would enable students to become enlightened in the ways of democracy that would empower them to practice their rights as citizens and people. I had the sense that were listening carefully.

Interestingly, and as a side-note, I was always treated with high regard wherever I went in the world just because I am an American. Given the results of the 2016 elections, I pray that this respect continues for Americans.

Our students learned so much about Russia during that trip. The scarcity of food and clothing. The high prices. Even at the largest clothing store in Moscow, Gums Department Store, what clothes they had were strewn on wooden shelves. The long lines for vodka, the medication de jour. The meat stores where they sold "half-cooked meat," at lower prices than the fresh meat. Half-cooked meant that the rotting parts were cooked a bit before sale rather than cutting them off to be thrown away. Black market cigarettes and rubles for sale on street corners. Broken elevators in the high apartments. Long lines out side the exits from the beautiful Moscow Metro with people selling everything you can imagine, even their own bodies.

One day, one of our students had a very painful ear ache. When we took her to the hospital, the resident doctor examined her ear, then asked her to lie on a table, the bad ear up. He went to a drawer and took out a bottle of vodka. He poured some of it into her bad ear, and told her to lie still until he came back. It worked!

I guess this is about as good a way as any to drop the curtain on my visits to the old USSR and the new Russia.

XXX

Just before these trips to Russia, I became involved with a group called Heal the Children, a remarkable organization that flew children from Guatemala with cleft palate and cleft lip malformations that occur during pregnancy to New Milford, Connecticut.

After volunteer surgeons from the area operated on the children, the healing process took many months while local host families acted in place of their parents back in Guatemala, sometimes for up to a year. Other volunteers then accompanied the children back to their parents.

This is where I came in, in 1987, when I was asked to escort one of the children to Guatemala. He had been away from his family for a year. In return, Heal the Children arranged for me to stay with a well-to-do family for a week. It would be a week of great adventures for me, a time when I saw real poverty and what it could do to people.

I remember arriving in Guatemala, the capital city. Michael's entire family and friends were there to greet him in the lobby of the airport. I walked him by the hand to them. They engulfed him with yowls of joy, screams of love! The poor guy didn't know what to make of it all. He was about three years old, and

I wasn't sure if, at that age and being away for so long, he even remembered his parents. I just stood back in awe watching this great demonstration of love. And then he was gone from my life.

It is hard to unreel the thread of that week, as so many things happened to me.

Each day there was a limo and driver to take me wherever I wanted to go when I was not otherwise involved in trying to give a women's organization called "Advash" a boost in opening a home for abandoned baby girls in the city. At this time of my life, I was becoming more and more involved with women's issues, so the chance to help these female babies who were left on the steps of Catholic churches was appealing to me.

What struck me hard about the villa I lived in and the available limo was the striking difference I was living every day between the rich and the poor. It was an eye–opener. Every morning when I got up there was a plentiful breakfast waiting for me, along with an old man who was always at the table waiting for me so he could talk to me.

I never understood him, too fast for me though I had taken a few years of Spanish in school. I would mimic his facial features. I just kept on eating. When he smiled, I smiled.

When he frowned, I frowned. He seemed happy with the arrangement. I spent a few of my days exploring the city, but mostly going to hospitals where I would visit the children's wards. These experiences left an indelible mark on my soul.

As the poor had to boil water in pots to get hot water, sometimes the little children would knock over the pots on themselves. So there were many burn victims. And there were many with bloated stomachs who were kicked there and beaten by drunken fathers.

We were asked one day by our Guatemalan leader representing Heal the Children if we would each chip in $10.00 and go to the barrio with her to give the money to a man whose young daughter had just died. He would use the money to bury her. To get to his tin hut we had to walk down a slimy path in the dark. The insides of the tin shack were covered by news-papers. His 13 year old daughter was breast-feeding her baby. The room was lit by a candle.

We stayed a while before walking up to our small bus. "Where do they go to the bathroom?" I asked. The guide laughed. "You're walking in it," she said.

A few days later we learned that the dead girl's father took the money we gave to him to bury her and went on a drunken bender with the money. I felt sorry for him, for her, for us all.

I didn't realize when I was there in 1987 that the civil war would still go on for another nine years, mostly in the countryside where I spent a few days at a home in the jungle for children whose parents had been murdered by the military, the killing arm that supported the dictatorial government which was backed by the U.S. government.

Many peasants who supported the insurgency were "disappeared," perhaps 50,000 of them many, as I have mentioned, in the countryside. Unknown to me, some were being "disappeared" when I was there! I was so naïve that I didn't even know that I didn't know.

I was asked one day by a woman named Angelina if I wanted to go with her to a place about 150 miles north on the Pan American Highway to the Rio Dulce (the Sweet River) to the Gulf of Honduras where she had set up the aforementioned home in the jungle for about 30 young children whose parents had been executed, some in cruel ways.

It was a trip that changed my world. We were pulled over on the highway by a group of men who commanded us to get out of the car so they could fumigate the inside against us bringing germs into their area. As soon as they started to spray this orange agent into the car, I remembered that we had four puppies in the back. I opened the back door to get them out of there while the men spraying the car angrily yelled at me. Thus, our first adventure!

We then found ourselves for about the next 50 miles behind a truck-load of young soldiers, each carrying a rifle across his chest. Every time I looked at them, so close in front of us, I became apprehensive. Driving behind a truck full of armed soldiers on a pitch-black highway in a foreign country known for a terrorist government backed by the military will do that!

I finally gave Angelina a reason for stopping, anywhere I hoped, to get from behind the guns. I had to urinate, so she stopped at a roadside bar that seemed like something out of a Clint Eastwood movie.

"Be sure to buy a beer or a soda before you leave," she told me. "Don't talk to anyone. Drink and leave." I had to walk on a long wooden footpath that ran along the length of the bar to enter. I swear if I had on cowboy boots with spurs, I would have been Clint's doppelganger. When I entered the bar, every face turned to look at me, the gringo.

I asked for a Coca Cola, hoping that it was sold here. It was. I paid for it and asked the bartender for the whereabouts of the bathroom, a word I knew from several years of Spanish in High School. "Banjo? Banjo?" I asked with raised hands and a rising cadence in my voice. I did my duty, drank only a bit of the Coke so I wouldn't have to reprise this experience. "Adios, Amigo," I whispered and got out of there as fast as I could.

Accompanied by several young men, we spent most of a day going up the Rio Dulce in a narrow dugout propelled by a strong outboard engine. It rained on us for many hours, but fortunately we were covered by a canvas tarpaulin.

I must tell you that I am a bit afraid of dogs, having been bitten many times by them in my childhood. When we got to the dock at the home in the jungle which Angelina called "Casa Guatemala," we were greeted by a man and nine German shepherds running towards us from about 30 yards away. I will never forget that image of the big dogs running on the long wooden dock towards us, hoping against hope to greet their Angelina.

"Angelina," I nearly pleaded, "I am afraid of dogs." "Don't worry," she replied, "they will not harm you unless I say so." I stood rigidly still with my hands at my side as several of the dogs greeted me by jumping to my chest with their front paws.

I stayed away from them during my visit as much as I could. My hut was in the jungle about 50 yards from the nearest bathroom. I knew that the dogs roamed the compound at night, so I would pee in a soda bottle. I could see the headlines back in the U.S.: *Connecticut Teacher Bitten to Death by Dogs in Guatemala.*

The man from Bolivia was Angelina's boyfriend. He was a nice man, and often invited me to accompany him to shoot arrows into a nearby lake. I never asked him about anything personal, as I had a sense that I might be getting into something I didn't want to know about.

On my second day there, she asked me if I wanted to sit on the porch while she gave haircuts to each of the children. "Many of them do not need haircuts," she told me.

"I will use the excuse to ask each of the children about their parents who are now dead, executed by the military. I will translate. Do you want to do this?"

At the designated time, she met me on the porch where she proceeded with the haircuts. She first warned me not to touch or pet one of the German shepherds who was pregnant and very close to where I was sitting. "She doesn't like to be touched when she is expecting. She might attack you!" So I sat back to my introduction to the world of evil.

She was very good with the children, first engaging them in small talk, then asking each of them in turn what happened to their parents. I was shocked, as I listened to the translations from Angelina. In their unsophisticated ways they told her about their parents and their families who lived in the countryside, and in the hills of Guatemala where many of the insurgents lived or hid out in the supported huts of the ordinary people. It was one of the ways of the death squads to cruelly execute innocent people in order to scare others. It is estimated that 200,000 civilians were killed in the civil war, 50,000 of them "disappeared."

I had read a lot about evil in the world, but this was the first time I was even remotely near it. There was a part of me that wanted Angelina to stop, the same way as I wanted the survivors of the A-bomb drop in Hiroshima to stop when they told me their stories of August 6, 1945.

Most vividly, I remember the little boy who told her that a death squad tied his parents to chairs inside their hut while they took him outside as they poured gasoline on the hut and set it aflame while he was forced to watch them die.

When I went to bed that night in the jungle, I knew I was agitated which probably was responsible for the most frightening experience, real or imagined, I have ever had in my life. I've had a few nightmares in my life, but the one I had that night was beyond terror. In the dream, I had no context of why I was terrified. You see, in every dream or nightmare I had ever had there was a context. By that, I mean the dream was always grounded in a place, something I could see or feel or touch. Something to stand on.

It is hard to explain, but in this one there was nothing to see, feel or touch. No context at all. Only raw, naked fear. As much as I tried in the dream to place the fear, I could not.

This is what really scared me as there was nothing to be frightened of! Thankfully, I woke myself up, put my hand under the mosquito net over me to turn on the light bulb hanging loose from an electric line to my left.

And here was a tarantula, about as big as my hand, on the net just outside my face! An experience such as this would normally really frighten me. Yet, coming immediately after my unhinging nightmare, it did not seem scary, a piece of cake in the pantheon of fear. I simply flicked it off the net and watched it scamper off to safety.

In the morning, Angelina took me to a native village, about a 20 minute walk through a path in the jungle. I remember how primitive it was. When the women saw me coming they covered their bare breasts. Several small barques, I think they are called, like slim row boats, hewn out of trees and looking very old, stood on the shore of the lake.

Mostly, though, I remember a large hole in the ground which once served as a well that they showed me. They told me a story of a young native girl who recently died after drinking from this well. Guinea worms lived in the water imbibed by the girl. Once inside the human body, they come out the anus as well as plugging up the breathing system. She died from asphyxiation. I was stunned and later took this new knowledge back to my Youth Ending Hunger group as well as my classes in Readings and Writings in Contemporary Issues when we studied water conditions around the world. Needless to say, they were also stunned by the photos I showed to them, as well as being motivated to do what they could about access to clean water.

As I look back on that trip, I realize how grateful I am for the ways it took me to new places in my soul. I used to think that I had come from poverty. In light of what I saw in Guatemala, I no longer think that because I know now that it is a relative condition.

The day before I left, I had a chance to meet the Minister of Education, the first of many people of consequence I have been lucky enough to spend a bit of time with in my life, a teenager who once only wanting to see the world some day.

When I got home, I received a letter from one of the founders of the new home for abandoned baby girls in which she said, ". . . we consider you a part of our "ADVASH," the acronym for the new home.

XXX

My travels took on a certain "busyness" during that early period of visiting countries. Sheila and I honey-mooned in Hawaii, a most beautiful string of islands.

Most memorable for me was visiting the monument to the battleship Arizona where I and Sheila were so deeply moved that we missed our ferry boat ride back to Pearl.

And then we went to Ireland. As I was brought up "old school" about a man's role in a marriage, I thought I would establish myself as the protector of my woman.

As we were about to land at the airport in Shannon, I thought I would tell my bride how we would handle it if it were again attacked by terrorists as it had been a few weeks before.

"If we hear the sound of gunshots or explosives, I want you to fall with your face towards the ground, and I will cover you with my body." She looked at me with a kind of disbelieving grin. "Get real," she said.

We rented a car in which we frequently flirted with danger, as it took some getting used to driving on the left side of the roads in a driver's seat on the right side. The "roundabouts" were so difficult to negotiate that we once drove around one eight times before figuring how to safely get off! And the roads were dark at night.

It was not difficult, though, to negotiate our lives with the Irish people, warm, kind and generous. Kissing the Blarney Stone was a hoot. As we did this during the outbreak of the aids epidemic, we had second thoughts.

Some day we will go back.

XXX

After I got married to Sheila, the circumstances and context of my life began to radically change. I was becoming more involved with the world at the same time as wanting to fulfill my life's dream to see more of it. I also wanted my youngest son, Jay, to be more experienced with its affairs. So, in early 1989 I took him, when he was eleven years old, into New York City to participate in a rally against nuclear weapons.

I was very pleased as we chose to march with the Japanese contingent. You see, I had a long emotional history with the Japanese dating back to when the A-bomb was dropped on Hiroshima. I was a young boy when I heard the news. And when I did I was upset.

I don't know why or how someone so young could be upset when I knew from my ultra-patriotic father that they were the enemy, the enemy responsible for my older brother's crash off New Guinea in 1944.

When I learned that some 80,000 Japanese were killed by a single bomb, I was very upset at the horror of it all. Along my journey in life, I've had a few people tell me that I was a phony, that a kid couldn't possibly understand this. But, I did. I even told my playmates that whoever made this ought to be damned to hell. This wish of mine came to haunt me for a long time because I had been taught that God made everything, something I completely misunderstood. So I became haunted as the kid who condemned God!

In any case, I've had a life-time of being adamantly opposed to the decision by Truman to drop the bomb. I truly believe it was immoral. I've even in later life had academics try to wear me down about the efficacy of the decision and how it saved thousands of American lives that would have been lost if the A-bombing of Hiroshima and Nagasaki had not happened. Even the eminent General Douglas MacArthur told Truman that there probably would not have been more than 25,000 American casualties if we put boots on the ground in Japan. I remember once telling two World War II sophisticates, after two hours of heated discussions, that they could cite books and opinions about the matter from men of consequence about the decision, they could talk at me from here to eternity that it was a good decision, but that they would never change my mind. Never.

As Jay and I walked in the peace march, I realized that he was about the same age as I was when the bomb was dropped on Hiroshima. He began to notice that some of the Japanese men and women were disfigured, and asked me why.

I told him that they were survivors of the August 6th bombing, that they are called hibakusha, meaning "survivors of the A-bomb." He asked me more questions and seemed to be troubled. Perhaps it is true that the apple does not fall far from the tree.

One of the Japanese reporters covering the stories asked me if he might interview Jay for the Hiroshima Chugoku Shimbun newspaper. He eventually wrote the story about Jay and the rally. He also invited us to come to visit him in Japan.

I did not know it that day, but our meeting with the reporter would set me off on a journey with the Japanese that would change my life. You see, I went to Japan five times over the years, several times over six years to initiate and help organize the 1995 International Students Peace Summit.

It all started in a sort of casual way. I was, of course, very excited to be invited to Hiroshima, the place that had enlivened my soul so many years before. It seemed like a dream to be going there that summer. Jay was too young to go.

I asked the Japanese reporter if I would be allowed to place 1000 paper cranes made by the Youth Ending Hunger club at Staples at the Sadako Sasaki monument in Hiroshima. He told me that the Japanese would be delighted. Sadako was a national hero, a young girl who developed leukemia, the result of being caught in the blast years before. The nation had watched her health slowly ebb, during which time she used the labels from her medicine bottles to try to make 1000 paper cranes, the making of which is called *senbazuru*. According to Japanese legend, if anyone made 1000 paper cranes his/her wish would be granted. Sadako did not complete the required number before she died, but students across Japan made far more than the thousand which were then buried with her. There is a beautiful monument to her in the Peace Park where visitors from around the world place their paper cranes which are, too, a symbol of peace.

The reporter also set up a meeting for me with the new principal of the Hiroshima Jogakuin High School, a man well-known for his peace efforts. His *sensei*, that is a deeply respected teacher and principal, met with me. He wanted to thank me for bringing the paper cranes to Sadako's monument.

Something happened in the next minute or two which I had not planned. "Is there anything we can do for you?' he asked through a translator. I had a simple and unexpected impulse. "Yes," I answered, "would you held me set up an international peace conference here in 1995 to commemorate the 50th anniversary of the dropping of the atomic bomb?"

Without hesitation, he said he would be delighted to do that, and promptly introduced me to Mr. Shinichiro Kurose who would be taking his place as the new principal of the school who would later direct the Japanese efforts for our peace conference six years later.!

He also arranged a dinner for me with half a dozen peace activists who had been helpful in pressuring the local government who wanted to dredge the Motoyasugawa River of the remnants of the Aug. 6th explosion. Sometimes the Japanese do not want to recognize a painful past, and I suspect that draining the river would be a way for them to shut down the pain of that awful day. The peace activists, though, organized students across Japan to take action to keep the bottom of the river a repository of the relics blown into it by the force of the bomb – roof tiles blistered by the heat of the bomb, hotter than the sun; vases from living rooms; twisted pieces of metal from bridges blown apart, and on and on.

I knew about the river and its tributaries. I knew how thousands of Japanese threw themselves and their babies into the river to try to stop their bodies from burning, which it did not as practically every one who did this died, many by drowning. In fact, when I first arrived on the shinkansen, the high-speed train, from Tokyo, I put my bags in my hotel, asked where the Moto River was, then sped to see it, about ten minutes away.

When I got there, a found a set of steps leading to the water, where I knelt and prayed a Buddhist prayer that the 80,000 killed on that August day might rest in peace.

The peace activists were so excited to talk with me over dinner about their efforts against atomic weapons. They asked me if I wanted to go down to the river at eight in the morning with high school students to "fish" in the low tide for residue of the A-bomb drop. Of course, I said yes. Two of the men were so excited that they high-hurdled over the dinner table to make a few calls to set the morning into action. I was amazed. And very keyed-up as I realized how much this was making a difference to them, an America, their former enemy, trying to set up a students' peace conference in the city where we dropped The Bomb.

I was totally fatigued from the long flight to Japan, but I was being drawn into their commitment to peace. I was also hungry, as I was quickly learning about the Japanese diet, thin by our measures. I thought the small bits of food were the appetizers.

No, they were the meal! As they escorted me to my hotel and I fumbled with the bowing protocols before getting into the elevator, I knew I had to get something more to eat, so I got off at my floor, and waited in the hallway until I figured my new friends were gone.

I got back on the elevator so I might find somewhere to eat. And guess what I found?

Mcdonalds! After two cheeseburgers and a soda, I found my way back to the hotel and a much needed sleep before getting up to meet a dozen or so high school students who would help me dredge the low tide for remnants of the bombing. They gave me about a dozen blistered roof tiles, melted glass and an assortment of household artifacts. I saved one of the roof tiles for myself and gave the rest to high schools in Connecticut and California where I had friends I knew would appreciate them.

I spent a day at the Memorial Peace Park which is quite large and located at the epicenter of where the Bomb exploded a few thousand feet in the air, purposely calculated so as to cause the most damage by percussive wind, thermal heat and fire.

And, as we know now, radiation poisoning.

It is an exceptional park dedicated to the memory of August 6, 1945. The memorials are many and comprehensive, the museum extremely sad as it bears witness to the horrors of the day. It is criticized by Americans because it is slanted towards the Japanese point of view, though from my point of view it is unreasonable to expect anything different.

Several of the students and Kazuo Yabui, the reporter who interviewed Jay in New York City, escorted me to ring the Bell of

Peace. Ringing the bell was a memorable moment, one I was to replicate with Jay 20 years later. The bell is inscribed: "May it ring to all quarters of the earth to meet the ear of every man."

Over the next six years, many of us in each country worked very hard to raise funds, to gather support and to pick students from several schools in Connecticut and New York who would accompany us. The great actor an philanthropist, Paul Newman, gave me a most generous grant to pay for some of the conference expenses, including round-trip air fare for the Americans going to the conference. Elie Wiesel, the Nobel Peace Prize recipient, agreed to be on our board of advisors, as did several college and university presidents and noted educators.

My daughter, Suzanne, an art major and school teacher headed a group to oversee thematic works of art by elementary school students that we sent to Hiroshima for display at the conference. It was a big hit with the Japanese that children so young could produce art so powerful.

And so time went by, and all almost coordinated. I flew to Hiroshima during my school vacation in April to finalize arrangements. I wanted to do this on the telephone, but the Japanese are precise people and wanted me to go there to make sure we were on the same page.

Sometimes, cultural expectations are without substance as their insistence that I come to them in person was somewhat a waste of time. I remember addressing the Japanese conference committee, about 16 of them, in the faculty room at the Hiroshima Jogaquin School as they sat on plump couches. Within a few minutes, the room was filled with sleepy people. As the sound of 16 snorers echoing around the faculty room hit my ears, I realized what was happening. There was no one to turn to for help, so I simply continued to talk. I felt I might embarrass them if I started to shake a few. It was a sight one could see replicated in Japan as they do overwork themselves.

Yes, it was a waste of time, my time, not theirs, or so it would seem. As I discovered more and more of the Japanese way of doing things, it was not a waste of time. Going there was a courteous thing for me to do, and courtesy counts for much in the Land of the Rising Sun.

On my way back home, though, I did stop over on Okinawa for a few days. Battle sites have always been of great interest to me, as each of my brothers served in the armed forces. Bob in the navy, Wallace in the army and Kenny in the Marines.

It was easy to get around the large island by bus. There were lots of war sites to visit in a battle that lasted almost 3 months, and where 12,500 Americans died. Lots of Japanese memorials to see, pictures of their heroes to buy. Seeing these memorials gave me a unique opportunity to witness the other guy's point of view, to gather a more balanced point of view about war in general. To know that everyone, friend and foe, suffers. I had a chance to explore "The Cave of the Virgins," where high school girls were entombed. Caves where young Japanese men blew themselves up with hand grenades so thy could die for their emperor. And to sit on a bench surrounded by fresh grass, peace and flowers at Shuri Castle where thousands of young men, friend and foe, were killed in 1945. I could look out over the water near Naha, the capital, and see where we first learned about kamikaze planes. An indelible image of the battle of Okinawa kept popping into the picture-taking mechanism of my mind. One was of the little Okinawan boy, often in documentaries, about two years old, nude, his tiny body shaking with fear as a G.I. tried to give him some food.

XXX

And then finally, a few months later I, my colleagues, including my dear friend, Dr. Richard Elliott, without whom we would not have had the conference, and about ten students, were on a plane to Narita Airport in Tokyo, then another to Hiroshima Airport where we were met by conference representatives and a few reporters for a 30 mile bus ride.

Everyone was a so excited. In typical Japanese custom, a ceremony that was covered by television was planned at the bus terminal. Mr. Kurose made a welcoming speech, then each of the Japanese parents took his or her respective American student in their own cars to the home they would stay in for the next week. They had two days to settle in and get to know their wonderful new families while visiting a few sites in the city.

I remember with fondness meeting my family, the Uedas. How I got there is a story worth telling, as they are an extraordinary family. You see, I do not smoke, while most Japanese men do. So, I did not want to stay with a family that had a smoker. As none could be found, I was scheduled to stay in a hotel. Lo and behold, out of the blue I received a letter from a high school girl names Noriyo Ueda, inviting me to stay with her family. She acknowledged that her father smoked, but that he would smoke only in their small garden in the back. I demurred because I did not want to step on the customs of the Japanese family where the father ruled. Noriyo told me not to worry, that all would be OK. And it was. Mrs. Ueda drove me to their home where I was met by her husband's mother, her sons and Noriyo. A musician with the Beatles portfolio greeted me, along with a translator and several friends of the family. Plus a table filled with delicious hors d'oeuvres. I knew right away that it was going to be a wonderful week in Japan.

There was a bit of tension in the air as all waited for the arrival of Mr. Ueda, a prominent man in Hiroshima and the owner of many businesses, including the only golden Buddhist hearse in the city. He arrived about an hour after I did. When he opened the door to the big room where we were all partying, the musician stopped playing, and all grew silent. How would Mr. Ueda present himself to me? I must say that my heart skipped a beat or two.

He came into the room and did a curtsy bow to me! This, of course, I learned later, was typical of him – courteous, generous, funny. It was, to steal a famous phrase, the beginning of a beautiful friendship that has lasted to this day, some twenty-two years later.

I did give a gift of friendship to him that day, a beautiful engraved switch-blade knife. Yet, I can never thank him enough for his kindness to me on that visit to his home, and two more later. He always makes me feel wanted.

When the guests left, I gave gifts to the Uedas, and they filled me in on the routines of my stay. We would eat breakfasts and dinners together, including grandma with whom I became great friends. She told me one evening after I was there for a few days that she had been kind of depressed but since I had come to their home that she wanted to live again. It was, perhaps, the kindest thing anyone ever said to me in my life.

Each morning before we all sat down to eat, she would put her right foot next to my size 12. And each time her gesture would draw yowls of laughter. You see, she had had her feet bound as a child!

Back to the routines: the upstairs bathroom would be for my exclusive use; Mrs. Oeda would drive me to the conference center each day and then back to their house; every second day she would serve a Japanese style dinner and what did I like?, and on the other days an American dinner and what did I like? I was to put my dirty clothes at the bottom of the bed each day before leaving for the conference and they would be cleaned, pressed and packaged, to be found at the foot of my rented American-size bed when I got home, usually late afternoon.

Can it get any better than that? She would even clean my underpants, press them, and fold them before packaging them. I took one package home to show Sheila, saying, "I'd like you to start doing this for me." "Don't hold your breath," she responded.

Mrs. Ueda has a bachelor's and a master's degree, but her goal in life, she told me, was to be the link between the old and the new. I must tell you she did this with impeccable taste.

The conference began on the 3rd day. The auditorium of the Jogaquin High School was packed as Mayor Hiraoka made a stirring opening speech. Both Mr. Kurose and I addressed the gathering, including, guess who? Grandma Ueda, although I learned later that she did not feel well. I told her later how much I appreciated that she came.

Sadako Sasaki's mother taped an address to the students, as did Samantha Smith's mom.

Samantha was a young girl who was internationally famous as a peace advocate when she wrote a sweet letter to Yuri Andropov, the president of the USSR, asking for peace. She has since been killed, along with her dad, in a light airplane accident.

I clearly remember standing at the podium and thinking about the past. About the day after the A-bomb was dropped on Hiroshima, how horrified I was that this could be done to a city populated with families of innocent women and children. And here I was, 50 years later, speaking to an audience that included the grandchildren of survivors.

Each of the students from the various countries (and six continents) were assigned daily to a mixed group that would meet in a classroom. The topics included, of course, peace and hunger, as well as the environment and others worth exploring.

What was most pleasing to me was that the focus and end goal of the conference was for each student to identify a practical/ do-able project they could take away and work on. It didn't have to be a big project. Our intention was to allow each student to identify something that he/she could do, something that was possible. Each one could throw his/her pebble into the pond and watch it ripple out. We wanted them to empower themselves and others.

Our purpose was not to debate the past, but to plan for the future.

It was truly a week of fun, growth and excitement. I think it was the international involvement that I am most proud of, as it affected a lot of bright teen-agers on both sides of the Pacific. Who knows where their individual pebbles might have rippled out?

Besides, I have always thought that dropping the atomic bomb on Hiroshima and Nagasaki was a sin against children. Because of its transformational character, dropping it was, to me, the Second Original Sin. Just as the Original Sin changed the nature of man, dropping the Atomic Bomb is a sin because of its capacity to change the very nature of how the afflicted die. I felt fulfilled to be a part of awakening the sensibilities of the young about atomic bombs. The genie came out of the bottle on August 6, 1945 and we know now what it can do.

On the night of August 6, each of the students and their host families were invited to attend the annual ceremony at the Ota River branch of the Motoyasugawa River to float lanterns past the Atomic Dome. The candle in each lantern was to be lit, but only after each one was dedicated to someone especially related to the atomic bomb drop. It is a wonderful, even inspiring, sight to see the candles floating down the river towards the dome. I have a framed photo of the floating candles hanging in my study.

Mrs. Ueda handed me a Sharpie pen and asked me to write the name of the one to whom I would dedicate my lantern. I wrote: *To the loneliest man in Hiroshima on August 6, 1945*. And so floated the lantern.

I learned later that our last night in Hiroshima was spent in different ways by the Japanese families with their American students. The bonds of friendship had grown strong. Very strong. A few had dinner out, most had dinner in with their last Japanese home-cooked meal. The Uedas wanted to spend a quiet night with me, just talking, sharing memories. As usual, the entire family was present at dinner: mom, dad, grandma, Noriyo and her brothers.

As the Japanese are always polite, and sometimes unrevealing, I had to wonder sometimes what they really thought. So I asked them this question at dinner, thinking that I had earned their trust over the past week: "What do you really think of Americans?"

There was a long pause as they looked at each other, I guess wondering who would answer the question. Mrs. Ueda motioned that she would. She raised her right hand in the form of a pistol, and pulled the "trigger." She then put the barrel of the fake gun up to her mouth before blowing away the pretend smoke.

It wasn't rude, and it wasn't a message. She is too polite for that. Long before the outbreak of gun killings in America, she saw us as a nation of gunslingers. "No, not really," I responded. But, I felt like a liar because I had just recently done some research about guns in America. On average, there was slightly more than one gun per American at that time, 1995, in our country!

It is a cultural habit of the Japanese to wave goodbye until they can no longer actually see the departing person. I have experienced this sweet gesture many times, and it is symbolic to me of how hard it is for them to say goodbye.

You can imagine, then, how hard it was for everyone, especially the teen-agers, to say goodbye the next day. We all met at the high school where the Americans would be taken by bus to the airport for the flight home. I especially remember the tears. It was a wonder to me that the Japanese who seemed reluctant to show their feelings were now profusely crying. It was with a certain relief for me that we got on the bus after having said our last farewells. I didn't think I could ever say goodbye that many times again.

Lo and behold, a parade of cars was following us! And so we re-did the hugs and spilled the tears once again, as the bonding that had taken place was quite real. We boarded the plane, and as we looked out the window we could see the Japanese standing on the viewing balcony waving their *sayonaras*. I had a window seat and as we took off I could see them sadly waving goodbye until I could not see them anymore. The sight has left an indelible emotional mark on my soul.

I was to return there again in two years.

XXX

In the meanwhile, the Youth Ending Hunger group was raising funds to build a water well in Sanda Wadjiri, Cameroon, Africa, where one of the original members of YEH, Tim Hartman, was serving in the Peace Corps. I knew from my experience in Guatemala how important it is to have a real water well available, rather than just digging a hole in the ground that probably contained the guinea worm. Tim is now the Peace Corps Country Director in Botswana.

We also initiated during this time "The Week to End Hunger in Connecticut," a program we kept for several years. We wanted to have a school in every one of the state's 129 towns do something about hunger in their own town. The significant difference, we hoped, was that every dollar raised, every can of soup collected, every winter coat donated had to remain in the town where it was collected. In this way, each town could take pride in its efforts to help its own people. The overall effect would be a coalition of students giving leadership and direction to a most worthy effort, to feed and clothe the hungry and homeless.

Our governor at the time, Governor William O'Neill, cooperated by declaring the week of March 12, 1990, "The Week to End Hunger in Connecticut." In the first year of doing this, 44 schools participated, and in the second year 65. As a requirement for participating, a school had to agree to show a short film that we would provide that made the distinction between famine and chronic persistent hunger. And, they had to create a do-able project in their own community to alleviate hunger and or homelessness.

Over the years, thousands of students across the state participated with bake sales, shanty towns on the front lawn of their schools, soup kitchen work, student assemblies, food drives, adopting needy families, classroom presentations, hunger banquets, food baskets, etc.

We did this for 6 years before we ran out of steam and my availability was growing problematic. Not all the teachers in the English department, of which I was the Chair, agreed with some of my time taken from them!

XXX

Before I went back to Hiroshima again, I took an eye-opening trip to France to visit a few of the iconic battles of WW II. For the past fifteen years or so, I have been my own travel agent, mostly on my home computer. Back in the day, though, I used a travel agent who was very talented at what she did and always got me what I wanted.

"I want to go on a trip that will take me from D-Day on Omaha Beach to the historic battles that ended the war." And here's where her expertise came in: "And I'd like you to get me with a group of men who actually fought in these battles."

Within a week, she called me to say she had booked me with a group of about 30 veterans, many with their wives or grand-children, who were taking the exact trip I wanted! I would soon leave on a journey that would change my life. Until that time, I knew about war mainly through stories told bit by bit by my brothers who served. Now, I would be with these men 24/7 as they sometimes point out to me the exact place where they had experienced death and the stupidity of war whose mantra seems to be, "If we disagree, kill." I sometimes think that if there is a god, this God must look upon the earth in deep disappointment and wonder if there is a word that could express the self-righteous anger in man that prompts him to kill those with whom he disagrees.

The disrespect for the mystery and sanctity of life seems to me a sign that there might not be a God, for if there was one he might have ended life as we know it long ago.

I was about to get a deeper look at the hearts and minds of men at war as I got to know *these* men and why men go to war.

These were good men, really good men, and I would grapple with how that goodness in them had been compromised back when they were young, idealistic and gullible. I remember the evening at a small hotel in Port-en-Bessen before we were to visit Omaha Beach in the morning as I walked by myself on a golf course that overlooked the landing on that beach, and thought how the very bluffs I walked that night would have been bombarded from battleships a half century ago. And now it was a golf course!

Confusion and excitement set in that night before Omaha against the back-drop of our morning visit to the British cemetery at Bayeaux, the final resting place for thousands of British men of the Second Army who made the assault on Gold and Sword beaches. I was struck harder than ever at my disgust with war. In the British fashion, personal messages are engraved on each headstone. The parents of W.L Cross, killed on August 2, 1944, at the age of 20, let me repeat 20, wrote: "Life is eternal, love will remain, in God's own time we shall meet again." To another, age 19, "A loving son, only lent," and to yet another, "At the going down of the sun and in the morning we shall remember him." He was 21. I could only think of the prophetic words of President Roosevelt who said about the impending war, "Men's lives will be shaken by the violences of war."

I spent that night talking until 2 a.m. with a soldier who came in on the 3rd wave at Omaha Beach. He told me that his commanding office yelled at him to get onto the beach. When he turned to respond, the officer was standing upright but without a head!

He showed me the next morning where he remembered it happened. Such is the violence of war.

Another man, whose name I remember, for a reason, as Wendell, was spared death four times by my count by what seemed an inconsequential decision – sort of a road not taken. I later told him that "Doing a Wendell" might have been a substitute for getting lucky.

As I lay in bed that night trying to go to sleep, I wondered about the men waiting on the night of June 5th so long ago and what they might have been feeling and thinking.

I was trying to go to sleep in a nice warm bed in a hotel that sat atop a bluff that was once so fiercely pounded with the killing shells of war that I felt the fear. I was beginning to feel a new identity with the ravages of war. Academic knowledge was being fleshed out in my psyche by experiences with men who made history.

The morning broke to a beautiful warm and sunny day. As we approached the remaining big guns at Longues overlooking the channel, the same guns where the Germans first spotted the invasion fleet, the men could no longer contain their excitement. Some ran up the bluffs to see the water, others to begin their own bombardment with the peaceful noises of cameras clicking off nostalgic photos instead of the deafening roars from the huge guns spewing death. Like little kids, the men and many of their wives climbed the metal ladders to look inside the huge bunkers.

I wondered what the Armada must have looked like to a German peering out of the narrow slits enveloped by concrete so thick that the most powerful bombardments from the navy ships mostly bounced off the walls. I didn't have to wonder about the wives in whose eyes I saw love and admiration for their mates, the same love and admiration I see today in them at the local supermarket whenever I introduce myself to a WW II man who wears his pride of service on his hat.

I remember, too, the couples who walked hand in hand past poppy fields lining the road. And I think now of the many men whose graves we visited at the American Cemetery at Omaha Beach, men who never had that chance.

Their 9,384 white crosses are symmetrically placed with geometric exactitude. It is a beautifully tended place. The west wall of the cemetery says it best:

"Their graves are the permanent and visible symbol of their heroic devotion and their sacrifice in their common cause of humanity."

As we were leaving, I overheard an American girl, about age 11, say, "It must have been sad to watch all those people die." Yes, indeed. No argument there with the men, several of whom had buddies long gone, resting in that place until the sun goes down and the shadows are no more.

We walked on Omaha Beach, the killing place for most of the men buried on the bluffs above. It was a bit hard to tell what it must have looked like in 1944, the place has changed so much. The bluffs overlooking the famous beach are studded with summer and weekend houses. Life goes on.

We all lingered as long as we could on the beach, each person letting the waves of the imagination wash over his thoughts or, with a few, memories. I wondered if for some it was a letting go.

Point du Hoc was our next stop. The 25 foot craters dug by the massive bombardment from U.S. warships were still there. Neither sleet or snow or the rains of the years have filled them in. It was tempting to try a slide to their bottom, but no one did. Our men had to climb the cliffs with grappling hooks to get to the top where it must have been easy for the Germans to fire down on them. Ninety of the 225 Rangers who assaulted the Point survived. The sad irony of the attack is that the big guns they were after had been moved further inland.

A quick bus trip took us west to Utah Beach which had been a less heavily defended section. When we got there it looked like any section of a Long Island or Cape Cod beach. The battle that took place there on D-Day was far less dramatic yet, it seemed to me, more somber to the men. Perhaps they were comparing the slaughter on Omaha beach with the relative ease of the conquest on Utah. That could make a man wonder.

We moved on to the little town of Ste.-Mere-Eglise which was made famous that day by the ill-fated airborne drop into the center of the town. For the German soldiers, killing the paratroopers dropping down into the square must have been like a shooting gallery. One of the paratroopers, John Steele, famously landed by the bell tower where he watched the slaughter below and lived to tell about it.

We had put in a long day. Our guide asked if we wanted to skip a planned visit to the German cemetery at La Cambe where 21,600 German soldiers are buried, two beneath each flat tombstone. The graciousness of the American GI's with me that day lives in my mind. They insisted on visiting the graves of their enemy. Perhaps a half century of space enabled them to walk a walk of peace. I don't know what their thoughts were, but one of the men whispered to me, "They were only doing what they were told to do."

We stopped at the Belleau Wood cemetery the next morning. There was something magnanimous in these veterans of WW II tipping their hats in tribute to the dead of the Great War. It was also sad. We were the only ones there. I hoped that they had not been forgotten. So we said good-bye to the boys and were on our way down the road rushing past poppy-speckled fields of wheat, red on gold.

At the "Little Red Schoolhouse" in Reims we saw the place where the Germans surrendered. Everyone seemed to remember where they were on that wonderful day. The Russian interpreter for General Omar Bradley, Leo Ushkoff, was with us. Once in a men's room, he told us, while the Russian general and Bradley were urinating side by side, that the Russian asked Leo to tell Bradley that "he must stop pissing on my shoes."

Even in jest, the Cold War was beginning.

I copied the name *Mario Pallazzolo* from one of the gravestones at the Luxembourg American Military Cemetery. I never knew this young man, yet looking at his unusually unique name I was hit with the strong realization, perhaps for the first time, how unique each one of us is, and how his potential was cut off at a young age. I began to think, yes, really think about how special each one of us is. And yet we resort to killing unique others in battle. How primitive, I thought.

The philosophy student in me sometimes takes over, as it did that evening while I was trying to go to sleep. I thought about the 100 billion galaxies and the 100 billion stars in each galaxy, that we all live in the galaxy called The Milky Way on the star called Earth. In its own right, how lucky we are to be on the star that has the specific physical calculations that can support life as we know it.

And I thought about the 200 million sperm that the average man releases in an ejaculation, each trying to make its way up the "Amniotic Sea" to implant itself in the mother's ova. And out of the 200 million only one makes the existential cut. How unique is that one. How unique was Mario, now lying beneath a gravestone in Belgium. My heart ached for him that sunny July morning. Ah, Mario!

It was a trip that was an awakening for me, a realization of the senselessness and tragedy of war. To see the waste and to be with men who were a part of it helped me to grow as a man with a social conscience. I realized that I hate war, and that I love and admire the courage of our military. Deeply.

Saying goodbye to these men was hard. I was keenly aware that I had just spent time with real heroes. Not the ones we are asked by the media to honor those who throw a ball, catch a ball, nor rock stars or movie stars whose glitz will fade soon enough. The men I was with had answered the call and in the response knowingly risked their lives.

No greater love has any man.

XXX

Only once, recently, have I gone abroad without an agenda. Mostly, the journeys were with a meaningful purpose. Once in a while, a trip was with and without a strong purpose. For example, I took a trip to Austria in 1990 with Sheila that didn't have an overriding agenda. We wanted to live in the Alps overlooking Innsbruck. There is nothing like that in America that I am aware of. The mountains were so beautiful that it seemed like looking out a window in the apartment we rented was like looking at a painting.

I realized after we got there, though, that I did want to see the German concentration camp, Dachau. Sheila did not want to go with me, as she is emotionally smarter than I am.

The trip was an all-day affair and I did not get back until 2 a.m. Unexpectedly, the experience was a profound one for me, and the beginning of a lifetime quest to see if I could wrap my brain around the Holocaust. I could not understand what I saw there. I was still an emotional innocent, naïve about mankind. How could anyone do the things that went on there escaped my brain. It was as if I was smacked over the head with a hammer. I was naïve about humans, yet now growing in experience and maturing in the realization of evil in the world. I was not the same person as I was the day before.

In fact, I became so interested in the Holocaust experience, I visited Auschwitz and Birkenau a few years later and then, over time, wrote a trilogy of historical fiction books about it.

The first book, "The Illustrator," is about a young man whose extraordinary talent as an illustrator is aligned with the integrity of his soul. When the commandant of Auschwitz, Rudolf Hoss, commands him to illustrate his face for the future history books about the thousand year reign of the Third Reich, his life changes.

The second book, "Oh, Israel My Heart Yearns for Thee," tells the story of the illustrator, Tyszka Dunajski, and his wife, Cecylia, as they journey to Israel, he for community, she for the founding of the new state. In the midst of the many battles between the Israelis and Palestinians for autonomy, their relationship goes awry. Yet, after years of separation and new relationships, their undying love brings them together once again.

The last book of the trilogy, "Waiting for the Red Cow," is based on a Hebrew myth that is read in synagogues once every year, about the arrival in Jerusalem of a perfect red cow, never yoked and with red hair only. With its coming, the conflict over ownership of the disputed land will end. But, at what price?

People sometimes ask if I take a trip in order to write a book about it. The answer is no. I have never taken such a trip. However, I often have experiences on trips that I write about. The Holocaust trilogy is a good example. Each of the three books is historically researched. Yet, if I hadn't at some point gone to the death camps, I don't think I could have written as authentically as I did.

I am not a believer in signs from the universe, for example. Yet on my trip to Auschwitz I had an incident that pushed me hard into wanting to be authentic in my writing. I was standing outside Block 10 that looks like a simple condo from the outside.

It was the block where outrageous experiments were performed on women's bodies.

We were not allowed to enter the block. As our female guide was talking us through its history, I began to pray to the women who had been tortured and killed there, telling them how profoundly sorry I was, and how ashamed I was that men would do this.

While I was praying, out of the blue, literally, a white feather floated down to my face and fluttered around it like a butterfly. I am not much of a believer in signs, but something happened to me then. I don't know what but something happened.

It is not easy for me to reveal this, as I am an intellectually trained man, perhaps what might be called an empiricist. I do not understand why Thomas, the follower of Jesus, in the Bible, e.g., is so scorned for wanting to put his hand into Jesus' wounds to see if He was real. After all, like everyone else, Thomas was born with faculties of the mind, including that of judgement. So, he simply wanted to see for himself what proof there was that this man sitting before him, was truly the Son of God.

I find no problem with that, and cannot accept that he did anything wrong. I find it hard, in fact, that some religions put such an emphasis on what is called faith, that is, believing without proof. In the God I hope is real, I cannot fathom that this One would put such an emphasis on believing without proof. I will speak more about that later in this book.

XXX

In 1997 I was asked by the Connecticut Education Association if I would represent the state in Beijing at the China-US Conference on Education. Of course, I agreed. I was asked to give a speech on the differences between old-fashioned teaching and what was called post-modern teaching. I remember how hard my Chinese translator and I worked to get it right. And the argument that broke out in the audience between Inner and Outer Mongolia teachers. I didn't know the details of the argument, heated though it was, but I got the gist of it from my translator: old vs. new ways.

I had a chance now and then to sight-see, but mostly I remember how boring it was to be stuck in a conference for a week. I did, though, see a Muslim temple for the first time in my life, not knowing that way off in the future I would get to know many Muslims in the mid-east.

Each day while there, I would get up early to do tai-chi with the women in the street. I felt odd as I was the only man in the group. The women took me to their own each morning and watched over me to make sure I was doing each step of the exercise the right way.

It was on one of these mornings that I met a very old man who always was going somewhere pushing a wheel barrel. He waited for me every day and on my last day in Beijing he gave a piece of paper to me that he had gotten a message translated on.

It was a Mao Tse Tung saying he thought would be useful to me: "Do something to change the world, even if you must die." I think of him now and then, as he left his mark on me. He was a grand old idealist even to the end.

XXX

I went from the chaotic airport in Beijing to Osaka to meet the Uedas who would take me to their home in Hiroshima.

The Uedas had plans for me. Oh, did they have plans! Noriyo was there, too, a surprise to me as she was supposed to be in school. The Japanese love surprises! They also introduced me at dinner to Mr. Ueda's half sister, Yoshimi Shimada, a most beautiful and spirited young woman with a medical doctor's degree as well as a Ph.D.

A few months before I was to visit, they asked me what I'd like to do on the visit.

I mentioned this and that and, being people of their word, they took me to every this and that I had mentioned.

They took me to the Ryoanji Temple with its Zen Garden, a thing of meditative beauty. And then to the Nijo Castle, the residence of the first Tokugawa Shogun Ieyasu in the early 1600's. The floor boards in the castle were purposefully uneven, so if enemies were to infiltrate the castle during the night, the boards would creak their warning that an intruder was in the castle.

Our trip to Kyoto was most memorable. The Gion Festival, a centuries old procession of colorful wooden floats pushed and pulled through the streets to appease the gods, was something to see. It reminded me of our own Thanksgiving Day parade. Each year the festival is held on July 17th and the 24th. The street are as crowded as the streets of New York on Thanksgiving day. No cars are allowed, the women wear traditional yukatas while cooling themselves with paper fans. Kiosks selling food stud the streets – barbecued chicken, *yakituri*, and *okonomiyaki* flour pancakes, with cabbage, onions, eggs and pork, are sold everywhere (except, I might add in Connecticut!).

I was taken on a ginrickshaw ride for three hours through the streets of Kyoto, a most beautiful city that was on the original target list for the first A-bomb. Secretary Stimson who had studied there as a young man warned Truman to take it off the list, as it is the cultural center of Japan. "If you bomb Kyoto, the Japanese will never forgive us," he warned.

The college student who pulled my rickshaw took me to the bamboo forest, the like I had never before seen. I remember, too, the Rock Faces gardens which had hundreds of rock-hewn mildewed faces, each different, sticking out of the soil.

We took the shinkansen speed train to Nagasaki, a city I had always wanted to visit. It is the place where the second atomic bomb exploded on August 9th, killing about 50,000 Japanese, mostly civilians, in minutes. I went to the house of Takashi Nagai, a revered saintly man who wrote about love and forgiveness in his book, "The Bells of Nagasaki."

And then to a one hour visit with the famous Dr. Hamasato, a young medical student in 1945 who discovered, with an old microscope, that the symptoms of the victims in Nagasaki manifested a dysfunction in their white blood cells. Leukemia! I took notes and Mrs. Ueda translated. I was kind of mesmerized in the presence of this great and humble man who also established a mobile medical team of his young colleagues in the days after the bomb exploded.

And they took me to Hagi, the artistic center of Japan, where I spent a few hours with Miwa Eizo, perhaps the most famous pottery maker in Japan. He ended our visit by showing me the very large kilns he used for his pots that are sold all over the world.

Before we left, he gave me a copy of a large book that contained photos of his work. He eventually signed it, a treasured book I keep in my study with other books given to me as gifts by authors.

Before going back to Hiroshima, the Uedas insisted that I create my own pottery, called "Hagi Yaki," at Yutaka's. Coincidentally, while I was at the potter's wheel, a magazine photographer showed up to do a story on the establishment and took a photo of me turning the wheel. I soon appeared in a Japanese travel magazine.

Mrs. Ueda arranged for me to interview several women who were in a special hospital for survivors of the A-bomb strike on Aug. 6, 1945. It was an excruciating experience to listen to their stories of that beautiful morning that instantly turned into a dark hell. At one point I was so moved by their stories of suffering that I had to excuse myself for 15 minutes before resuming the interview.

XXX

Years later, in 2007, I visited the Uedas once again, this time with my youngest son, Jay, to climb Mt. Fuji with Noriyo and a few of her friends. I remember how wonderful the Uedas were once again, even though Mr. Ueda has suffered a stroke and was doing therapy to regain speech. He was so gracious with Jay and me. He and his entire family went out to dinner with us one evening, the first time, we were told, in over a year that he left the house. Jay and I felt honored. We missed grandma who passed away several years before.

Jay was deeply moved visiting the Peace Museum. He asked me if I would leave him alone while in there. I guess he didn't want the teacher in me to take over. I don't blame him, as a visit to that museum is a time for reflection. We rang the Bell of Peace as we held hands with Noriyo. I was happy to see how well Jay and she got along. She is, quite simply, the best. Sheila thinks there is no one worthy of Noriyo, and because of that she will probably never get married.

I remember mostly from that visit the breakfasts that Mrs. Ueda made for me and Jay each morning. No 5-star restaurant in the world could match her. None! I was sometimes embarrassed at the morning buffets of bacon and eggs, breads, juices, yogurts, and more. It was Mrs. Ueda's way, and Jay and I did the best to accommodate her!

Our attempt to climb Mt. Fuji, probably the most historically revered place in Japan, was held back by me. We went there on a new national holiday, The Day of the Sea, honoring the bounty given by the sea to Japan over the years. And so, the climb was very crowded, the pace set by the guide strenuous, at least for me.

You see, I was not well-prepared for the climb, which was uneven, rainy and cold the higher we got. We wore headlamps so we could continue to climb after darkness had set in. But I was growing more and more fatigued as time went by.

Before I tell you what happened next on the mountain, let me explain two characteristics of Japanese culture. The first one is *Wa*, that is the keeping of harmony which is very important, especially in formal affairs. The second in *kaigi*, that is consensus, also very important, especially to keep the *Wa*. I first learned about this one day when I was invited to a Japanese delegation at the United Nations after the Hiroshima Students Peace Conference in 1995. A *kaigi* was called to decide what restaurant we would go to. The conference lasted what seemed to me for a long time, until everyone was satisfied with the choice, I believe it was pizza. *Wa* was honored, and consensus had been reached!

Now, back to the mountain. As I started to crawl over some of the rocky climb on the mountain, I realized that I could not go on. Literally, I was drained.

In my attempt to keep harmony, I told Jay and Noriyo that I would try to get a bed in one of the many huts along the way and they should go on to the top. I would meet them in the morning. By this time, it was raining quite hard and we were getting soaked.

I was trying hard to attain *Wa*, so I thought my offer would do it. We tried several huts, but there was no room. I was by then the most tired I had ever been in my life.

Ever!

"Do you see that johnch over there?" I asked. Without waiting for an answer, I said, "I am going over there and going to sleep. You two go ahead and we'll find each other in the morning."

"But you will be wet and sick," they said. Such sweet kids! Somehow, they found us wooden beds and food in a hut. I think Noriyo bribed the host. A young Japanese man who was on vacation from a college in Vermont got us tatamis (mats) and hot soup. I restrained myself from kissing him! I was never so happy to go to bed.

Unfortunately, it was so dark that I jumped in on top of a Japanese man who shouted something at me, fortunately in Japanese. How do you say, "Hey, Stupid, get off me" in Japanese?

XXX

In 1991 I went to Alaska for the first of three times. I was visiting one of my sons in Portland, Oregon for 10 days and decided to take a little time to go to Glacier Bay National Park. I stayed for a night at an inn in Gustavus where they told us to be careful, as there were bears in the area. We were showed a coffee pot that a bear had smacked at a nearby camping spot. There were four distinct and large holes in the pot from its claws, leaving me convinced. We were also encouraged to wear a bell around our necks when walking from the cabins to the restaurant where I ate crab legs for the first time in my life before hustling, bear scared, back to my room.

The long boat ride the next day was a powerful introductory experience with nature for me. For a city boy, it was something. I saw ice bergs calving (breaking off)) chunks of ice as big as city blocks. I can only imagine now as I write this how the earth warming is doing more and bigger damage to the polar regions that will result in rising seas that will overwhelm islands and coastal cities.

The seals came so close to our small craft that I was awed. Their faces are so pretty and they seemed so vulnerable to the larger predators. I felt very protective.

We saw a few of their predators, large whales, perhaps hump whales but I am not sure.

As I left for the bus to take me to the airport for the flight to Portland, I went into a small jewelry shop and bought a silver ring with the image of an Alaskan totem on it. It was to be the first of about175 rings I have collected from around the world.

I try to buy indigenous rings or rings that reflect the culture of the country I am shopping in. How and where and when I bought these rings would make great stories, perhaps another book of memoirs. Enough for now. I am even starting to give away some of the rings. When I taught a class called "Readings and Writings in Contemporary Issues," I would tell my students that they ought to notice what ring I had on that day, and I would tell them an interesting story about its purchase. I could almost always find a way to weave the story into a contemporary issue.

XXX

I went again to China in 2005 to teach summer school at Dongguan University, about 100 miles north of Hong Kong. I think back on it as one of the most enlightening and exciting adventures of my life. I had a few briefings from Chinese friends before I left home, and was told that they are very family structured, so I should bring family photos with me. One of the first things I did was to tell them about my family, our home, our little town, my wife, our cats. There were 16 students in my class, mostly older people who wanted to learn beyond their rudimentary English language skills in order to enhance their business opportunities. As I showed them two albums of family photos, they seem to be engaged and excited. I thought immediately, and I was right, that this was going to be a great summer.

My curriculum was simple: English pronunciations, especially those that were seldom used in China, perhaps not ever. You know, the ones that don't have the tongue and palate meet, the *l*'s and the *r*'s, American culture (as some in the class owned a business whose products might be bought in America); writing in English; creating an English newspaper for the university; putting on an abridged version of "Romeo and Juliet" which played before a packed auditorium; giving short talks in English before their classmates; and having an e-mail exchange with my youngest son, Jay, who lives in Los Angeles. He gladly took on the mission to write each one back. In turn, each would have to read their original letter to him and his return letter to the class, and comment on what they had learned from the exchange.

It was a custom in the school, I soon learned, to give each of the foreign teachers a Chinese nickname. I told them that to do this, I would leave the class for about 15 minutes. In that time, they should pick one of their fellows to lead the class in order to choose my Chinese name.

When I came back in, there it was, on the blackboard, in English and Chinese:

"Qiang Li Ma" or "The Winged Steed." I have a pony tale, so I think they were infuenced by that. The Winged Steed was famous throughout the land, as he could fly 1000 miles a day! They did, though, continue to call me Teacher Jerry.

Part of my duties was to plan evening assignments for the teachers, mostly talks to the other teachers who attended, along with a few Chinese teachers who heard about these opportunities. My time began to get crowded, as the teachers picked me to be their chairman.

I soon got into a few problems such as asking permission for our male teachers to wear summer shorts in the classroom, decidedly against Chinese mores, not modest.

We were, though, granted permission. However, it did not sit well with all the English teachers as they thought I was disrespecting Chinese culture. I did notice, though, on the next day that the dissenting teachers wore shorts.

I also drew some disfavor among the Chinese leaders when I got wind that our favorite caretaker, Helen, had been missing work time because of a heart condition that sometimes flared up. I got to know Helen and would sometimes take her to the hospital for treatment, which usually consisted of hydrating and rest in the hospital for a few hours.

To combat the administration's intention to fire her, I asked the teachers to sign a protest letter that Tracy wrote to Mr. Mao. As Helen was a good worker who quickly met out needs for the everyday things in life, soap, toilet paper, blankets, phone cards, she was well-liked and everyone agreed to sign. I wanted to make it public that we were behind her so I gave the signed letter to Mr. Mao's assistant, Angel, at a morning faculty meeting. We saved her job.

At one point, too, the teachers thought that they were being overworked and threatened to quit, a really stupid move in my opinion. So, I checked the contract that the teachers had signed and, lo and behold, they were not being overworked.

I tweaked a few things in it with the administration's approval and brought the compromise back to the teachers. A few holdouts, so American, thought I had sold them down the river. But, I think I saved the day.

The teaching was a great experience. The Chinese are really eager to learn, and I was eager to teach them, trying out some new methods, while mostly relying on the old. I did make a mistake by introducing the class to the card game of "Old Maid,"

It was then that I discovered that they, too, would like the easier and softer way. They wanted to play every day, so I had to take some measure to keep control of the learning process.

After a week or two, several of the students wanted to take me shopping in Dongguan City. I started to wonder if the fraternizing would not be a good thing for my role as teacher, that the respect I wanted as "Teacher Jerry" might be compromised. It was not. In fact, it probably was enhanced that day when I took them to a book store where we discovered a copy of *Chicken Soup For the Teacher's Soul*.

I had an essay in it, both in Chinese and English, called "Chuck," about a beloved student of mine who died very young of cancer. Of course the word spread that Teacher Jerry was famous! Or, as my students would say, *famorse*.

We took some great trips on weekends, sometimes to old villages still with the remnants of 1960's and the Cultural Revolution posted on the door frames. It was kind of eerie to think about the cruelty of those times, especially to the teachers who represented the old to the young students, not realizing that Mao Tse Tung was just using them to regain control of the masses.

I got a good look, too, about what it means to "Lose Face" in the Chinese culture, as I was causing it in the way I was teaching by handing out work sheets to be completed in the class, with immediate follow-up questioning by me. As they were used to being given a day's room on assignments like this, they could find out the answers at home, thus never losing face the next day.

That Chinese families stick tight became evident when I asked a very bright student, Aline, why she never went to college. She told me that she went to work immediately after high school to support her brother who was in medical school studying surgery. I thought it a shame that she never had a chance to enhance her own education by what I thought was an act of supreme self-sacrifice.

She came to class one morning very excited, telling anyone who would listen that her brother had performed his first surgery, amputating a mans' leg! I was so impressed with her generous spirit that I started to make inquiries about how much it cost to go to a first-rate college in China. It was about $1600 U.S. per year for tuition, books, dormitory and food. Not a bad deal, indeed.

I asked Angel if it would be appropriate for me to approach Aline about my paying the cost. She said I would have to get approval, of course from Aline, and also from her husband and her parents, brothers and sisters.

So I asked Aline and her girlfriend if they would have lunch with me at MacDonalds (yeah, Micky Dee's) to go over this. "Aline," I started, "how would you like to go to college?" She looked surprised that I should ask such a question.

"Of course I would," she answered. "But I cannot afford it."

"OK, I know. But I'm about to get into some tricky stuff here. I am willing to pay for you to go to college. How do you feel about that?" I remember how her face became a kind of redish brown flush.

Before she had a chance to answer, I thought I would spare her the agony of responding, figuring it would be a Yes. "I know that I've got to get permission from your husband and parents, but as they live far away from here, I wonder if you would do that for me."

As soon as I looked at her face the next morning, I knew the answer. She was admitted into Guangdong University in the School of Foreign Studies, and is now an English translator in one of the leading companies in China.

Leaving was hard. They sang an original song for me the last day of class.

I cried. And the class took me to dinner and speeches the night before I left.

XXX

Hurricane Katrina hit the day I came home from Dongguan University. Even though I was a bit tired from my summer work and travels, I was drawn to help. I first asked Sheila if she would mind my leaving again. I'm happy to say that we were never "locked together at the hip" and so she was really OK with it.

I am Red Cross trained for disaster services. "Can you leave tomorrow?" they asked. "How about giving me two days. I just got back from China." I was ready to go.

I flew into Montgomery, Alabama, where the Red Cross had a huge staging center. The next day I was on my way with nine other volunteers to Tuscaloosa, Alabama where many of Katrina's victims were either heading north to new homes or waiting it out to go back.

I called us "The Team of Ten." Ed Welch, a retired army colonel, was "the Old Man," a term of respect and affection we soon gave to him. Quentin, a young Air Force enlisted man assigned to the Pentagon, took his vacation time to be there. We chose Gwenn as our team captain. The list went on.

One of us was always assigned to do shelter work at the University of Alabama.

Three others did outreach, that is, finding those who needed help from the hurricane but did not know where to get it. I remember that they found 23 people looking for help.

The rest of us did case work which, in a disaster of that magnitude included listening to their stories for the first time, assessing their need for food, clothing and shelter, and referring them for medical assistance where needed.

Our group handled evacuees from Louisiana, Mississippi and seven counties in Alabama, including Greene, the poorest in the United States. Each evacuee was a client. Ironically, my first client was a young woman whose name was Katrina. I asked her how people were reacting to her name. "Are you sure you want to go there?" she asked. We had a few laughs.

I remember it took me a few days to get the hang of the paper work, and managing the ways that people wanted to talk, some a lot, some not. Their stories were compelling.

There was Winny, a 63 year old grandmother who lived two blocks from one of the levees in New Orleans. She told me that she got out a few hours before it burst.

And Harold who was not so lucky. He watched his wife slip away from him as New Orleans flooded. We got him food, fresh clothes, and shelter before placing his wife's name on the national hot line of Katrina's missing persons.

I had to convince the diabetic couple to buy healthy food with the money the Red Cross gave to them. I found out that they had been eating crackers for three days, afraid to spend the money.

One of my clients had come face-to-face with an alligator as he swam in the flood. "I was lucky it wasn't hungry," he told me.

There was a woman from Mississippi and her child who clung to a tree to prevent from being blown away. All she remembered was screaming to her daughter, "Get out of here!" as a tree fell on her mobile home. She didn't have time for niceties. "My daughter is retarded," she told me. As I fumbled for the correct term to put on the forms, she said, "Just put down retarded."

My oldest client was Lucille, 84, was a woman of great dignity. Each time she she began to tell me about the horrors she witnessed – dead bodies of people and animals floating by – she cried and released the floodgates of sorrow we all knew.

Most of our clients described the sound of the wind as a jet plane or a loud train.

Trees "popped" as they were ripped out of the ground, and telephone poles, as a man from Louisiana explained, "bowed to the ground."

One amazing lady told me that in the middle of the fury she began to be curious about what was going on outside. When she opened the front door, the window panes on the first floor blew out!

A 24 year old woman with four children came to us after wandering about for over a week. She seemed dazed and in need of medical help, which we got for her right away.

Downed structures and trees also made millions of bees and insects homeless.

I noticed that many people who came to us had bite marks on their faces and arms.

There was a couple, Ramon and Elizabeth if I remember well, who struggled to get through the flooded streets of New Orleans when they heard the sound of a barking dog. Ramon wanted to put him on high ground, but "Poncho" placed both his front paws around his neck and never let go! We got Poncho to a vet for a checkup and shots. He was one of the lucky pets. Actually, Ramon and Elizabeth said that they were the lucky ones.

I was touched by the blank stares on the faces of many of the young children.

One child took the hand of our crisis counselor and walked her around every part of the center, opening doors. I asked her what she was looking for. "The boogie man," she said.

My heart will forever be captive to the black grandmothers who came through our doors. They are fiercely loyal to their families, and outrageously loving of their grandchildren. With all the suffering and upsets they had experienced, they talked to me about the goodness of God. Many of them said to me, "Mr. Jerry, what can I do for *you?*" I would invariably say, "Ask the Man upstairs to keep me in mind," because I knew how spiritual they were. "I will" or "Count on it, Mr. Jerry," they would say before leaving. I do believe they have kept their promise. They are my heroes.

The "Thank you's" we received were endless. Hugs and kind words were common place. One man left us a note that said in part, "You have shown us light in a dark time." And I will never forget the woman who, after her daughter nudged her that her name had been called, jumped out of her seat and ran to me as if I were an old friend.

She hugged me and hugged me some more as she tried to tell me that she was deaf.

We cried. In front of everyone. It didn't matter. I think she knew that I was really her friend.

I often think of them, hoping that things are better for them now. I am grateful for having known them, if only for an instance in time, as they taught me much about how to grow in graciousness while still in the fires of life.

XXX

Over the years, Sheila and I have visited sixteen islands in the Caribbean. I have little to say about these trips, as they are all similar, except that they were always fun and relaxing, and that being with Sheila is always a delight. I love being with her. She is the comfort of presence, the delight of companionship.

Our week in Antigua, though, is memorable, kind of nostalgic for me. You see, when I was a young monk and waiting for my first assignment on the mission to teach poor children, I wanted so much to be assigned to Antigua or Africa as they seemed to me to be far away and quixotic. Besides, Br. Driscoll, the monk I modeled myself after, had been given his first assignment there. I was, though, assigned to a poor boy's school in New York City.

When we got to Antigua, I called them and asked if I could visit the mission school. Of course, Br. Driscoll was not there. I think by this time he was the President of Iona College. I loved my visit with the monks that day. They were gracious and kind to me, and at last I did get there.

XXX

We decided to go to Kenya, Africa, for a safari in 1994. It was to be an extraordinary growth experience for me in getting to see the beauty and wonder of animals. My first lesson had come years before when Sheila talked with me about my indifference to the feelings of our cat which she had seen me brush aside in the hallway with my foot. "She has as much right to be there as you do. Please do not push her aside." It was an epiphany for me to realize that animals also had rights and were deserving of kindness. It was probably only because of the love, high regard, and respect I had for Sheila that her words sank deeply into my soul. I have since loved animals as an abiding part of who I am. I am impressed with their intelligence and sensitivity, their ability to love. One of the deeply moving times in my life is when Chloe, our younger cat, and Sheila get on what I call a "talking riff." They sit on the floor, about two feet from each and communicate, Sheila with human sounds, Chloe with cat noises that have the nuances of human talk. It is something to behold.

I learned so many things on the way to Nairobi. Our wait in Rome was scheduled for one hour, yet we had to wait for eight. You see, our plane from Rome was scheduled to stop in Jeddah to land a few hundred Saudis coming from Washington, D.C. and a World Cup soccer game. The game went overtime, and the airline decided to wait for them in Rome. Ah, the power of money.

I was quite surprised, too, that many of the Muslim men on board were drunk, as I thought, in my innocence, that Muslims do not drink. As one of their elders told me, they were drinking as much as they could on the plane because they would not get away with it at home. Ah, the power of hypocrisy.

When we landed in Jeddah and they got off after numerous reprimands from our pilot, six or so plain clothes men boarded and checked every overhead for what I assume was a bomb. It was all very serious. When I got out of my seat to go to the men's room, the captain bellowed at me, "Sit down." Ah, the power of terrorists.

We were told to be careful in Nairobi, as the streets were a bit dangerous. I don't know why, really I don't, but I thought the danger might be less on side streets. So we took a walk on a side street, and were surrounded in a few minutes by a crowd of locals trying to sell us indigenous necklaces and bracelets. They began to press in on us and it got very noisy. I sensed danger.

"Sheila, I'm going to grab your arm by your wrist. I'll count to three and then let's run. I'll go first to clean out space for you. And keep on running back to the hotel, if we can. OK, ready?

"One, two, three" and off we went, running, running, running – until we couldn't run any more. Fortunately, the crowd stopped following us, probably because we were now on a main street. Except for the afternoon when Sheila gave a drunken mother and her crawling baby on the side of the main road a bag of food we had and called the police, we did not leave our hotel again until everyone on the safari had arrived.

From that day on, it was like being in the pages of a National Geographic magazine on assignment in eastern Africa. We were taken to a lodge built on eucalyptus trunks high over a waterhole. Imagine a somewhat muddy hole about 50 X 50 yards beneath you in the middle of the jungle. You are looking down on it from your hut perched in the trees. Every kind of animal is walking around it in peace with each other. I guess there was an implicit agreement that this is where we water, not fight.

We watched a little drama going on: a mother elephant trying to convince her baby to follow her, but in order to do so the baby would have to cross in front of a buffalo, a really big buffalo. Every time her mom would beckon her, the baby would start, then quickly felt the fear of crossing in front of this big guy, who seemed at the moment to be quite peaceful. We kept on rooting for mom and her baby for about 15 minutes until, finally, the baby crossed to her mom.

We also had an underground observation post which put us at eye level with the animals. When one of them came close – elephant, rhino, buffalo – it was almost surreal.

Especially for a city boy like me.

As we drove into the Rift Valley, I could only think of Leakey and his discoveries about the beginning of man. Having read much about this, I was in awe. And I crossed the Equator for the first of many times to come on my travels.

We spent a few days in the Masai Mara. How extraordinary. We were taken on to the savanna for a few hours each morning after an early breakfast, then back to our tent for lunch and a nap, then out again til 5 o'clock when we had to be off the savannah. Our guide and driver, Matthew, mis-timed this one day and we were stopped by the patrol guards wielding machine guns. They checked Matthew's papers, gave him a lecture and let us go. Whew!

We saw every kind of animal – giraffes, elephants, leopards, lions, and on and on.

Wild flowers galore, ant hills, wild ostrich, so big you could ride them! One afternoon we saw three lions getting really antsy with each other, a bit frenetic nipping at each other's backsides. "Matthew, what's going on?" I asked. He gave me his binocs. "Look way out there," he instructed, "and you'll see a zebra. The lions are getting ready for the kill."

Now, you know how much Sheila loves animals. Watching three lions maul an innocent zebra was not what she wanted to see. She asked me if I would call upon the good will of Matthew and the two other people in our jeep to skip the slaughter. They were all very gracious and generous to not wound Sheila's soul.

We went into a Masai village. What an experience! The men in red robes did their classic dance, jumping up and down. As I tried to take a photo of a women carrying her infant, she hid the child johneath a blanket. I was told that it is the Masai belief that a photo would steal the child's soul, that the baby's soul would go from its flesh into the photo. However, if you gave an American one dollar bill to her, the photo would not steal her baby's soul! I gave her a dollar. So be it!

A very tall Masai woman made a splendid beaded ring to add to my collection.

I wear this ring with pride and I love the symbolism of the colors she chose. Green is for health, red for bravery, white for peace, and black that I might be able to fight against life's struggles. I remember, too, how the children wanted to touch my white arms.

One of the men invited me into his tiny hut. I was first struck by the fact that it had but one ventilation hole in it, the size of a golf ball. And yet they lit a fire in the entrance to cook and for warmth on a cold night on the savannah. There was a hanging cloth that separated the hut in half, the left side being where one of his wives slept, and the right where he and his wife of the night would sleep together. Large rocks were used as pillows. The children slept at their feet, heads on rocks also. And one of their cows slept to the left inside the entrance.

Next time you think that your house is crowded, think of the Masai!

Monkeys were everywhere. We could hear them playing at night on the roof of our hut back at the camp. During the day, they would like to jump on our lunch table to take the lemons in our drinks. We loved it, great photos, but it drove the waiters crazy.

They would come to the tables with small whips to shoosh away the little critters who would see them coming and spring back into the trees above. We were always amused and would sometimes put lemons on the table to entice them. Bad!

In fact, wild animals were all around us everywhere, even crocodiles in back of a rock wall where we ate outdoors. After dark, the line where the jungle ended and our huts began would be held by men carrying bundles of flaming sticks which, if needed, would scare off a lion or wild dog.

One day we went back into our hut to get my camera for the morning's outing.

I got it but when we turned around there was a baboon in the doorway waiting to come in the room. We had been warned against them, as they are fierce with long, sharp teeth that could do real damage.

I whispered to Sheila, "What do you think we should do?" "I don't know," she said. We watched, hoping it would go away. I was anxious, so I threw up my arms, and lunged towards it while screaming as loud as I could – RAHHHH! It ran away. I screamed so hard that my throat was sore for a day or so. Matthew told me later that screaming at it was the worst thing I could do, so assertive that a baboon would normally attack such a militant outcry.

I had an experience one morning with two herds of elephants that changed forever the way I would see animals, in fact, all living things. It was early one morning that we spotted two herds of elephants, each led by a matriarch. I would say there were about a dozen elephants in each herd. They were about two hundred yards away from each other.

Now, remember this is a city boy talking here. Matthew stopped our jeep so we could observe. Each of the two matriarchs apparently ordered their respective herds to remain where they were. The two then ambled slowly towards each other. It seemed like a long time, as they walked slowly. I was really enjoying this, as it seemed as if I was watching a TV documentary, two big elephants marching towards each other in the distance.

To my surprise, they welcomed each other, or so I thought, by touching their heads while at the same time intertwining their trunks while rocking back and forth.

The experience struck a deep chord in me. It was an anthropomorphic moment turned inside out. What I had at first interpreted as a peaceful demonstration was, in fact, I didn't know what! I knew right then that I didn't know.

What I did know with the certainty of insight was that I had always interpreted animal actions from my own perspective. In grander terms, from man's point of view.

Suddenly, I realized that these wild animals have an existence of their own, that they are their own reference point, unique to them as mine is to me, or yours is to you. It was a lesson that I have never forgotten. I realized how unique each living being is, and have extended the lesson as my life went on to realize that each of us carries a cross that no one knows about and that I must respect.

On one of our last days at the Mara, we took a camel ride with a few of the natives out to one of the rivers about 40 minutes away. As we got off the animals, I asked them why they were carrying spears. One of them who could speak some English told me that a woman washing her clothes in the river "was killed by a lion, right there," about twenty feet away! Yesterday. Now, this got our attention that we really were in Africa in the wilds of the savanna.

The next part of our journey took us to the Sambaru National Reserve, home of the Sambaru tribe and herds of elephants. It presses hard against my ability to write as I grope with describing the wonder of the herds, the magnificence of their bodies, the maternal instincts of the matriarchs. I know it might sound hyperbolic to some, but I think about the ways that elephant mothers watch over their babies is at the essence of motherhood. They are watchful, yet demanding, solicitous yet trusting. We've all heard the phrase "It takes a village." Regarding elephants, I say "It takes a herd." It was obvious after a while to note how each of the members of a herd, whether brothers, or sisters, aunts or uncles, and mom, especially mom, keep their eyes on the babies who wander about under their feet, always under their feet. They wait when the baby wanders off, guide her back, and steer her straight, and never lose track of her. It is an impressive thing to observe.

I inadvertently supplied laughter to those in our jeep one afternoon as I was standing while looking at a herd of them close by with my binoculars. One of them, a big bull, let out with the classic elephant deep rumble roar and started to take quick steps towards our vehicle. I swear it was going to get me, and I fell on my back, much to the delight of my friends. "It was the binoculars, I yelled in self-defense. The binoculars!"

One night after dinner, we were invited to go to the back of the restaurant to observe one of the waiters putting out the left-over meats in the middle of the garden.

He kind of waltzed out with a huge plate of meat. Suddenly, we could see eyes peeking out from the lip of the jungle. As soon as the waiter was safely into the restaurant, out came the jackals, wild dogs to grab up the hunks of meat in their mouths before speeding back to place the meat in the confines of the jungle. They would do this over and over until the meat was gone. They didn't fight or bite, yet it was clear that the bigger dogs ruled.

One of the last things we did was to go to Lake Nakaru, a place where up to one and a half million pink flamingos migrate each year. Their droppings dry into pink algae which they eat, reinforcing the pink as in pink flamingos. We were there at a good time as there was pink everywhere.

It is a strange thing, an almost mysterious thing, that I have read about many times – that many people who go to Africa seem to bond with it quickly. I was beginning to feel this way as we were getting ready to leave the savannas for Nairobi and our flight to Rome.

I was feeling nostalgic already as a host of images began to play on the picture–taking mechanism of my brain: the vistas of the flat grasslands, the family of lions sitting on boulders as we passed by, magnificent elephants and their babies, monkeys in the trees, giraffes mock-fighting, baboons along the dirt roads picking insects off of each other, antelopes, the rhinos rambling, the hippos snarling. And the rising up of the sun in the morning and its going down in the evening. There is something special about that in the preserves of Kenya, perhaps because it is not cluttered by cement.

I think, though, that it was karma that got me this way as we were getting ready to leave. You see, there is a part of me that believes in this tit for tat business of karma.

Let's go back in time a bit. I once told Sheila that I would like to have a tie dye shirt, you know, one of those hippy shirts. Not long thereafter we were at one of Long Island's beaches when she saw a piece of cloth, about 4-5 inches sticking out of the sand. She pulled it up and up and up. Lo and behold, it was a beautiful tie dye shirt, yellow, blue and red splotches. I took it as a karmic sign, sort of for fun, sort of real. We washed and dried it. And I wore it a few times.

"I've got an idea. Let's take the shirt with us to Africa and find someone to give away the shirt, a sort of karma-giving, passing it on." So we took the shirt to Africa, and decided to find a young person along the road out of Sambaru. I just knew that we had to find someone who would like the colors in the shirt. The road was a dirt, lonely one.

Now and then, we spotted someone walking, but it usually was someone quite old, and I wanted to give it to someone younger who might one day pass it on to his or her son. And on and on. Yes, I am a romantic who imagines such things.

There he was! "Stop," I urged our driver. We had caught the eye of a young boy dressed in a short red cape, a shepherd watching over his flock. I beckoned him to come get the shirt, but he seemed afraid. He just would not come, yet he seemed to understand that I was trying to give him this gift. Finally, I balled up the shirt as best as I knew how, and threw it to him.

He ran to get it, and the last we saw of him was the image of a very happy boy waving the shirt over his head while running home, I suppose, to show it off to his parents and friends. The sight of him so happy expanded my soul while capping off my memories of Africa. I, too, have bonded with Africa. One day I will go back!

XXX

Sometimes a trip is just a trip, as it were, or so I thought at the time when Sheila and I went to Cancun, Mexico, in the fall of 1995. It was for R & R for me after the responsibilities of the Hiroshima Peace Conference in August.

It was just that, too, as we put in many hours on the beach relaxing, though we also did a few adventuresome things. You see, I think of traveling as the most expansive experience anyone could have, better than all the college courses one could ever attend.

I have, for example, five earned college degrees, yet not a one of them taught me as much about life, the world, and others as my travels have. In so many ways, these trips have expanded my life, my way of seeing. In this sense, the trip to Mexico, though touristy, was like, to use the college courses metaphor again, a short one credit seminar. A real life seminar that introduced me to Mexican history and culture that in some subtle, yet real, ways, influenced me in gaining my respect for the Mexican people. The respect has had a practical value, too, as the town next to us, Danbury, has a large Mexican population many of whom I have had the pleasure to meet in different contexts. They are a hard–working and reliable people. It makes me sad that I even say this. In the 102 countries I have visited, I have never encountered anything different.

Little things influence my soul, my growth. The mother and her young child, for example, who hid behind the vast structures at Chichen Itza, hiding because it is illegal there to sell to tourists. I gave them some pesos and they gave a hand-made handkerchief to me in return. I still have it, a reminder to me how lucky I am.

XXX

"Hey, this is just like Iceland."

That is what Neil Armstrong said after his famous utterance, "That's one small step for a man, one giant step for mankind." They had trained in lunar-like Iceland.

I recall my 1996 trip to Iceland with my daughter Jessica so well, it seems like it was yesterday. I remember stepping into the plane at JFK for the direct flight to Reykjavik being greeted by a steward. "Follow me, please," he said as he took us to a first class accommodation. I don't know why we were given this privilege, but it was really something, perhaps a presage of what we would find in Iceland, that they are, quite simply, very nice people. The seats were made of plush leather, all very roomy, with a curtain that could provide privacy, if wanted.

We had an immediate visitor, a stewardess who wanted to know if we wanted a drink or something to eat. Not a bag of peanuts, mind you, but a cheeseburger, if you will.

Ah, we were off to a good start. As it was Jessica's first airplane ride, I thought I better clear things up about the seats. "Jess," I said, "it's not always like this. This is what is called "first class," and probably costs 4-5 times as much as I paid for our seats. Today's our lucky day." And so it would be for the days of the next week.

Except for my trips to the polar regions, Iceland is one of the spots on this earth that is what I would call *raw, beautiful naked raw.* I mean this in the most complimentary way. It is a small island, with aspects of primitive nature mixed in with the ambience of its cities. It does not take long to get from one of its small cities to a beautiful waterfall such as the Gullfoss where layers upon layers of water falls. Or to the larger stereotypical one called Skogafoss.

I had seen a few glaciers in Alaska, yet I had never walked on one as Jessica and I did at Solheimajokull, a glacier that imperceptibly continues to move. We tippy-toed about, as it can be a bit dangerous if one is not careful.

We also walked in a trench that had been formed during an earthquake when tectonic plates collided. It provoked my imagination to think that if I were in that trench during the earthquake I would have been crushed like a bug underfoot!

To add to the wild ambience of this island nation, there are four active volcanoes on the island!

It got dark at about 10:15 p.m. in April when we were there. It's sort of different to be walking about at that time of night. We did not see this, but the nights can be dangerous for puffin birds in August when millions of young puffins set out for the sea where they will spend two years. They navigate to the sea by using the moon but many of them get confused by the streetlights of Heimaey in the Westmann Islands which I visited, off the coast of Iceland. The puffins confuse the lights with the moon and, unless they are rescued, they will be killed by the dogs and cats of the town. So, to prevent this from happening, they have a wonderful annual custom called "The Puffin Patrol" wherein parents and small children search the town at night for stranded birds which they put in boxes until the morning. The children then release them in the right direction of the ocean where they will mature and return in two years. It is a delightful family custom, I was told, that has been part of the ways of Iceland for many years.

Ironically, the puffins are also a main dish in Iceland.

It was also part of the draw for me to be intrigued by this place where women with babies still leave them in the carriages on the sidewalk unattended while they shop!

Can you imagine doing this in an American city?

I found it interesting when one of the librarians told me with pride that Iceland has the highest incidence in the world of library books taken out per person.

Alas, I found out when I got home that as a nation the consumption of alcohol per capita was also on the high side. It can be extremely cold in Iceland, so it's easy to picture its citizens sitting around reading and having a few drinks on a cold winter's night. Sounds cozy, doesn't it?

One day while there Jessica and I decided to split up. She wanted to ride the famous Icelandic horse and I wanted to take a half hour prop plane flight to the Westman Islands. The Icelandic horse is small, almost pony size, yet it is registered as a horse. It is, too, well protected. No horses are allowed in Iceland from outside the country, and once one of its own leaves the country it is not allowed to re-enter.

As for the Westman Islands, its largest island, Heimaey (mentioned before re the "Puffin Patrol") is the only one inhabited. In 1973 its volcano erupted suddenly and all of its 5000 inhabitants had to be quickly evacuated as the lava began to eat up people's homes and stores, while also clogging its harbor. As it is a fishing community, it was only with the help of the U.S. navy that the harbor was set free.

I had a wonderful day there, as I was warmly embraced by the locals. I met the local librarian who first went there as a college student some 30 years ago at that time, fell in love and never left! She told me much about the local mores and I am indebted to her for spending so much time with me.

As I was having lunch in one of the local restaurants, I noticed three young ladies at a table nearby. As I often do on my trips, I introduced myself and asked if I might sit with them. Usually, it is a way, especially with teen-agers, to get the real story about the place in which they live. So, I met three of the students at the local high school who invited me to visit their school, which I did late in the day. As I remember, they told me that there wasn't much to do on the island, something that teens everywhere seem to echo.

When I got to the high school, they were there to greet me and gave me a gift: a good size piece of lava glued to a piece of porcelain as big as my hand. It was signed, Greetings *from Lava, The Edge, and Harp*. It hangs in my study.

I took a small bus ride into the volcano that fired the town in 1973. It was a bit spooky as steam was still coming out of seams in the black sand. For whatever reason, I decided to sit in it to see what would happen. For the rest of the day, I walked around with wet underwear! I took it as an act of faith that there was no imminent danger but then I realized that the 1973 blow came as a surprise to everyone. I was glad when the bus came to take us back down into town from what I thought of as a "hot" volcano.

There have been several volcanic eruptions on the mainland since the big blow on Heimaey, but none as destructive because of the lessons learned from 1973.

We never did get to the Blue Lagoon, a popular spot where locals and tourists bathe in the thermally heated waters. In fact, geothermal energy heats homes and supplies hot water to the people of Iceland. It is as simple as using the heated steam coming from underground to power the turbines that supply the heat. Ironically, the fishing boats, cars, and busses of Iceland still use traditional methods of producing power for its motors.

Given my disappointment with formal religions, I was interested to discover that the people of Iceland believe in a spiritual force yet do not necessarily practice religion.

XXX

I had always wanted to go to the Galapagos Islands. To do it with Sheila in 1996 was a total joy, for she is my best friend, and my best companion. To go to the Galapagos is to go to animal heaven, and to do this with the great animal lover, Sheila, is to go to Jerry heaven.

On the first night in our hotel room in Quito, 600 miles off the coast of the Galapagos, we knew this trip was going to be different, quite different. Out of the massive window in our room, we could see the lights of hundreds, possible thousands, of homes built closely to each other on Mt. Antisana. I wondered why people would choose to live there because immediately above them on the top of the mountain at 16,000 feet is an active volcano, Guagua Pichincha, that hadn't blown in over almost 400 years. A year after our visit, it rumbled hard and had a big eruption of ash, but no explosion. To this day, it continues to huff and puff and lately, as I write this, it sounds ominous. Yet, the people of Ecuador have a saying: "Volcanos nor earthquakes will kill us. Our government will."

In the morning we flew to the Galapagos and boarded our small yacht, the Corinthian, which held 48 tourists. I think we visited five of the thirteen main Islands.

Generally, we would spend most of the day visiting an island, then sail at night as we slept, to wake up on a different island, have breakfast and explore some more. Each day was a sensual and visual delight, well, almost every day. Sometimes, a sea lion that had twins would let one of them die of starvation, as she could only feed one.

We saw one of these one day abandoned by its mother. Poor baby. Poor Sheila. The same with a red-footed booby. Our guide called it "an obligatory murder." I guess we were learning some of what Darwin called the survival of the fittest, although I don't think the obligatory murders were really part of that, as he was theorizing about natural survival.

Actually, I thought a lot about Darwin when I was in the Galapagos, the place where he gathered a lot of his evidence for his theory of evolution. We were told to never touch any of the animals, as they were used to the protective environment of the islands, and might grow scared if they were ever mistreated. Yet, every time a finch would come up to me I felt like putting out my hand for it to jump into it, as it is the finch and its evolution that seems to have attracted the most interest in Darwin's work. Probably because it is the easiest to explain. One class of the finch evolved a long beak on one of the islands in order to drink water from splits in the rocks.

Another, on a different island, evolved a short beak in order to crack the plentiful nuts found there. I even asked Sheila to be ready with the camera one afternoon when I saw many of them on a beach. When it came time as a lively one approached me, I could not go through with it. To disrespect the rules of protection was something I could not do, even though I always wanted a bird to land in my hand. But not this one, not here.

We saw so many extraordinary animals. Fur seals sunning on rocks and beaches, and do they stink. Big and cute, but very stinky! We walked so close to the nests of red and blue-footed boobies at our face level that it would be easy to simply touch them. I thought one of the mommas was going to kiss me. Sheila sat next to one of the turtles we saw while walking through a village. She spent some time petting it on its head that he stuck out for stroking – yes, they seem to sense an animal lover. It was sweet to watch them bond so quickly. Iguanas were everywhere. They love to be petted under their chins we found out later as we watched one pet owner do in the village. Lizards, too.

And Sally Lightfoots, the large red crabs that hang out together on the rocks by the sea, always making a colorful splash for the eyes.

One day we went to Santa Cruz island to see the famous "Lonesome George" who was thought to be the last of his sub-species. It is a myth that George was never interested in mating. More than once, he was successfully mated, but each time his mate's eggs became inviable. Oh, how they tried at the Darwin Research Station.

George died in 2012, probably about 100 years old which is not *very* old for a tortoise.

I tried to swim with the wild seals, hoping to get a few photos with an underwater camera I had purchased. They were too wild for me, bumping me and pushing me around was a little too creepy for me. But, yes, I watched Sheila, the Animal Whisperer, calming them down and petting them.

When we got back to the mainland, we took an excursion to the Equator Monument where we took photos of each other, one foot in the northern hemisphere, the other in the southern hemisphere. Not too many people can be in both of the hemispheres at once!

XXX

I suppose that culturally we are more aligned with the English than with any other nation. Same kind of art, music, literature, architecture. Same kind of militarism, although the British have been at it longer than we.

So, I went to England in 1996. When I got into my room in London, I put on the T.V. to relax a bit before exploring this great city. There it was: TWA flight 800 had blown up over Long Island Sound a few hours after my flight took the same path the evening before! It gave me the creeps when the speculation began that the plane might have been the victim of a ground to air hand-held missile, or an accidentally fired missile from a military installation nearby. It could have been me. The misty ghosts of fear of flying wafted through my mind a few times.

The highlight on the trip was visiting Stratford Upon Avon, the birth and death place of William Shakespeare, perhaps the greatest ever of all writers. I never did like the mandatory teaching of his plays, as I think the plots about murder, deceit, infidelity, and the other dark sides of humans are too mature for adolescents. The medieval language, too, makes it quite difficult to understand. Yet,

I think that his ability to say something swift and powerful about the lives we lead is extraordinary. "To be or not to be," "This above all: to thine own self be true," "Cowards die many times before their deaths." On and on. I have been in two books citing quotes with some of the great ones, including Shakespeare. Compared to his, my words are those of a first grader.

I learned when I was there that saying "Let's have some crack" means "Let's have some fun." It was more difficult to know the meaning behind Stonehenge, those huge rectangular boulders set in a circle. Scholars place many theories behind it all, as a place of healing fraught with religious significance. Each of its stones weigh on average 20 tons. As the site is possibly 5000 years old, many mysteries surround it, including how the boulders might have been lifted on top of each other back then. As the mystery behind its purpose, its existence, is shrouded in speculation, I think maybe it was built by a bunch of guys who liked rocks!

XXX

Sometimes a cigar is just a cigar. And sometimes a trip is just a trip. And so the trips I took in 1997 and 1998 to six countries were more than trivia in my life, yet less than impactful. I do not, of course, say this as disrespectful to these countries. I always learn much on any trip to satisfy my curiosity which is why, in the first place, I take many of my trips. I learn the sights and sounds and people of each one, something no book or course work could ever do. Perhaps it is more accurate to say that I never left a part of my heart in any one of these six. Perhaps, too, it is close to what I am trying to say here that the trips sharpened and maybe excited my brain rather than my heart. So, I will simply put down the highlights of each trip in its turn.

Greece: seeing the original Olympic stadium while suddenly hearing, "Hey, Brooker," the voice of my friend from college days whom I hadn't seen in a long time. Turns out he was on the same ship as Sheila and I.

The island of Mykonos with its white, bleached houses, windmills, lovely shops and restaurants.

Wondering why so many people were staring at me and Sheila as we walked the streets of Crete eating from cardboard boxes and talking excitedly. It was Good Friday, a day of mourning in the Greek Orthodox church. "Sheila, I'm noticing that people walking on the street are not talking. Maybe we ought to keep it down."

Turkey: the super aggressive men. Visiting the house where the Blessed Virgin allegedly lived after the death of her Son. Looking into the eyes of a female statue created in 1600 BC. Why did she bring tears to my eyes?

Netherlands: visiting Anne Frank's hiding place in Amsterdam. She wanted to be a great writer. Without knowing it, she was.

Checking out the marijuana restaurants and the Red Light District – a different world. Sweden: the boat trip around the many small islands in Stockholm. Watching President Clinton on T.V. in our room telling the world, with determination, "I did not have sex with that woman."

Denmark: saw the iconic "Little Mermaid" statue in the Copenhagen harbor. I thought she had a forlorn and dreamy look.

My youngest son asked me if I would take a photo for him in Denmark of a pretty young woman. It took me many walks past two blond beauties sitting on a bench before I approached them. "My son asked me if I would take a photo of a pretty woman in Denmark. Would it be OK if I took a shot of both of you?"

They looked at me as if I were a scoundrel. "Yeah, right!" they answered.

Tivoli Gardens, the biggest and most classy amusement park I've ever seen, was also a hoot.

Norway: Of course, I remember it as being naturally beautiful. What engaged me the most, though, was the day I visited the City Hall in Oslo. You see, Elie Wiesel had just been awarded the Nobel Prize for Peace, right there in the tundra of the city hall.

I am not one who worships heroes, most of whom are not worthy of the crowns placed on them by the media. Yet, he has always been one of my heroes whose book, *Night,* I have taught many times. And I have visited Auschwitz where his dad was killed by two drunken guards and where he was imprisoned as a young man. He always put his time, effort, and voice to keep the memory of the Holocaust alive. This takes commitment, whose beck he answered whenever it called.

I took many photos that day, and even asked a stranger to take one of me standing at the rostrum where Wiesel gave his acceptance speech, a superb one in which I remember him saying about the millions of his fellow Jews killed that if we forget, "... we are guilty, we are accomplices."

Little did I know when I was in Oslo that about a decade later he would agree to be on the Board of Advisors of the 1995 Students' Peace Conference which I arranged to be held in Hiroshima, Japan. He also was kind enough to write a letter in support of my candidacy for inclusion in the 1998 National Teachers Hall of Fame.

He called me an outstanding teacher and human being. After speaking with me, he wrote, "I learned of his deep commitment – to peace and to young people." I have always struggled to let his words in.

XXX

The United States Information Agency sent me to Ukraine for two weeks in 1998. Here's the story behind that invitation: as the Soviet Union broke up, Ukraine became an independent nation, one of the Newly Independent States (NIS). When President Clinton paid a visit there, he asked what he could do for them. One of the problems with the education system, he was told, was that it had been "old school" for generations. That is, it was teacher-centered.

This kind of a system and its implicit teaching methodology placed the emphasis on the teacher as the all-knowing dispenser of knowledge. Only his/her thinking processes were honored. The students' role was to take notes, ask no questions, and spill out the contents of the notes on quizzes and tests. The more accurate you spilled, the better would be your mark.

Student input was, by and large, forbidden. There was no students voice, no way for any of them to sign their signature, so to speak, as a student and a person. There was no sharing with each other, questioning the teacher was rare, no real creativity was going on. In a word, there was no democracy in the classroom. That was the way of an autocratic society. Be seen and not heard!

The answer to the president's question was, "Send us teachers who will show our teachers the methods that will allow our students to be full participants in the classroom."

The way I got it was that the Ukrainian officials knew how important that was for them to develop an open society by starting in the classroom with democratic teaching.

I passed the required bar of the USIA and was sent to Ukraine.

My first inclination that I was heading into an area of the world where I would further my development was in the airport in Vienna where I was waiting for my flight to Kiev. I met a man who would be working on the hardshell of the atomic power plant at Chernobyl that had blown twelve years before. I immediately wondered how far the city of my posting, Poltava, was from it. I found out it was about 150 miles away. When I got into Poltava, I began to ask how I would get to Chernobyl, as I had read that there was a bit of safe tourism going on, hand held Geiger counters, that kind of stuff. I was told by the officials at my school that they would not support my going there, that it was still a very toxic place. Putting my responsibility to them together with meeting the guy at the airport, I concluded likewise.

A few days later, I was asked if I would like to visit the Poltava fire department in town that had a connection with the Chernobyl disaster. In the immediacy of the explosion, its fire department rushed a company of men to help put out the fire, thinking it was an electric fire. No one told them of the real nature of the fires, that they were nuclear reactor explosions. The men were rushed to the rooftops. Most of them died soon after of acute radiation sickness.

The chief of the firehouse was most gracious and generous to me. He gave a large medallion to me, a medallion made in the image of two firefighters, one with a rescued baby in his arms, the other fighting flames. Its inscription is in Cyrillic which I have had translated: "Our job is to put out fires." Indeed. He told me that the medallion that he gave to me was the last one. It is in a prominent place in my study.

Going back bit, I was met at the airport in Kiev by a lovely couple, Ivan and Nina, with whom I had a wonderful and warm relationship. Ivan was an assistant principal at the school to which I was assigned as my home base, sort of my guardian angel while I was there, always watching over me to make sure I was OK. It was good to have someone to lean on when I needed to lean, as I was very busy giving talks and lessons at schools of every level.

I was invited to a reception with the U.S. Cultural Attache who was not as gracious. She asked me where I was from and then inquired about my children, asking me where they lived, how many children they had, and so forth. When I told her that my oldest son, Kevin, lived in a little town called Post Mills in Vermont, she lit up. "I'm from Vermont!" She went on to let me know that she knew every town in Vermont, and that "There is no such town in Vermont." We went back and forth on that one until I finally gave up. "I guess I've been going to the wrong house all these years," I said. She harrumped and spun off, never to talk with me again.

I was assigned to live in an apartment with one of the teachers.

I had made it known to the agency that I wanted to live in a place that had a shower.

Well, she had a shower and a full complement of bed bugs! I was so tired the night when I first got into her place that I wanted, after the introductions, to go to sleep. As I pulled down the covers to get into bed, I was met with a horde of bedbugs, literally hundreds, running for their little lives to get out of the light. When they finally were out of my sight, I shut out the light, got into the bed and pulled the covers up on myself.

Fatigue trumped bedbugs!

When I got up the next morning, she made me a breakfast, as I remember home fries with eggs and toast, a harbinger of the many fabulous meals that she would make for me over the next couple of weeks. She was exact in her ways. One day, for example, she slept in late. I tip-toed about and left for school, alas, without my breakfast.

I was in school for about a half hour when she showed up with a full breakfast in a bag for me!

Back to my first morning there. I ate, then went into the bathroom to take a shower. When I pulled the plastic curtain over to get in, I was met again by the bed bugs, now crawling on the sides of the shower stall. I got in and used the shower spray hose to wash the stampede down the drain. Word must have gotten out in the bedbug community after that, as they no longer showed up anywhere in the apartment.

Ivan assigned me to the English department at my home-base high school. They were a wonderful bunch, always solicitous to meet my needs. Every day or evening one of them volunteered to take me somewhere . . . a private visit to a museum, a comedy club, the circus, an evening of conviviality at one of their apartments with their friends, accompanied by guitar and songs.

Ah, yes, how I remember the circus. Apparently, they knew I was a guest from America because when I arrived an usher asked me to follow him to a chair that was was placed immediately outside the big ring. It was a little scary when a scantily clad woman accompanied by a full-grown and beat up looking lion entered the ring, and stopped about ten feet from me. Its mouth was taped shut but, oh, the paws. When the circus ended, the lion lady asked me if I would like to accompany her and her lion back stage. I told her that I was honored but I could not as I have a lot on my plate (including the will to live).

The lives of teachers in my school was a potpourri of misery. On average, English teachers taught seven classes a day, sometimes eight. This compared to the average of 3.2 classes per day at Staples H.S. They were paid in vodka, sweat socks and sugar as supplements to rubles, which they blamed on Yeltsin. There was a saying going around at the time: "The difference between your president and ours is that he (Clinton) did it with one person. Ours did it with the nation."

Yet, they seemed to take great pride in their teaching. Perhaps that was why their school was chosen for an American teacher's visit. They seemed eager, even creative, in listening to my talks about post-modern teaching methodologies. I remember telling one group about alternative seating instead of the old ways of lining up desks and chairs one behind the other: "There is a way to use the desks and chairs so that the students can see one another." It was not a big deal, as it had been my way for years – a large circle!

One of the teachers came to see me the day after the desks and chairs talk. "I want you to come right now, to see the ways I use the chairs." I did as he asked. In a most remarkable way, he put most of the chairs in a circle, except two sets. These he placed inside the circle facing each other. I asked him how he would use that kind of configuration. "Oh, I don't know right now, but we will figure a way." How I loved that guy. "We will figure a way," he had said. Not the old "I will figure a way." He was really incorporating his students into the work of the class, such a contrast to one of the teachers who told me, "Sleeping is my hobby."

I noticed, though, when I spoke with university teachers that they were not interested in teaching methodologies. They wanted to know about salaries and contractual matters in America, and how difficult it is to get a visa that would allow them to go to America. It made me kind of sad to think of how good teachers had it in Westport, and I wondered if many teachers there realized it.

One of the Ukrainian teachers invited me to dinner at his parents' apartment. His father, a major in the army, told me "You are an owl." I found out later what he meant: that I was a wise man to reject offers of vodka, wine and beer.

On one of my last days there, Ivan rented a car and driver to take him, me, and his son to Kharkov, about 70 miles east of Poltava. In most respects it was a beautiful city except for one entire block which had sunk. I had never seen anything like that and was filled with awe. They took me to a water show in a setting that was quite deteriorated.

There were three other people there to see the show that featured a single dolphin. Ivan seemed so proud of it all, even paying for me to have one of the dolphins leap out of the pool to kiss me.

I taught some classes at the school, and so knew many of the students. I cleared it with the principal and several teachers to raffle off some of my winter clothing in the classes. I wanted to be sure that this was a good move, one that would not humiliate anyone. We had a lot of fun with that. They gave me tons of gifts when it came time to say goodbye. When I got home, I spread the gifts out on the floor to show my wife. In all, they took up floor space in two rooms! I eventually gave several exhibitions of them back in America. The remaining few days in Poltava were emotionally closing in on me. I had made so many new friends. I knew it was going to be hard on me to leave. I am like that. I had grown in so many ways just by being there. The conditions reminded me of my childhood when we lived in a cold water flat. And I saw how dedicated the teachers were, especially Elvira who took such committed care of me, fed me, introduced me to her friends, and gave her room and T.V. to me. On my last day there she invited me to sit in on her class. I could see how nervous she was, yet how dedicated to teaching her 3rd graders. She impressed me by the way she incorporated her little ones into the procedures of the lesson, letting them sign their names in the process of learning. I would have been proud to be her supervisor.

The English department had a lunch party for me. I knew that once the speeches and gifts started that this was going to be difficult for me. They gave me a beautiful sweater and the wooden *bulova,* their national symbol that looks like a medieval club with wooden spikes. It had hung on the wall in their faculty room. It is a symbol of faith and courage, qualities needed in Ukraine as I write this. I have written to them several times since the Russian intrusion to the east of Poltava but have not heard back.

I didn't know what gift to give back to them, so I went for simplicity, a fresh rose to the elder of the department. I gave a little speech, thanking them for their abiding kindnesses to me, something that I will always remember. And then, dammit, I cried.

They simply allowed me to do that.

Ivan took me to the train in the morning, as he would accompany me to Kiev. I couldn't believe how many new friends and teachers came to say farewell.

They gave me more gifts, ever so sweet: bags of potatoes and vegetables that they had grown in their own gardens. I was deeply moved by this as I know the historic role of potatoes in the lives of the poor.

The train was about an hour late, which reminded me of the only joke I got at the comedy club: little boy's tooth falling out, dad ties a string to the tooth and attaches the string to the local train which would pull out the tooth for the Tooth Fairy when it leaves, probably within the next hour. It took three days!

Every time I looked out of the train the group was still there waiting to say good–bye. So I would go to them for more hand shakes, more hugs. I thought it would never end.

Yes, I left a part of my heart in Poltava. It was becoming more and more clear in my travels that I was becoming the Other, and the Other me.

XXX

In 1999 I took a trip to Spain, Morocco and Portugal. In a way, they seemed dim compared to the intensity of Ukraine. Dim, but not dark. So, a few notes on how the trip pushed forward my awareness and growth about the wonders of life.

Spain: I saw Picasso's *Guernica* in Madrid. I did not think it a great work of art but, hey, what do I know about art? The old Toledo Bridge is a sight to see, but the story surrounding its rebuilding is the interesting part. Apparently, the original was poorly built and beginning to crumble, thus ruining the reputation of the architect who designed it. However, his wife, smart cookie that she was, waited for an electric storm to come upon it one night and, taking advantage of the storm as a cover, burned it down. Point, I guess, is that behind every stupid man there is a smart woman. My point: Melania Trump, where are you?

Morocco: seeing Gibraltar from the ferry trip to Africa. A business sign in Tangier that Said, "Brooker, S.A." I looked it up when I got home. The "S.A." stands for "Societe Anomyme," anonymous partnership.

Walking through the Medina in Fez was unlike anything I had ever done. It is a walled-off city within a city. 15,000 residents live in this nest of apartments, hotels, kiosks and forbidden looking alleyways. Our guide scared us with stories of people disappearing in the dark corridors, so dangerous, he thought, that he hired two extra guides for our visit, one at the head of us, one behind. We were never to leave the line, lest we, too, might disappear, never to be seen again!

The walls were sometimes so narrow in the medina that we were instructed to hug them when a donkey, laden with goods, wanted to pass. There are up to a thousand shops (kiosks) that sell everything plus more that one could find in an American mall.

There are smells of every kind, some good coming from flower shops, some not so good coming from the tannery shops. We soon found out not to put our hands in any of the many holes in the walls, as they were occupied by feral cats, some mean and hissy. There is, too, a respected university, U. Al-Karaouine, in the medina. According to UNESCO, it is the oldest degree granting university in the world. It offers a diversity of courses, but is mainly known as a center for Islamic teachings.

The Arabian horsemen in Marrakesh were extraordinary. When I went to see them perform, I sat in the first row on a curve. I was so close to the horses as to touch them. It was the best of rows and the worst of rows. The riders were athletic and very talented as they rode in extreme positions, backwards, heads on saddles, feet in the air on fast and powerful horses. I can see the horses now, rounding that bend in front of me, in their glory, muscles rippling, nostrils flaring as they picked up speed, spewing dirt and dust on me. I felt like I was watching a movie.

Portugal: we took the ferry back to Spain, and then a bus to Portugal where I saw my first and last bullfight in Lisbon. I hate bullfighting, as killing a vulnerable animal is immoral in my book of values. It is also the act of a coward. But I went to this one because they do not kill the bull in the ring in Portugal. What I did not know is that they torture them before the event is over. It goes something like this: the bull is relentlessly lead about by a man on a horse. He eventually sticks a long and thin javelin into its back three times as the bull bleeds and the audience cheers, for what I have never understood.

It is very noisy when this happens allowing me to cheer for the bull, "Toro, Toro!" The rider now goes off, and eight men with silly looking caps confront the raging bull, trying to make his efforts look silly. The bull got his revenge the night I saw him fight in Lisbon, as he knocked one of these men half way across the arena, bleeding and unconscious. As the hushed crowd stood and waited, an ambulance came into the arena for him. Eventually, the half crazed bull was led off by three cows. Ah, yes, those romantic Portuguese.

I am now a fallen away Catholic, yet I still have a great respect for its liturgy and many of its practices, including the veneration of the mother of Jesus. So, I was quite excited to visit Fatima, the site where she appeared several times to three peasant children in 1917. A long time ago when I was a monk I dedicated myself to the mother of Jesus, asking her to watch over me. At the same time, I said to her if there is such a thing as good works would she kindly take any good works I might do in my life and, if they are worth anything, would she apply them in any way she liked, perhaps to another who needed it to get back into the good graces of her son, Jesus. I renew this request annually in the presence of a statue of her that was given to me at Christmas time in 1958 by Brother Gus Galway, a great man and my superior at St. Cecilia's community and school in Harlem, NY, to which I was assigned at the time.

There is a smooth marble pathway, about three feet wide, that runs for a hundred or so yards at the holy grounds where she appeared. It is a place where devotees get on their hands and knees to crawl from one end to the other. I looked at it for a while, wondering if I, too, should do some penance for my sins by crawling on it. Crawling on one's hands and knees is not an easy thing to do. I figured I had earned the right to ask for forgiveness, so I did it for about 15 yards before I began to feel self-conscious, yet satisfied that I had participated.

XXX

I retired from teaching in June of 2000, then immediately took a very long trip to Australia and New Zealand. Sheila gets ill on plane trips that last for more than eight hours, so this one was not for her.

My trip to Australia encompassed the entire east coast beginning in Sydney, the largest city in Australia, but not its capital as most Americans think. Canberra is its capital. I knew immediately that I would like the Australians, as they are very friendly and have a great sense of humor. In fact, I think they are the friendliest of all the people I've met on my travels.

I took a flight north to Cairns, pronounce "cans". From there I went to the famous Great Barrier Reef where there were so many things to do from an observation station called *Quicksilver*. You could simply swim or snorkel or take a semi-submersible submarine which I did twice. I couldn't make up my mind about snorkeling. The reef seemed a bit wild and I am not a strong swimmer. I finally decided to snorkel, an amazing visual discovery at once and a bit frightening at another. You see, I got so lost in seeing the colorful fish life and reef that I forgot to take a look now and then to see where I was. I do remember seeing a 3 foot shark. In fact, the tide was strong, so when I finally came up to take a look I was about 200 yards from the observation station.

It frightened me that I was alone and far from safety, wondering if the tide would take me further out with no one seeing my predicament, if it might be called that. My first thoughts were about the tide, and if I should immediately begin to shout for help. What came to me is a simple thought, *Don't panic.* And see how it goes if I start to do the breaststroke. I got quite clinical about it. I'd do the breaststroke and begin to calculate how much closer I would be getting to the *Quicksilver* every 2-3 minutes measured against how much weaker I was beginning to feel. I decided that if my strength weakened faster than the distance I was closing in to safety, I would then start to yell for help. I closed the distance more quickly than I thought I would to get back to home base.

Adrenaline will do that.

After that personal drama, I went to Kuranda where I took a five mile skyrail trip over the rainforest canopy. It is a most extraordinary look at a rainforest from above. I then flew back to Sydney.

We were told never to try to pet a kangaroo, as they were apt to flash-kick, a powerful move that can eviscerate a human. I saw a few in the open at a zoo, and kept my distance. I went to the famous Opera House, and took the walk on the Sydney Harbor Bridge, a great experience. Each person was given a locker into which we had to put our belongings, as a falling object, even a hairclip, from the top of the bridge can go through the roof or wind shield of the moving cars far below. A "jumper" type garment was then put on. The climb is not as dangerous as it might seem, as we were each strapped to a heavy-duty cable throughout the walk. Naturally, the sights beneath us were amazing. After that, we got to see the soon to be Olympic stadium and the village where the athletes would stay.

My awareness of critters was awakened again when we were told the story of the Olympic frogs that had recently occurred. The story: there was a huge frog pond which the Olympic committee wanted to replace with a large parking lot. A public outcry ensued. So the committee decided to move all the frogs to a new and "fitting" pond site down the road a bit while keeping the plan for the parking lot at the original pond.

Sounds like a good compromise, right? Well, the frogs didn't think so. They were carefully moved late one night, as the story goes, to the new pond. However, when the morning sun came up, guess what? The thousands of frogs that had been moved the night before were back in the original pond! The parking lot would be built on the replacement grounds. "No problems, Mate!"

I flew to the South Island of New Zealand to Christchurch where I visited the International Antarctic Center, a kind of museum where the conditions of the Antarctic were replicated. I was fascinated and decided that one day I would visit the Antarctic.

I remember when I visited Queenstown how impressed I was with the peace and quiet I felt there that I wrote an e-mail to Sheila saying, "Sell all, come at once." Of course, I was kidding.

I hired a pilot to fly me around Milford Sound in a Cesna 207. It was as if I was on a magic carpet flying in, out, and around the mountains and over the beautiful lakes.

The North Island of New Zealand was our next destination: Rotorua and the Maiori Cultural Center, a major meeting place for the aborigine Maiori Indians who have been nicely integrated into the two-island nation, unlike other nations (see the United States of America) that have not done a good job of this. Our guide called us aside to tell us that there would be a ceremony that the Maiori held sacred and we were to select a leader of our group. The elected leader would be confronted by the chief in the ceremony. Even though it was a kind of "touristy" ritual, we were told that the native participants ask that we hold the rite seriously.

As a rite, it would mark our acceptance or rejection by the Maiori. It was emphasized that there should be no laughter, especially by the leader who happened to be yours truly. I'll tell you it was not difficult not to laugh, as the chief was a very scary looking and well-muscled guy wearing very little. I was instructed to stand still, arms at my side, as he would persistently get close up in my face while making grunts, groans and yowls. He would back off, do a sort of threatening dance while holding a spear, and then come back at me again. After a series of these moves, he came in close and, voila, rubbed noses with me, a sign of acceptance, a greeting in the Maiori culture. We were all relieved and could now get on with a wonderful meal, at the end of which I was given a necklace with a traditional Maiori wooden mask attached, "for withstanding the fierce chief."

At one point we sailed across a lake to visit a sheep station where we'd see sheep shearing, a mainstay of the island. What is note-worthy about this trip for me is seeing a beautiful beach on the lake shore, the kind of a beach that New Yorkers of my youth would die for. Not only was it beautiful, it was deserted except for sheep who were using it as a toilet. The sight of this inspired me to write my first book, "A Gathering of Doves," about a rogue president of the United States. Here is the introduction:

"It is a beach so removed that animals bathe in it waters and crap on its shores, a crescent shape that cups the blue lagoon. Overlooks splay out into green hills where sheep graze while keeping their covenants with nature.

The vista from the hills is clear, yet double-edged, an immediacy of sunshine against distant rain that falls like a black bridal veil, as the bleatings of lambs break silence.

Suddenly, a fox streaks out of the trees, sheen of its red fur caught by sunlight, snatches a lamb by the throat and, before the flock knows, escapes into the maw of woods nearby. The lamb's mother, watching now, backs up a step or two before continuing to eat. Nothing changes. Except doves begin to whirl in tightening circles, looking for a place to gather."

In Auckland, we went to the America's Cup Village where we motored on a yacht that supposedly was the famous "Endeavor' which competed in the 1934 America's Cup. When we were asked who would like to pilot the boat, I volunteered.

It was a thrill to steer her, but I don't think it was the Endeavor.

XXX

In 2001 Sheila and I took a trip to Italy and Switzerland. Our first stop was Rome, in some ways the birthplace of Christianity. It is so rich in historic sights that I probably will not do justice to it. One merely has to simply walk in the city and its history will find you. We did that one day as we broke away from the group. The Spanish Steps, the Trevi Fountain, and the Pantheon found us.

Over a few days, we saw the Pieta and the Sistine Chapel where Michaelangelo over 500 years ago painted the famous biblical scenes, the most famous, of course, being God reaching out to touch the hand of Adam.

We spent time in the catacombs outside Rome. They are almost 2000 years old, and are usually about 50 feet under the ground. These underground burial places are laced with twists and turns, and they are very dirty and dusty. It was not unusual for Sheila and me to see bones sticking out from behind the walls. Their origin is a narrative filled with many reasons. The one that "sticks" for me is that it was unlawful to inter in the city, so these catacombs, forty in all, are outside the city walls.

Our trip to the ruins of Pompeii was exciting, as we could see Mt. Vesuvius which erupted in 79 A.D., smothering the city and its inhabitants. It, too, was a bit spooky as the casts of victims were placed exactly where the city dwellers were overcome by ash, dust, and fire. It is really thrilling for me to actually see places that I have read so much about.

On to Venice where we had a room overlooking the Grand Canal. Not everyone had such a delicious placement. So we invited others, whose rooms were on the outside of the canal, to come to our room and see the gondolas gracefully plying the still waters under our window. We took our own trip on the Grand Canal, a different kind of experience, like walking along blocks of beautiful homes belonging to the "beautiful people," except this time on water.

Of course, the Leaning Tower of Pisa was something to behold, as well as a great image for hokey photos, you know the one with me in the foreground holding it back from falling with my hand.

I've always wanted to go to Switzerland, probably because it always seems to avoid war, perhaps because it is a safe as an anonymous depository of international money, some ill-gained. Who would want to bomb their own money?

So, we went to Lugano for a day and did a little shopping, including a very nice green enameled ring for me. It is a very neat and clean city. I am happy that it is my lasting image of a Swiss city.

Before we left Switzerland for our flight home, we took a boat ride on Lake Como where many notable people, now and in the past (see Mussolini) had homes.

XXX

One month after 9/11 I decided to go to southeast Asia to visit as much of it as I could in three weeks. Some of my friends thought it not smart of me to travel so soon after 9/11, yet I thought it might be the safest time as security, especially at airports, would be on a high state of alert.

Thailand was different from other trips I had taken. Reclining Buddha, Golden Buddha, feeding monks in the morning as they passed by me with outstretched bowls in their hands, the Bridge over the River Kwai, the cemetery for young British men who died building the bridge – "In the going down of the sun and in the morning, we will remember him" – the baby elephants: I so yearned for them to be released into the wild instead of being taught to dance for tourists.

And the Yao hill tribe that I spent an afternoon with, a day that opened my heart more to the world than ever. I had a chance to play games with them, to give them lolli–pops. I even danced the indigenous dances. When I left the hill tribe, I stopped in my jeep for a minute or two down hill to see some strange flowers when I heard voices. Here is a poem I wrote about that day:

Sound tends to echo in the feedback
chamber of a jungle gulley. Once, after
leaving the Yao hilltribe of Thailand,
I stopped in the seashell of such a setting
to sigh, a way to feel my heart, to wrest
it from the mountains that tried to steal
her for its own.
In that very instant I hear a chorus of greetings
from the bowels of trees
encasing my car. *Hello* resonates
to itself and back again.
I see patches of yellow, green and gold
in a clearing far above.
The children are calling to me, their
thin aves affection to the yearning
of who I am.
Cupping mouth with hands, I cry back
my own *hello.*
Our greetings mix in this pan of
lives, bouncing off each other
like molecules in the cosmos.
But I must go.
So I yell *goodbye.*
It echoes too much for me,
And I cannot tell if the sound
is theirs or mine.
It is the story of lives.

And then it was on to Cambodia and the town of Siem Riep where I went to see some of the skulls of the 2,000,000 Cambodians killed by the Khmer Rouge during the time of "The Killing Fields," 1975-79.

In an uplifting part of my trip I went to Tonle Sap Lake from whence came the Cambodian family that we adopted for a year in our home. They are the Bunleuts who had an extraordinary and dangerous journey to get out from underneath the Khmer Rouge.

There are many floating kiosks on the lake. I went into one and actually paid for a boa constrictor to wrap itself around my shoulders for a photo. I can't believe I did that.

Next up was Angkor Wat the name of a religious temple there, the biggest in the world. It is not the 500 year old temple that attracts visitors. It is that 500 acres of jungle land at the temple are studded with the most beautiful buildings that have been overgrown by the jungle to create a most spectacular setting. The images of jungle trees growing through the roofs and windows of architecturally creative buildings built and then abandoned hundreds of years ago is something to behold.

We did a quick trip into Laos where we spent an afternoon on Donsao Island.

I was frustrated that I could not find a ring for my collection. That is, until I came across a small shop where I was shown a pinky ring. They wanted $20 U.S. for it. I thought it was Cracker Jack plastic ring, so I declined. As I pride myself at having a ring from every one of the countries I visit, I offered $10, only because the boat was waiting for me to get on to explore the Mekong River. "OK," she said after conferring with her boss. It was only on the plane heading home that I took the ring out of my back pack and it clicked against my wedding band that I knew it wasn't made of plastic. In fact, I found out back home that it was 18 caret gold. For $10!

I remember buying a watch at a kiosk in a border town in Burma which was pretty much closed off for us. I paid $2 dollars for it, and wear it regularly now, years later.

And then on to Vietnam, not knowing that I would be back there in a few years, the organizer of a peace and development conference.

Hanoi is a beautiful city. What most amazed me was how friendly the people were to me, some even expressing their condolences for 9/11. As I walked through its streets, I couldn't help thinking about the war years when Nixon decided to bomb the city. I grow sad in my travels whenever I am in a city that has been bombed. It is so primitive that on a planet, unique as it is with possibility for wonder and fulfillment that humans resort to violence to settle their disagreements. To say we are childish to be that way would only dignify the violence because children have a dignity that wars do not.

I went to see the Hanoi Hilton, the prison where captured American pilots were held during the war. Most of the scenarios presented in the prison were of the horrendous tortures that the French inflicted on the Vietnamese during the French War from 1946 to 1954. The torture procedures were inventive, cruel, and diabolic. It is a wonder the human mind can conceive ways to inflict such pain.

The water puppet shows are historic in Vietnam and quite funny. It was a relief to see the show on the night after the prison visit.

One of the highlights of the visit was going north of Hanoi to Halong Bay which is in the Gulf of Tonkin. I was intrigued to see the Gulf of Tonkin because it was here that President Johnson used a made-up story in 1964 that North Vietnamese torpedo boats had attacked a U.S. navy ship called the Maddox in order to get congressional authority to start the war.

We took an all-day outing on Halong Bay. It has hundreds of islands, and lime–stone rock formations and caves. It is a photographer's delight as there are lots of classic "junk" boats, usually with one large sail which, when placed against the setting sun, makes even an amateur's shot look ready for the front cover of a magazine.

The day ended with a stay in one of the bay's many hotels, and a morning breakfast before leaving for Hanoi.

XXX

In July of 2002 I took a two week journey that I had waited to go on for a long time, the Arctic. I went on a ship called the Academik Ioffe, a Russian research vessel during the Cold War that can carry 110 passengers, with a crew of 53.

Before sailing we met in Manitoba to take a cruise on the Churchill River in motorized Zodiacs to see the numerous white beluga whales that congregate there in July. We could hear their breathing, a soft hissing in the wind. Churchill is a town that is called "The Polar Bear Capital of the World" as the town is taken over in October and November by the bears when one dares not walk the streets. During those times, tourists rent special busses to see them up close.

We then sailed for a day across the Hudson Bay towards Baffin Island, a huge land mass that lies parallel to the west coast of Greenland. The next morning we set out in the Zodiacs for Walrus Island, the first of many exciting trips into a world that was new to me, a city kid who vowed he would one day see the world, all the world.

A polar bear greeted us as we were about to land on Walrus Island. He looked young and friendly, happy to see us as he rocked back and forth. Naturally, we waved good bye to the bear and motored away. After dinner that night, we were called to a meeting by our expedition leader, an extraordinary man whose love for the polar regions was evident, to tell us that from now on certain members of the crew would bear (no joke) a special kind of shotgun that would be used on an animal only in case of an emergency. As I remember it, the gun would first make a loud banging sound, then a rotating flare of sparks would shoot out and hover over the animal to scare it. Only in a dire circumstance that might endanger one of us would the animal be shot. It was made emphatic that the islands belong to the animals whose guests we were.

On our way to Coral Harbor, we spotted dozens of walrus frolicking on the ice floes. The feeling of being in a previously unknown part of the world was upon me.

Coral Harbor is an Inuit village of some 800 people. They put on a show for us that included drum dancing and throat singing, an ancient cultural expression where two people stand face to face and alternately grunt mild explosive sounds from deep in their throat for about a half minute. There is something primitive and noble about it.

Young children and their moms staged a fashion show for us of beautifully sewn and decorated sealskin garments. The adolescents demonstrated unique Inuit games. Caribou meat, dried, barbecued or baked was served as an after-show snack before we went back to the ship for dinner.

Dinners aboard the ship were exceptional. Served in a nicely appointed dining room, it was diverse, attentively cooked and plentiful. Desserts were of the type found in fashionable restaurants.

After Coral Harbor we were up early to ride around Digges Island to see the 600,000 thick-billed murre birds. They are small, yet hefty, and live in the rugged cliffs of the island. It was a spectacular sight to see the birds coming and going to their nests.

They are quite heavy so they must leap from the cliffs in order to fly. I can still hear their collective shrieking sounds.

We next went to Eric Cove, an island that used to be the site of a Hudson Bay trading post on the Ungava Peninsula. Seeing the abandoned little cemetery was sad and nostalgic for me. The gravestones of people who died in their early 20's are historical markers of how difficult life must have been there. I remember drifting into a kind of little funk about this, being buried at a Hudson Bay trading post.

How undignified and lonely it seemed to me.

Not too far from the cemetery our guide asked us to kneel quietly when he spotted several caribou in the distance heading towards us. In a few minutes two large and handsome caribou came so close that it seemed as if we could reach out and touch them.

Cameras clicked, startling them and they pranced away slowly like show horses on tundra.

The next day we went to High Bluff Island where we separated into one of three groups of our choice: the fast walkers, the moderate walkers, or "pick the flowers" group.

A nice touch. I think I chose the moderates.

Layered clothing is a good approach for walking in the Arctic. You can peel or add, as one's unique body temperature requires, and the temperature can change extremely quickly. On this day, we saw lots of animal bones strewn about, as well as an "inookshook" which is an elaborate pile of stones about ten feet high that function as guideposts to lead caribou and as markers for inhabitants to follow in the heavy snowfalls of winter. They have become a symbol of the High Arctic.

The summer tundra on the island teems with flower life: orange and black lichen which is called "reindeer moss," food for caribou, white and yellow poppies, little willows and fireweed flowers.

Kimmirut is a village of about 250 Inuits. It has a small school, staffed mostly by teachers from mainland Canada, and a small food market. It was good to mingle with the children who were excited to see us and to show us their parents' snowmobiles, the main source of mobility.

We cruised off the southern coastline of Baffin Island in the heartland of Nunavut, the newest Canadian territory, formed in 1999, and governed almost exclusively by the Inuits with help from the Canadian government.

Soon we entered the Davis Strait which separates Baffin Island and Greenland. We then were at sea for three straight days before crossing the Arctic Circle at 8:45 P.M.

As we were in the middle of constant daylight, it was still quite light out. We celebrated with a champagne toast and three blasts of the ship's horn. Some danced away the night on the ship's bow and, with much fanfare and laughter, tried to imitate Inuit games.

We finally spotted land, Godhaven (God Haven), a village under the umbrella of Denmark. It had several small supermarkets, a Danish bakery, a beauty parlor, and a two man police force. We didn't see many Inuits in the morning, as they tend to stay up late during the summer months and, of course, sleep late.

And then we sailed to Uummannaq, a town of 1200 inhabitants, a new school, a wonderful small museum, and shopping opportunities. Icebergs surrounded the town, giving it a sort of mystical look.

That afternoon we had one of the most exciting experiences of the trip when we cruised in the zodiacs to Qilaqitsoq, the island where eight mummies were discovered in 1977 in a small cave. The island is an ancient Inuit burial ground where numerous stone mounds, each with a round stone cover, contain the skeletal remains of an Inuit.

It is difficult to get access to the island, and one hopes that tourists do not desecrate it.

We arrived in the morning at the largest of the Greenland Inuit towns, Ilulissat, where about 8,500 people live, surrounded by many of the amenities of modern life.

It is situated among hills next to the Jakobshavn Glacier, the fastest moving glacier in the world. Each day, the glacier calves icebergs as big as city blocks. I took a 94 year old fellow tourist to see the glacier. We made it by unusual means. Helen was her name.

She gave me a customized ring that her brother had made for her. I want to be like Helen when I grow old.

We spent several hours that day in the Zodiacs, cruising among the ice bergs and ice floes. The experience was kind of surreal because at times we could see only the blue-tinted ice against the sky as far as the eye could see.

On our next-to-the-last day of the cruise, we visited Itiudleq, a tiny village of 160 people. Each of the tiny wooden homes is painted in bright pastel colors that make them easier to spot in blizzards.

Many of the little islands in the area were occupied by husky dogs, kept there so they could run free during the summer months. Each time we approached, they would rush to the water's edge, hoping for a handout, though we had to keep our distance, as they are not domesticated.

Our day ended with a long walk on an isolated island of soggy tundra that was rich with pink, purple and red flowers, as well as with desolate scenery, special and pretty in its own way.

After a final night of sailing the Sondre Stromfjord, the longest fjord in the world, we disembarked the Peregrine at Kangerlussuaq where we took a bus to see the great hairy free-roaming musk oxen before boarding our flight back to Ottawa.

XXX

My second trip to Vietnam was in 2003. Of course, it was going to be an exciting experience for me, as I was in charge of an international peace and development conference which took me two years to organize. The war had ended 28 years earlier.

Like so many other Americans, I had my opinion about the morality of the war, and took my own small measures to say so, sometimes alienating myself with others as on the Sunday at Catholic Mass when the priest asked the congregation who we'd like to pray for. "I'd like us to pray for all the Vietnamese children we are napalming," I shouted out. Of course, faces turned to see who was the guy who didn't know that God was on the side of the good guys, the Americans.

When I went to Vietnam for the first time in 2001, I became friendly with my Vietnamese guide, Nguyen Van Nam. I told him about how I had set up an international peace conference in Hiroshima in 1995. I remember as clearly as if his response was this morning: "Why don't you set up one here?" As simple as that, and so I did with the help of St. John's University where I had received my doctorate and, once again, with the generous financial help of Paul Newman.

Nam was in Hanoi to meet me, the ten students from St. John's and one from Iona College, along with three staff members from St. John's. It was so good to see Nam. I knew very well that without his faith in me that I could not have succeeded there, as I was not certain if my efforts would be appreciated by our former enemy.

Along with several dozen Vietnam students selectively chosen from the Institute for International Relations, a school for the best and the brightest who would study diplomacy, we held a tight schedule for five days of guest speakers, large group sessions, and small groups that were always action-oriented with projects that were expected to have results, short and long range. The bonding that took place between and among students was extraordinary, a delight to see, as it has always been my purpose to unite students whose parents were once enemies.

As always during any of the conferences I have organized, we had exceptional times outside the formal rooms of diplomatic exchanges. On our second day in Hanoi, we were taken to Ho Chi Minh's mausoleum where we saw his embalmed body. And then to his home and museum. It was an "Uncle Ho" day!

I went one evening to a home for young blind musicians who played for me.

When I asked the Vietnamese student who took me there what had cause their blindness, in her kindness she sort of deflected the question. I learned later that it was caused by agent orange. The student who took me there is Thoan (Nguyen Thi Thoan). She and I have become great friends over the years. She has asked me to be her grandfather, an honorific in the Vietnamese culture. Several years ago she came to stay with Sheila and me in Bethel for a few weeks. We took her to many of the sites in New England, to Washington, D.C, and to the 9/11 site in N.Y.C. She is now a teacher, is married, and has a son, Bao. We keep up on a regular basis, and I did get to see her again when I went to Hanoi with Patch Adams to clown at hospitals for children who are victims of agent orange. Small world!

We stayed in what is called "The Old Quarter" of Saigon, now called Ho Chi Minh City. It was exciting to simply walk the streets, as there is so much going on: shops of every sort, restaurants, artists, street "salesmen" who were annoying as they follow you for a long time to sell their wares, usually packets of post-cards. I think they have concluded that all Americans are rich.

The evenings, too, are exciting, as it seems to be the time of day when families and friends gather on the sidewalks where they sit on tiny wooden seats to share their food with each other, as well as to sell it to any interested person.

We had much fun in the evenings sitting on the streets, eating, and sharing with the locals. It was always a favorite time for me.

Being there and listening to the sophisticated Vietnamese guest speakers, mostly professors, was truly an eye-opener for me about the plight of nations. Being among the Vietnamese, talking, exchanging ideas, listening to their concerns about the residual effects of agent orange on the environment and people, especially children born with the genetic defects from this poison, brought a new awareness to me. I was becoming evermore aware of the essential one-ness of all people, each of us, with the exception of those who seek the sources of power, wanting only to fulfill our potential on this earth, and to find our way to sign our signature that can enhance all those with whom we have contact. I would love to send a birthday card to everyone telling him and her that the world became a better place on the day that they were born. Unfortunately, this is not the reality of the world in which we live.

I especially liked to get up early when I was there to do a tai chi class on the street. I would first buy a couple of deep-fried crullers to eat on my way to the women's class. I had a choice of being a part of a women's or a men's group. I chose the women, as its version was far less militaristic than the men's.

I noticed that at the end of each session many of the women would sit and chew on a kind of nut. I inquired about it with lots of hand and mouth gestures before, of course, I was given one. This was met with lots of laughter, as the women knew what I was in for. It was a beetlenut that was used as a kind of teeth cleanser, tooth paste, so to speak. I didn't realize it while I was chewing as, of course, I did not have a mirror.

The more I chewed, the more the women howled with laughter. You see, beetlenut colors the teeth a kind of deep brownish-orange. In old Vietnamese culture, teeth that color are desirable and considered beautiful. It took three days and constant brushing, American style, for my teeth to turn white again!

One of the many cultural practices in Vietnam is about the symbolism of the peach tree which bears dark pink peach blossoms right about the time of the Tet celebrations which are somewhat comparable to our New Year. I wanted to leave behind in Hanoi something memorable about our conference. I asked Thoan if she would use my money to buy a peach tree to be delivered the morning of our conference closing. The peach tree has long and deep roots in the culture, and stands for many things, especially keeping away bad spirits. The legend goes that a long time ago, the shadow of a huge peach tree covered the land. The gods Tra and Vat Luy lived in the tree, and protected its people from evil spirits. But at the end of Tet, they had to exit the tree, leaving the people on their own.

In making a farewell speech to the conference, I asked a Vietnamese student and an American student to come to the stage where the peach tree sat. I asked the two students to grasp one of the branches of the tree and squeeze as tightly as they could.

"Now, the essence of Vietnam and America has been squeezed into the veins of the tree.

The tree has been embraced by our two countries. So, as it grows to celebrate Tet, let us call it *The Peace Tree*." It was planted in the courtyard of the school with a commemorative plaque.

As the people and government of Vietnam recover from the war years, they have tried to place the push and pull between government and citizen in an amusing context:

"We have given you the hats. Now give us the rabbits."

XXX

As my political awakening coincided with the Cuban Revolution in 1959, I always wanted to go there. I had my chance in the summer of 2003 and took it. I was allowed entrance because I was involved in education. The other fourteen, who knows!

We spent most of our time in Old Havana, and a little in Modern Havana, as well as a trip for a few days to the colonial city of Trinidad, a showcase city southeast of Havana. Our schedule for the week revolved mostly around official visits to service organizations, hospitals and community projects, although we still had lots of free time, so we could mingle with the Cuban people, a good lot, I must say. On one of these days we were taken to a farm where we spent several hours talking with the members of this prototype Communist commune.

The architecture of Old Havana was exceptional, though the buildings were somewhat crumbling. The ambience was how I expected it to be: crowded streets, vendors and market places, old American cars made over to their original look, strikingly handsome. Even the police were easy to chat with, that is, once we had broken through the fear learned from the American press about them as being the henchmen for Castro.

The Malacon is a famous wall that has been built to protect Havana from the ravages of the ocean. It has become a meeting place for small groups, mostly teen-agers, and couples holding hands. The teens seemed to be a bit nervous around us Americans at first, yet once the wall of propaganda was broken, they welcomed our presence among them and were willing to talk about this 'n that. Seems to be the same wherever I have gone. I remember being in Iran when we were told that locals would demonstrate against us, whereas they gathered around us in the streets, eager to talk about our and their lives. One group of teens-agers asked me "Why do you hate us?"

Governments do such damage to their citizens, always trying to create fear of the Other.

There were photos of Che Guavera everywhere. The museum dedicated to him and where his embalmed body would soon be placed was not yet ready, yet his spirit was omni-present as Hero of the Revolution. One day, e.g., I asked our guide if he would stop the bus so I, and perhaps others, could relieve myself. He stopped the bus, told me to walk around a particular building where there would be the privacy of an alleyway.

I did what he asked. True, there was an alleyway, and there was privacy. And there was, too, guess what? A giant photo of Che Guavera looking down at me!

I learned that there were regular meetings in the evenings in the streets of Havana. The city is divided into zones, *Zonas* as they are called. We were invited to one of these meetings one evening to *Zona Nueve* (Zone 9). I saw it as an opportunity to get a deeper look into the way things were politically structured in Cuba. I was not disappointed. I asked about it and was told that it is a way to foster community among the people by dividing the city into areas, or zones that would regularly come together to be informed about issues, to eat good food, and to communicate with their neighbors.

Sure enough, when we arrived we were met by several men who seemed to be in charge. One of them found out that I was a poet. As poetry is revered in Cuba, I seemed, all of a sudden, to have status and was asked if I would like to address the crowd. Many children and women came forward to give me red and yellow roses.

I was kind of dumbfounded by all this sudden attention. And I had to think about what I might say.

What to say? Not so easy as it sounds in that America was in the midst of the George W. Bush presidency, a man with whom I totally disagreed. I saw him as an incompetent who was making very bad decisions for our country. So, the first idea that came to mind was to seize the opportunity to vent about Bush. However, I had always honored my conviction to not speak negatively while abroad about the U.S. I just think it is bad faith and cheap to do that. So, I would not do that.

I was put in front of a microphone on a stage. I asked my translator what his name was. "I am Hector," he said. I told him that I would talk slowly so he could feel free to translate whenever he decided to interrupt. I didn't have much time to think about what I wanted to say, as it all came upon me suddenly. I decided to just say something nice, not expecting that it would get the warm welcome that it did.

"I am grateful to be here and to have the opportunity to speak to you tonight.," I started. "I am also grateful that your children have just given to me bouquets of flowers which speak to me like beautiful poetry speaks to you."

At this point, I asked someone to retrieve for me one of the yellow bouquets from the table. "These wonderful yellow flowers stand for friendship, all over the world. So, I am in your debt that you have offered to me, an American, the gift of your friendship.

And how beautifully done through your children, the innocent ones of the world." The ovation was extraordinary. Quite frankly, I didn't understand why. I think I was still naïve about the politics of it all.

I then asked for the red roses. "And look at these gorgeous red flowers . . . ."

Before I could finish the sentence, a burst of enthusiasm broke out. I remember turning to Hector and asking him if he was telling the crowd that I liked Cuban cigars, that being the reason for the enthusiasm. He laughed.

I continued, something like this: "As you know, red roses stand for love. I am humbled that your children have offered to me the gift of love, the most powerful of gifts one can offer to another."

The enthusiasm was beginning to overwhelm me. I thought I had better end this.

But how? "I know that as sure as I am standing here now with you in beautiful Havana, that one day soon all Americans will be free to come to Cuba to be with you here. Be certain that I will take back to my friends in America the love and friendship that you have extended to me. *Muchas gratias.*"

XXX

Navajo Indian Reservation, 2003, Chinle, Arizona. I've skipped mentioning about a few trips, mostly because there was to me a sameness about them. After a while, most European cities began to cease resonating to my soul. It is not that they lack uniqueness or historic value. Rather, it is I who does not bring to the table the inner curiosity it takes to appreciate what these places offer to me. In this sense, I have little to reflect upon.

I was invited by Holly Shapiro to visit the Navajo Indian Reservation where she worked as a nurse the summer after she and I came back from the conference in Vietnam where she served as the nurse practitioner for our students and chaperones. Of course, I have read much about our treatment of the American Indian over the years. Here in Chinle, I had a chance, mainly by way of Holly's experiences, to see what it has wrought.

The effects of alcohol are rampant. Many car accidents, fights, stabbings, gunshot wounds.

I could see, too, the distrust that the Navajo adolescents had with the white man. I was given permission, for example, to spend some time in the reservation high school.

While I was there, I took the opportunity to talk with a senior class to give a little pep talk about the opportunity to go to college, and how this might enhance their career opportunities. I couldn't help but notice that not one student looked at me during my talk.

No one asked me a question, nor did anyone stay after class to talk with me about college. I think I embarrassed the students after class when I asked if I could take photos.

Their silence spoke. Holly asked me to back off, that they were a bit nervous around a white man. Just as I was about to leave, a boy from the senior class stepped forward and stood by my side. I was grateful. Of the thousands of photos I have from around the world, it is the only one I have with an American Indian.

The week I spent on the reservation deepened my understanding of the residual effects of the mistreatment of the American Indian, especially when I compare it with the humane treatment of other indigenous people I have visited around the world, for example, the Maori Indians of New Zealand and the Saami Indians of Finland who are well integrated into their societies. The fact that I have identical genetic markers on my mother's side with the Saami has influenced the depth of the experience on the reservation. It is something I wish I didn't have to live with that I am ashamed of America's grab of Indian land as its people moved westward. The dark shadows of this past live hard in my soul. Here is a poem I wrote about the reservation:

Reservation Man

I see you coming towards me
in the side view mirror of my car,
cinnamon red face flushed
as you stumble slightly
before regaining your dignity.

In that second, I see a young man
tall, fit and swift,

a leather bandana holding a stream
of hair that falls like shiny water
combed black.

I want to be back with you in time,
blood brothers running into wind
that sweeps across the prairie
like deer prancing
in deep canyon valleys,
like elk standing foursquare at
the edge of a rust-stained mesa
to watch eagles spinning high
like dust devils
in the afternoon sun.

You come closer now and
I look away, not wanting
to see you stagger,
or to smell
the unsupported sadness
on your breath.

XXX

The Antarctic, 2004

Once again, I boarded the Akademik Ioffe, this time from Ushuaia, Argentina, in February of 2004 to the Antarctic. As it turned out, it was one of the most exciting trips of all, quite possibly because I had never experienced anything like it before in my life.

Sheila and I were going to do this trip together. However, about a week before the trip her mom was hospitalized with an apparent heart attack. So, of course, Sheila cancelled her trip. I always felt bad about this, as I know she would have had a great time, what with all the close contact with animals.

Let me first tell you about one of our initial lectures, this one about how to dress while outside on the trip. It is possible, we were told, for the temperature to change drastically within minutes. By *drastically* they meant 50-60 degrees in minutes. They dramatized this by telling us a story of a U.S. Navy ship that anchored in the Antarctic during WW II. It was a beautiful and warm day, so some of the men decided to play a softball game on the ice, about 200 yards from the ship. The temperature suddenly changed, so much so that several of the sailors without shirts on died. The story sounded a bit exaggerated, yet it made the point.

The best way to dress, we were told, was to layer our clothing. In this way, we could take off layers if too warm, or add layers if too cold. So, here is how I, a guy who was brought up in a cold-water flat, dressed before getting into a zodiac for a trip:

1. tee-shirt
2. thermal top
3. J. Peterman shirt (cotton)
4. light windbreaker
5. thermal sweatshirt with hood
6. water proof jacket (Sheila's)
7. life jacket
8. ear muffs
9. woolen cap
10. scarf
11. thermal gloves

Now, that is just for the top half of my body. The bottom half:

1. jockey shorts
2. thermal leggings
3. jeans
4. rain pants
5. 2 pairs of sweat socks
6. Wellington boots

I also carried a light back pack for discarded clothing if it ever got hot! *Semper paratus!*

My room-mate, John, with whom I became a life-long buddy, told me that this was the first time in over 50 years that he hadn't gone out without a suit on. He was from the Cotswolds in England, and he was the best of men. His wife had recently passed on and his daughters bought him this trip to help him regain his vivacity. He told me later that the first sight of me, pony tail and ear-ring, set him to thinking how dreadful the trip was going to be. He had spent his working life, he told me, with business men without pony tails and ear-rings. I could not have been blessed with a more compatible room-mate.

On the way to the Antarctic from Ushuaia we had to go through the Drake Passage. It is one of the most difficult stretches of oceans in the world – churning seas, mighty waves. We did not experience its difficulty on the way south, but took our turn bashed about on the way north back to South America.

I had lunch the first day out with Toni Hurley, the daughter of Frank Hurley who took the famous photographs of Shackleton's expedition to the South Pole. I enjoyed talking with her about her dad and his exploits.

It was not long before we spotted our first ice berg. It seemed to me, city boy, to be surreal. I think the word *huge* down-sized the height and heft of it all. I got a few photos. Really, bergs of the Antarctic are so extraordinary that if one has eyesight to see and fingers to press the right buttons on the camera, the result necessarily will be great photos. I even got a national magazine, *Mensa Bulletin,* cover!

On one of our first outings in the zodiacs, three humpback whales allowed us to follow them for about 20 minutes. They spaced themselves evenly across and kept up a steady pace, making it easy to follow them. It was as if they were leading us on a merry chase. Needless to say, I got great photos before they dove under, to be seen no more.

What an experience!

We eventually stopped at four penguin rookeries. We saw adelies, chinstraps, gentoos, and macaronis. The first one we spent time on was at Petermann Island. They are adorably cute, and many quite small compared to the usual way they show up on film.

We were told to give them the right of way, three feet on all sides. Their moms build nests from tiny stones, each nest quite close to the next. The rookery had a pungent smell of ammonia from their urine. At one point in the year, the moms go off to the ocean to feed on fish and krill to bring back to their chicks. While they are gone, interestingly, the male penguin incubates the egg for months at a time, not eating and losing lots of body weight before mom comes home.

It was so much fun for me to watch the chicks chase their moms. "More food, Mom, more food!" All this as the moms resist giving away their hard-earned belly full too quickly. Food measurement is of the essence.

Penguins walk very quickly, as if they are in a hurry to get somewhere. One of the funniest things about them is to see one hustling along, especially when he is coming right at you, for an appointment, when suddenly he simply stops in his tracks and falls down to take a nap! They are truly funny little guys. I would invariably think of how Sheila would have loved them and their antics.

We stopped at Cuverville Island which was once a 19th century whaling processing and discarding center. It was sad to see huge whaling bones strewn about, and the rusted remnants of the machines used to extract oil and other parts of the great dead creatures over which the Bible gives man dominion as killers of the magnificent. It is no wonder to me that I do not believe in organized religion!

If one digs on the edges of the waters of Deception Island, one will find thermals.

To swim in them, as a few did in bathing suits in an otherwise very cold environment, is adventurous. I did not – brrrr!

The two wooden grave markers I found as I strolled about the island put me in a nostalgic mood, one heightened that late evening when our ship stopped in the Urlacht Straits to meet the Academik Sergey Vavilov, the sister ship of ours, in order to pick up the lost luggage one of our fellow ship-mates and bring it back to our ship. The Vavilov was about 300 yards from us as we watched our zodiac zip through the misty haze to her.

I found it exciting to see this as we interrupted our dinner to go to the railings to see the ship. Then, the railings of their ship were crowded with passengers to see us. We began to wave hello across the waters to each other when suddenly the Vavilov folks began to sing "Sing low, sweet chariot . . . ." And then the Canadian National Anthem. It was beginning to get dark as we returned the gesture with Waltzing Matilda, my all-time favorite anti-war song. It had all the trappings of the Canadians singing to the Australians in spontaneous song, a reaching out from one ship to another in the deep and freezing waters of the Antarctic. It touched me to realize how bonded we had come. And really, too, how vulnerable we all were in the middle of a freezing ocean with no one else around if we were in need of help.

On our last night at sea, I read poetry from one of my books to a packed library audience. And then the next day as we crossed the infamous Drake Passage on the way back to Ushuaia she spoke her might to us at lunch time. One of her giant waves hit the side of the Akademik Ioffe, splaying food and drinks across the room. It was a bit frightening, yet quickly apparent that all was well.

XXX

That same year I took a three week trip to seven or eight nations in Europe.

The trip is memorable as it resonated to many books I have read about their history, mainly during WW II. I will speak of some of these visits in snippets of nostalgic memorabilia.

One of the things I remember clearly is my visit to Slovenia and the Lipica Stud Farm which has raised and developed the famous Lippizan horses since the end of the 15th century. I went to their indoor show which featured the horses dancing to classical Strauss waltzes. It was so exquisitely beautiful that tears came to my eyes. I have never seen anything like it.

Our stay in Croatia brought home the reality of the Balkan wars as many of the homes we passed on our bus rides in the area had their roofs badly damaged and their outside walls pock-marked by bullets. Little did I know that ten years later I would become deeply involved in affairs in this region.

Having dinner in the Jewish Quarter of Krakow, Poland, sticks in my memory.

We had dinner in a café across the street from bombed out buildings of WW II which were left as they were as a sort of monument to the cruelty of war. The trio that played for us during dinner, the old paintings on the walls, the menu – all spoke to my soul in a most memorable way.

To be in Dresden was special as I have taught Vonnegut's "Slaughterhouse-Five' to high school students. And to visit the site of the Warsaw Ghetto was memorable. Lord knows how many books I have read about it.

And then to the places that spoke to my soul in the most searing way, Auschwitz and Birkenau. The houses in Auschwitz look like condos, though the houses are called "blocks," as in Block 1, Block 2, etc. For example, Block 24 was the brothel where mostly Polish prostitutes satisfied Nazi officers and rewarded prisoners known as "kapos," often Jews, who could be as brutal as the guards. Block 11 was right next to the "Shooting Wall," the place where prisoners were executed, sometimes for target practice.

Block 10, as I have said before, was the place where experimentations on women were performed.

It's an especially strange experience to be so close to evil. I remembered the day I visited the underground bunker at the Berghof, Hitler's residence at Berchtesgaden in the Obersalzberg Mountains when I sensed the presence of evil so strong that I ran out for my soul to be washed in the light. I am sometimes ashamed to be a member of the human race.

And then I entered one of the reconstructed gas chambers. More then a half century has gone by since the seven chambers were last used, then subsequently destroyed by the Nazis as the war was winding down.

As the door clanged shut behind us, I remember that I felt a bit dizzy. I think my mind was trying to shut down from the reality of it all. I just wanted to go on "Off" mode.

It wasn't so much that I didn't want to face the horror of the Holocaust, or the anger I was feeling. I think it was the bewilderment I was facing as I was standing in this killing room, waiting in my mind for the gas to waft down from the ceiling.

I have written three historical fiction books about the Holocaust. The writing was my personal attempt to give it some meaning. I thought that the more I knew about it, the more I might understand it and give it some meaning for myself.

As time went by in the pursuit of meaning, I finally realized that it would never make any sense. So, I turned to the question, "What is the meaning of meaning" thinking that I had been approaching my quest in the wrong way. Yet, the more I read about this shameful chapter in man's history, the more I felt baffled, especially by the killing of one and a half million children.

As time went by, I began to realize that it would never have meaning to me, as I am a rational man, wanting rational answers. Perhaps the pursuit of meaning is the meaning.

In my last book about the Arab-Israeli conflict, I created a character called *Jonah The Jew* who has a grasp on what mindless murder is, but had decided that because words are but metaphors for experience, he will use only one phrase each time an atrocity is committed by either side. He believes, as I do, that most words about killing "cover the blood." He simply says on a wooden box at the sites of wanton killings by either side, "What you have done is wrong." Nothing more. For this, fellow Jews spit in his face, and Palestinians throw rocks at him. They all know, in their hearts, that what they are doing to each other is . . . . *Wrong.*

As I stood next to my fellow tourists that day in the gas chamber at Auschwitz, I again felt bewildered why so many follow the voices of darkness. Without warning, I began to breathe as if through a gauze. A stillness lined my inner skin and inside its silence I could hear eerie shouts and the soft moans of humanity. It was as if spiritual tuning forks were echoing from my heart to the walls and back to me again as I waited for them to open the door so I could run out of there.

XXX

Sheila and I took a cruise in Alaska in 2005. Among several memories is watching the Hubbard Glacier calving about 200 yards from our balcony aboard the Oosterdam. The booming splashes are something to behold, a sort of precursor to the extraordinary calving we see now in both of the polar regions as global temperatures rise.

We also took a seaplane ride from Ketchikan to Misty Fjord, landing in a lake that was so far from civilization according to the pilot that if we had an accident we would never be found. I presume he was trying to add a little spice, inappropriate as it was, to our flight. I must say that the scenery was different in its beauty from almost anything I had ever seen.

XXX

I am being a little redundant here about teaching at Dongguan University in 1995.

It was so exciting for me in its particulars that I am going to take the risk. Most of my students were involved in the business world of China and wanted to up-grade their skills in speaking and writing English. One of my Chinese friends back home advised me to bring photos of my family, friends, and the town I lived in to show them, as they probably would be very interested in the kind of life I had. So, on the first day of class, I divided the students into two groups, one to write for me why they had signed up for the course, the other to look at my photo album and ask questions about America. My friend was right. Showing the photos helped a lot in getting us to know each other. That was important to me as I saw my teaching mission also to be as an ambassador for America which, indeed, it always is abroad whether we like it or not.

They did not serve coffee in the teachers' cafeteria at breakfast. No coffee at breakfast! They've got to be kidding. I always have coffee in the morning. In fact, my lovely wife has a cup of hot java waiting for me when I get up in the morning, first thing.

I was only half kidding when I told my students on the second day of class about my plight, that if I seemed to be grumpy at 9 a.m., the start of first period, it was because I did not have my coffee. I could not believe it on the third morning that there were two cups of coffee on my desk, and they would be there for the rest of the summer session!

How gracious of them, how generous of them, typical of the way "Teacher Jerry" was treated all that summer in China.

My son, Jay, who lives and works in California, agreed to read from each of my students an e-mail in which they could ask him any questions they would like about America. In turn, he wrote back to each one who was then responsible for reading their letter from Jay in front of the class and to speak about their Q&A with him. I tried to give them as many speaking opportunities as I could. We also worked a lot on phonetics as the Chinese tongue sometimes has difficulties in getting to speak English words. We also wrote and made available a newspaper called "Jumping Into The Swimming Pool." Each student was responsible to write a short essay on just about anything they had a handle on. One of the students wrote a powerful essay about the terrible working conditions in China. I was afraid that she might get into trouble, as the newspaper might get into hands that could make life difficult for her. She did not take my advice, so I asked one of the more advanced students to speak with her about notching it down a bit. She eventually wrote an effective piece about working in a restaurant as a waitress, "working for eleven hours and pretending to be a happy girl every day." This approach let her get the message across in a milder way, one that would not get her in trouble. She seemed to appreciate that, finally.

Over the weeks, I gave three evening talks at the university. "Listening Skills" was a bomb, "American Humor" got some interest, and "American Sports" was a hit, so to speak. The room was full and the questions great. Most of the questions were about baseball.

The university provided the American teachers and their students with wonderful trips on weekends. We went to the home of Sun Yat-sen, the Father of China. And to an old village, exciting in itself, yet more exciting to see worn-out posters of Mao Zedong on doorways, and old men playing mahjong in shady places. I could clearly imagine what it must have been like in this, and a thousand other villages during the days of horror under Mao. Our trip to "Pearl Land" was exciting to see, much the same as our amusement parks are. I especially recall spending time getting to know a men's group that was on an outing to the park. A few of them could speak English and so we sat together and talked. My brain was excited and my heart full as they seemed excited also to have some time with an America.

Flowers play a rich part in China, as it does in some other Asian cultures. I remember a Sunday when several of my students took me into Dongguan City, bought me breakfast (when the waitress places a small flower pot on your table it means you have paid your bill), then to the flower kiosks center. Quite beautiful are the collections.

I remember another little tidbit about cultural differences: yellow flowers stand for friendship in America whereas in China if you give a yellow flower to your boyfriend or girlfriend it means "We're through, it's over, Peng You." That last part means "friend."

Can you imagine walking up to your girlfriend and handing her a yellow flower? It seems so cold.

I will say more about this soon, but some of our time was spent preparing for my class's abridged version of Shakespeare's "Romeo and Juliet." They would be responsible for putting their play at the end of the summer session (by edict of Mr. Mao, I think as advertisement for the efficacy of Dongguan University's summer program).

We did have much fun, too, that summer, I must say, more fun than teaching back home. It was less prescriptive in its ways, and I had more freedom to do the kinds of things that I thought might enhance the skills they were trying to hone. I wanted them to know where the book stores in town were that sold books in English, especially novels as I have always thought that reading books in English and watching films and t.v. in English were a few of the organic ways to learn English. So, I took them to several book stores where I pointed out novels that might be light and fun to read while learning English.

Lo and behold, on one of the shelves there was for sale, in Chinese on one side and English on the other, the book "Chicken Soup for the Teacher's Soul." I was excited because I have an essay in that book. It is called "Chuck," the name of one of my students at Staples High School whose father was a famous radio announcer. Chuck used his influence with his dad to have commercials placed on radio about s few of the fund-raising drives I organized to feed hungry children. Chuck and I added friendship to our relationship.

I got a phone call from Chuck about half-way through his sophomore year studying writing at the University of Missouri, and that he would be coming home for treatment of lung cancer. When he got home, I went to see him, the last time I would see him, as he did not tell me that it had metastasized When I went to his funeral a few months later, his father asked me if he could have a few words with me.

He told me that Chuck had picked out six items that he would like to have buried with him. One of them was an essay that he had written for me a few years before. He told me that Chuck had always kept the piece because he liked the message I wrote to him at the bottom of the last page. In that little note, I affirmed his talent as a writer and urged him to be responsible for the gift, to be committed to it as something special. That encouraging post-script would now go with him across the great divide.

I was touched and grateful for the gift Chuck gave to me that day. His wonderful gesture gave the teacher in me a vital insight, one that would change my life. His taking my reassuring note with him into eternity offered to me a tremendous opportunity for impacting students' lives. I felt re-energized and with a sense of purpose that was greater than ever. Whenever I forgot my purpose after that, I think of Chuck and I am reminded of it once again: that teachers have the power to affect hearts and minds for a long time.

Some would even say for eternity.

My students, a very social bunch, took me to karaoke one evening. I sang "Unchained Melody," while they laughed and laughed as their teachers probably would never have done such an undistinguished thing in public.

As I've said before, my trips abroad have almost always enlightened me, made me more understanding of people. In a word, helped me to grow as a person.

A good example here in Dongguan was the night a few of them took me to a restaurant to get pizza and coffee! I gave the waitress a good tip, as she was very kind to us.

My students told me that in China the waitresses did not keep their tips but had to turn them over to the manager.

"See that man over there in the white shirt. He's the manager and he gets your tip."

"For doing nothing?" I asked.

"Yes, for doing nothing, for being the manager."

What a difference in cultures! Can you imagine in America if your waitress had to give your tip to the manager? I asked one of the students if she would bring the waitress back to our table. I told her in the nicest way that I did not agree with the custom and if it didn't cause any trouble for her if she would give my money back to me. She said it would not and gave the money to me.

Our presentation of Romeo and Juliet was a big success, not as in great acting or anything resembling greatness. It simply was unusual. The house was packed, and excitement was in the air. One of our many problems was that the theater did not have a curtain, so that when Tybalt is killed by Romeo (played by Horgen from our class, a 65 year old man), he must lie dead on the stage for the rest of the abridged play. Now, that would not do because the rest of the play does not always include a dead man lying on the stage. So, I came up with what I thought was a great idea.

"Horgan, how about every now and then when you think the audience is preoccupied with action at the other end of the stage, you roll over a few times towards exit left. I figure you will need to do this about four times before your "dead" body is off the stage.

This strategy did not work. Each time that Horgen did this, the audience would break out into howls of laughter. When he finally rolled himself off the stage, he received the biggest ovation of the night! When it was over, the cast also received a big hand, one at a time. Of course, Horgen again received the biggest hand.

I was so pleased that everyone had a wonderful evening. My students, friends, parents, everyone. It didn't matter that we were amateurs, that we screwed up in a few places. What mattered is that the Chinese actors did it in English, the very reason for their taking the course. I could tell, too, how happy my gang of sixteen was. Each one of them had taken a part in the play, had practiced together, had taken a chance together.

They wanted to celebrate, they needed to celebrate before they exploded. So, we went to do the karaoke I mentioned before.

Oh, how I knew the next day, our last, was going to be hard. Leaving is always hard. The time my students and I had had spent in class learning about each others' culture is memorable. I would miss the time I allowed them each day to teach me, their teacher, about the Chinese ways of leading their lives. The strategy seemed to increase their own earnest cooperation with me to learn English.

They gave me so many gifts that I had to leave some of my ties and shirts behind so I could get the gifts in my big bag. Even with that, I had to buy another bag to take all their gifts home.

Two of my students, Horgen and Aline (who is now the English translator for a large firm in Guangzho) were chosen to give the graduation speeches. I beamed with pride.

When we met in class for the last time, I played Andrea Bocelli's "Time to Say Goodbye" to them, but not before I was sure that they knew what the words meant.

And then they did what I hoped they would not, only because I am sentimental. They wrote an original song in English, got up in front of the blackboard, directed me to sit at a desk, and sang the song for me, rather *to* me. I held on as long as I could but the tears refused to stay in.

That night, our last night, they invited me to a restaurant in Dongguan City, gave me presents ands made speeches in English. Even some of them who struggled with English made speeches, halting as they were. I was so proud of them.

I received some good-bye letters. Cecilia, who has become a teacher, wrote:

"I walked almost the entire shopping center to select this gift for you. I wish you could put it on your desk, and when you are tired you can watch it. You'll find that it is smiling at you, and saying "Come on. Don't give up!""

When I left for Hong Kong in the morning, some of my students accompanied me to the bus station. Hugs and teary good-byes once again.

In the first year or two after Dongguan, my students and I shared lots of e-mails, about changes in their lives, marriages, babies. It was great. Several even called me long–distance. I was proud of how they wanted to show me that they could speak English.

Since then, though, they do not answer my e-mails. I suspect there is a crackdown on use of e-mail. Sad.

XXX

Two days after I came home from China, I volunteered with the Red Cross to help out with Hurricane Katrina. I ran it by Sheila, and I was off again, this time for 3 weeks, which would be 61 out of 63 days away this time.

I have already told the story of my participation for 3 weeks in Tuscaloosa, Alabama to help out the Katrina victims moving north to wait it out or to re-settle someplace new. Again, it was a great experience in my life, especially getting to know the black people of the south. I was especially enamored of the grandmothers, the extraordinary grandmothers, the glue who hold together thousands upon thousands of families in the south. To this day, I know there are many black grandmothers who pray daily for "Mr. Jerry."

XXX

Early the next year, Sheila and I went to Chihuahua, Mexico, for a few days to a friend's wedding to a Mexican doctor. We had a chance to roam about the city where we met many wonderful locals. It makes me sad now that our new president refers to Mexicans as "rapists and terrorists."

XXX

I went to India in 2006 for a few weeks. It was one of the great learning and growth experiences of my life. It was so different from other travel experiences: the smells, crowds, old ladies sweeping the streets, pollution, castes, dirty cows everywhere, women in bright dresses making pancakes from cow feces that would be used for heating their homes, history everywhere.

Let me begin with a few animal stories. When I was in Jaipur, I took an elephant ride up a steep hill to what is called the Amber Fort. When I mounted her, I didn't know whether she was male or female. I'm going to get anthropomorphic on you here, maybe.

It's probably the only way I can get across what I was thinking on the ride.

I remember that it was a very hot day. As soon as I asked the mahout about her age, I began to appreciate why she was struggling to get me up the hill. I was stuck in a caravan of elephants, each one carrying one or two tourists to the top. I don't know why I agreed to stay on her. Maybe the fascination of the moment, or not wanting to be a pain to everyone, getting trampled or maybe that I was afraid that if I didn't go along I would be vilified by the group. You know how tough it can be to stand alone in a group.

I wanted to give her a name, but then I didn't want to. If I did, I probably would remember her as she once might have been as the matriarch of a herd. She would have been given that place of honor by the others because of her age and her wisdom.

As she began to wobble up the hill, I began to think of the herds I had seen in Africa, how they tended to their underfoot babies who were always, or so it seemed, to be on the verge of being trampled. And when I thought of these things, I was ashamed of myself.

In Ranthambore, I went to a bengal tiger sanctuary where there were about 25 of these tigers. Our guide stopped our little van at a small natural pool where he said we might see one, as it is a place where deer come to drink. As much as I wanted to see a bengal tiger, I was relieved that none of them came that afternoon when five or six deer gathered to drink.

I was asked to ride the lead camel for about a half hour to a small village. Can you imagine doing this with about five minutes of instruction! I was shown how to get on one and how to get off one. With a magic touch from my guide the camel sort of bowed down in two consecutive motions so that I could climb on it. Then the camel did the two-part motion in reverse to stand. I was told that the camel knew the way to the village and not to worry, just let it lead me and the rest of the group.

When we got to the village, a man came to each of the riders, beckoned to the camel to do its thing to let its rider off. It was quite thrilling. The next time I rode one was on the Gobi desert in Mongolia.

As pigeons are honored by Hindus as the purification of the spirit, many people put bird seed on the top of their roofs. When I was in Jaipur, I was asked if I'd like to go up on one of these roofs. Of course, I said Yes. I was astonished when I got up and walked across the roof to see the bustling street scene below. The flat roof was covered with about 3 inches of wild birdseed. Imagine this conduct in Central Park!

I wanted to go into that bustling street scene. A "street vendor" tried to sell me a notebook pad, stalking me for a long time to get me to buy it. I didn't dare, as I thought it would be a signal to other "vendors" that here was a pushover tourist.

Interestingly, as I have a pony tail, the sight of it seemed to attract, probably because it's not a part of the culture.

When I finally dodged the vendor, I went into a crowded jewelry store to add to my collection (175) of rings. I was told beforehand that the price on gold was much less expensive than in America. Waiting customers sat on stools at a long table that resembled a NYC bar. I bought a decorative 22 k. ring for $151 American. It probably would cost about $500 in the US.

We had a bit of excitement after visiting the Jama Masjid, one of the largest mosques in India, that had three bombs in backpacks blow up in its courtyard later in the day after we spent a few hours there. It was front page news the day after.

Sheila told me when I got home that the tour company called her that day to let her know that I had already left the Jama Masjid before the bombs exploded. That was very thoughtful of them.

The centerpiece of our visit to Agra was, of course, the Taj Mahal. Made of marble, and taking 16 years to build, it is beautiful beyond compare. It is, too, quite romantic in its origin. The story goes that the Mughal emperor, Shah Jahan, had it built to commemorate his love for his wife, Mumtaz Mahal, who died in childbirth delivering the last of her 14 children by Jahan. Her body is entombed in the mausoleum section, the part we see in frontal photos. And when he died, his body was laid to rest next to hers.

A friend of mine had asked me to visit a friend of hers who was a university professor. This, too, was a great learning experience for me. You see, I think that authenticity ought to trump uncomfortableness. Of course, there are exceptions.

I thought, though, that when I questioned her about the garbage in the streets of most large cities in India, she was reluctant to answer and seemed uncomfortable.

I was asking because I think professors ought to be dedicated to the truth. And because my friend who introduced us told me that the professor was an "open" person.

Here is the question I asked her: "How do you account for the streets filled with garbage in many of your large cities? Is it just centuries of bad habits?" And then I added, "Or is there something genetic about this after centuries of throwing garbage in the streets?" And, "Why doesn't your government develop a public campaign against street garbage as a national priority?"

I went on to explain how a public all-out campaign against smoking in America had cut that bad health habit to manageable proportions.

To make a long story short, I learned, too late, that my questions embarrassed her, and that my desire for authenticity has limits. Perhaps, too, that friendship is more important than the dynamics of curiosity.

I will always remember, too, the rag-tag girl of about eight years that I met in the market place, her hand out for money. I simply knelt down to shake her little hand, not daring to give her money as we were strongly advised not to unless we wanted to start an avalanche of needy children to quickly come down upon our heads. I got up and said good-bye.

That afternoon as we were getting on the bus to leave, I felt a gentle tugging on my sleeve. It was the little girl! Her tug seemed like a genuine gesture of friendship rather than a request for a hand-out which is usually indicated. She will never know that her gesture stole my heart and re-energized my awareness about the poor children of the world.

I almost missed out on one the many cultural differences between India and the US. I was asked if I wanted to go to a famous movie theater that showed the latest what we call "Bollywood" movies. I told my guide that I'd rather skip it. He let me know that I would be passing up a great opportunity to experience the central place that movies have in the culture of India. I think I was being arrogant as I had six years previously received a Fulbright-Hays Seminars Abroad grant to go to India in order to study the role of movies as a unifying force in India. So, I thought I knew it all about movies in India, although I could not accept the grant because I retired from teaching. My guide, bless him, kept on giving me reasons to go to the movies.

I gave in and went, and had an exceptional night, not so much about the movie but about how the Indian audiences conducted themselves, quite different from Americans. Even after the lights went out and the movie started, late-comers would loudly greet friends as they looked for seats. Nobody seemed to mind. And when one of the featured actresses in the film made her appearance, everyone applauded, some standing. The respect and love for the older superstars, I was told, prompted this. Ohhs, Ahs and giggling are allowed.

When our guide asked us to leave with him at intermission, I was disappointed as I wanted to see the rest, even though I knew that the stereotypical, always dancing, lovers would live happily ever after.

He took us to a restaurant that resembled fast food places back home, except that your food was brought to your table. A surprise came a few minutes into our meal when all the waiters and waitresses came together in the middle of the floor and did a snappy sing and dance routine. Their leader gave me the group's card and asked if I would tell someone in America how talented they were. I think the pony tail I wear makes me look artistic to Indians.

We took a plane trip to Varanasi the next morning to see the many activities at the Ganges River. We went that night to see the "Sacred Light" ceremonies at the river ghats, long and narrow walkways down to the Ganges where Hindu ceremonies are held. The Sacred Light ceremony is called the Aarti. It is quite spectacular with the Hindu temple priests each taking one of the ghats, side by side. There is singing and dancing and worship rituals for the Hindi deities. Small denomination coins are thrown into the Ganges where children are allowed to dive into the water the next morning to search in the mud for the coins.

Our excitement was intensified when a beautiful young American woman tapped me on the shoulder to tell me that two men had been following her for the past two hours and she was alone and scared, wanting now to join our group for safety. I told her to come with me to find our group leader, a tough Sikh, to ask him if she could join our group. He not only said yes, he told her that we would escort her back to her hotel, but not before she joined the group for dinner. On the rickshaw ride to our bus, in itself an event, our new friend spotted the two men who were still stalking her. Our guide stopped our rickshaw and confronted them. They appeared very scared of him and quickly took off out of sight.

"What did you say to them?" I asked. He told me that he recognized them as ne'er-do-wells who had been in trouble with the law. He told them that if they continued to follow her he would turn them into the police. And that they would not want to tangle with him, telling them something along the line that he would not only knock their heads off, but would shove them so far up their butts that they would have to get a plumber to get them out. Ouch! I knew that he carried a very long and lethal pin in his Sikh turban.

I took lots of kidding the next day from the other tourists in our group because after we escorted our blond friend in our bus back to her hotel, she called our hotel to try to find out my name so she could thank me. In doing so she spoke with several of the group, asking for the name of the man in the group who had a pony tail.

She finally succeeded and thanked me.

Our last day in India was truly memorable. We started off early in the morning by taking a small flat open boat to cruise along the

Ganges. It is a very busy river early in the morning. People enter it to pray, to wash themselves, to wash their clothes.

Cremations take place at the end of one of the busiest sections of the river in Varanasi.

Typically, the oldest son dresses in white and oversees the cremation on the beach from a high chair. It is something to see a body doused with gasoline and torched.

I asked our wonderful guide if I could spend a minute or so before getting on the bus to take off my sneakers and sock to dip my feet into the Ganges. "Why?" he asked.

"Because I want to tell my friends," I answered. He tried again to deter me by explaining how dirty the river was. "I'll wash my feet and ankles as soon as we get to the hotel."

"OK," he said, "but make it fast."

It never happened! As I started to dip my bare feet into the river Ganges, a bloated dead cow floated by me about 40 yards away. I quickly put on my socks and sneakers, and said goodbye to India the next morning.

XXX

That same year Sheila and I spent a week in the Cotswolds in England at the invitation of John Rowden whom I met in the Antarctic. What prevails in my memory is what a wonderful man John, RIP, was and how I honor his memory. And the beauty of the Cotswolds, like going back in time a hundred years.

XXX

I first met Louis Elneus eigtheen years ago. He was just beginning his work in Haiti where he was born on the island of Gonave, about an hour's ride by ferry off the western coast of Haiti. He called me and asked if he could come to speak to a group I formed at Staples High School called "YEH"– Youth Ending Hunger – an up-beat name for a down-beat reality. He told me that day that he had recently committed himself to the children of

Gonave and asked if the club could help him get started. We did. In a few weeks we raised enough money to buy 100 back-packs, each filled with pens, pencils and note books for the children of Gonave. Louis and I have been fast friends ever since.

He asked me in 2006 if I would come to Gonave and give talks to teachers on post modern teaching techniques. No "Veni, Vici, Vidi" Caesar stuff here. Instead "I went, I tried, I failed." You see, there are few schools of higher education in Haiti, so the only way to get admitted is to get a certain mark on a government exam. If a student does not attain that mark, they have no further recourse, The parents on Gonave would not abide by any "newfangled" ways and wanted to stay with the old. I cannot find fault with that.

So far, I have visited 102 countries, some of them very poor. Yet, I think that Haiti is the poorest and most dysfunctional place of them all. There is garbage everywhere and smoke from burning it in backyards everywhere. Children die young, their little bodies stacked like cordwood in the mortuaries. There is chaos in the national airport, men grabbing at the luggage of visitors to have them use the beat-up old cars to drive them to wherever they are going. One must hold on tight to luggage.

The roads are terrible, really terrible. What was once asphalt is dirt, the asphalt being scorched through by the fierce and hot fires from lit tires, a favorite way to protest.

Unauthorized toll "booths" are set up. Cars can be stopped by purposefully dug potholes that prevent the cars from moving forward without paying the "tribute" fee. It is only after payment is made that the wooden gate is moved to let you through. Much of the island's tree life is de-nuded. Soil erosion is massive. Except for a few places which the locals use, the once pristine beaches are strewn with garbage. The room I rented rarely had water for a shower, and the toilet did not flush. I tried to beat the others by getting up early to use the bowl, which was flushed by someone at night using buckets of water, thus leaving the bowl clean for at least the first person to use it in the morning.

Robberies are common. The run-down hotel I stayed in the first night in Port-au-Prince was guarded by men with shotguns. Classrooms were sterile, the teaching mainly rote–directed.

I remember in one of the classes I visited a little girl of about ten showing her left hand, which was a claw, to the other kids, rather awkwardly I thought. She turned around to me to stick it quite near my face. I didn't know what to make of it. The other girls around her were watching as she did this. I took the claw and clasped it in one of my hands because I thought she was using it as a way to show others that she was an outcast.

I wanted to show her and them that he wasn't an outcast, so I held her hand for what seemed like a long time.

Giving talks to the children in the lower grades was always a happy time for me.

Seven and eight year olds want to know about my pets, how old my children are, what games they play. I would talk with them about working hard in school, the future, going after their dreams.

The upper grades, though, were quite different, as the realities of the state of Haiti had already hit them between their eyes. I remember one senior class in particular. I talked with this packed class of very mature boys and girls about going after their dreams.

They listened respectfully. "Do you have any questions?" I asked.

One of the girls stood and said she did. "What can you do to *really* help us go after our dreams?"

"What do you mean?" I asked.

"We do not have computers here. Can you send us computers? We do not have science labs here. Can you get us science labs?"

I was a bit stunned, as I never had really thought about how urging a group of poverty-stricken students to go after their dreams can be as useless as sounding brass and tinkling cymbals. It was the last time I ever spoke to a group of students in a poor country without first setting a context of hope for them, that I would be simply using words and ideas that might vivify their minds and excite their hopes for the future in the same way as a few New York City policemen from the Police Athletic League (PAL) had excited mine back in the day.

There is something profoundly sad about Haiti. The children are so lively, so talented, and have so few opportunities to fulfill themselves. The called me "Blonc" – "Whitey." Although I do not speak Creole which is a mixture of Spanish, French, English, Taino, and west African, and the children do not speak English, we got along really well. They would come in the evening to the house where I rented a room and stand in front of the gate waiting for Blonc. I would open the gate and come on out to be with them, reminding me of my childhood when my little buddies would call up to my mother to ask, "Can Gerard come out?" Or, as I remember fondly, "Can Garage come out?"

It is axiomatic that children are the future, so I hold it as a sacred obligation to treat them with the utmost care, to be for them what I would have liked from my elders to be for me. It is some of those early evenings that are the fondest memories for me of this, my first trip to Haiti.

The grim reality of Haiti and its children was brought home to me once again after our ferry docked on the mainland, and Louis pointed out the marshlands where Papa Doc had dumped about 100,000 Haitian he had murdered.

XXX

Yes, the year 2006 was a very busy one for me. I went to Iran on a citizen diplomacy mission run by Global Exchange. There were 16 of us on the trip. Basically, our mission was to follow an agenda set up by the Iranian government to show us a side of Iran that would be appealing. Our job, as I soon found out from our Iranian guide was to be informed about the wonders of Iran and bring back that news to America. Unfortunately for the Iranians, Global Exchange chose people of experience and consequence for the mission.

Here are a few of the ways that Iranian media tried to explain our reason for being there: "16 American Peace Activists Visit Iran." And, "A group of 16 Americans Lurking About Tehran, Motives Unknown." Another, "16 American Visitors in Iran Protest American Maneuvers in Persian Gulf." This point of view, I think, came from my naivety in choosing my words when I was interviewed and asked if I thought there would be any consequences by American warships being in the Persian Gulf. I went on to explain that, of course, there might be consequences for both sides. I was asked a general question and gave a general answer to which the press chose to feature its own point of view. I was truly a babe in the woods.

I certainly have learned a lot about Islam from subsequent trips to Jordan and Kosovo, yet I did not have a good grasp on its culture the day I got off the plane in Tehran. My guide, "Bhatman," and his female assistant met me at the airport. I shook his hand and then attempted to shake her hand. She quickly stepped back as if my hand might electrify her. He gave me a brief and righteous lecture about how women are treated in Iran. They are not to be touched. Actually, many of the women are highly educated and I saw from the week or so that I was there that many of them quietly revolt against the way they are treated.

The ways women dress in Iran is prescribed by the monotheistic government.

Generally, there are 4 prescriptions: cover your hair, cover your legs, arms must be covered, at least to the elbow, and cover one's bottom, at least to mid-thigh.

The women in our group always wore the *burka*, a head scarf, so we got to see their hair only once, in the bus on the way to the airport to leave Iran.

Actually, one of the ways that Iran controls women is having what I call "The dress police" whose job is to check the ways that women dress in public. We could see this in action as a way to keep liberated women off guard about how strict the police might be on any given day. If a woman's burka showed lots of hair, they might or might not be brought to the police station house for a lecture and/or a small fine, depending on the day.

Many of the women, especially older women, wore what is called the *hijab*, a garment that covers head and chest. Others wore a *chador*, a modesty garment that covers the body from head to foot. On some days while we were there, we could see the ankle part of dungarees showing on some women, on other days not so many. I guess it depends on individual risk-taking.

Too, women are required to sit in the back of public busses. No Rosa Parks there yet. They must enter public buildings through entrances for women only. There is a saying in Iran that is intended to describe being in a condition that is not good. They call this condition "Having a stick with shit on both ends." It might very well describe the condition of women in Iran.

As Mahmoud Ahmadinejad was president of Iran in 2006 and publicly denouncing Israel, our ally in the mid-east at the time, we were expecting to be treated with some hostility. Quite the opposite occurred on the streets and in the market places. One day, for example, while I was alone in a large shopping area, I felt the presence of someone following me. I waited a few minutes, then suddenly turned to see what was going on.

There was a young woman, about 20 I'd say. "I'm sorry that I am following You. I wonder if we might speak," she said in excellent English. "Of course. Where Is it OK for you?" She beckoned me to follow her while she found a place to sit and talk.

She kind of warned me that people would look at us, knowing that I had a non-Iranian look, pony tail and all.

She told me her story: that she was studying English every day, she could tell that I was an American and it would be great to talk with an English-speaking person.

She showed me her back-pack and the English grammar books in it. She told me that she took a bus at 6 a.m. five days a week to go to school to learn English before going to work. We talked for about an hour about my family, my wife and children, America, etc.

Perhaps she was an agent checking up on me. Maybe. I didn't care. As I told her that I traveled a lot and collected rings on my trips, she took off a ring that she was wearing and gave it to me. I was astounded by her generosity. I told her that I must return the favor. "What do you like?" I asked her. "Teddy bears," she said. I then asked her to take me to a store where I could buy her one. She protested, but eventually took me to a fairly large toy store. I bought her a nice one. When you pressed its belly, it sang "We are the world." Fitting, I thought.

She seemed very pleased. I asked her if she did e-mail. She hesitated to give me her e-mail address after I gave her my card with e-mail and address on it. "My father is a policeman and he could get in trouble if I e-mail you." She then wrote her e-mail address for me on a piece of paper. I tried to e-mail her several times, but it always came back as undeliverable. Oh, well!

There are billboards everywhere of the then religious leader Khamenei, as well as his predecessor, the famous Khomeini. It reminded me very much of the many posters of Guevara in Cuba. Public distaste for America is evident. In fact, there is a large painting of the American flag on the entire side of a 20-25 floor apartment building in Tehran. The flag is being bombed, and the saying in Persian, the official language, is "Down With America." I never did, though, get the idea that the people in the streets felt that way. November 4 is called "The Day of Students," a day in Iran to commemorate the take-over of the American embassy by students in 1979. Do you remember the song, "Tie a yellow ribbon round the old oak tree," a romantic song hijacked by the American people to protest the take-over? The take-over day is now an annual student holiday in Iran. We were asked to stick together in the streets that day, as there would be lots of noise over loudspeakers, police and students marching with signs that tried to denigrate Americans. Of course, we wanted to see the action by leaving our hotel together. I remember how we stood on a street corner as high school students came marching towards us carrying the ever-present signs about America.

We watched them grow closer and I figured they knew who we were, "the Americans wandering about Iran." They did know. They stopped marching, some of them put down their signs and many of them came over to shake our hands. It was a wonderful moment that said much to me about governments.

The same thing, more or less, happened when we visited Persepolis, the ancient Persian city. I was surrounded by a group of college students who wanted to talk with me.

"Why do Americans hate us?" one of them who could speak English asked. I thought the question in itself said much about how governments around the world lie to the people in order to make us a part of their agendas.

"We do not hate you," I answered. "How could Americans hate you when most of us do not even know you? My government tells us that you hate us, and your government tells you that we hate you. Do not believe them. My experience of Iranians is that you are wonderful, kind and generous." They clapped. And I expected that I might get arrested.

Many Iranians speak English so it was not hard to get to know them. I found myself comfortable talking with students and with families in the streets. I was often invited to their homes for a meal, although in some cases we had talked for perhaps only 10 minutes. I didn't know what to make of it, as I had never met with such graciousness anywhere in the world. Even the young men who used the hookah, an instrument to smoke tobacco that passes through water and a long tube before inhalation, would invite me to sit on a blanket with them to have a smoke. They call the smoke "hobbly-gobbly."

Iran is one of those countries that do not respect intellectual property rights.

This was evident in a chain of McDonald look-alikes that resembled the ones in America in every respect except that your burgers are delivered to your table. These fast food restaurants are called "Boofs."

And the coffee shops have plagiarized Starbucks, including the unique coffee cup design. These shops are called "Starcups."

"Bhatman" explained to us that, in spite of public rhetoric, Jews were accepted in Iran. So, he took us to what I learned later is the only Jewish synagogue in Tehran.

I call it "The Showcase Synagogue."

There is a good standard of living in Iran. It probably is why organized protests go only so far and then fizzle out. Creatively, the young (60% of Iranians are under 25) find subterranean ways to counter strict rules that govern drugs and alcohol. If found drinking alcohol, the victim can get up to 70 lashes. Though on the books, I was told it is not often inflicted. Possession of 5 or more kilos (1 kilo is 2.2 pounds) of coke is punishable by death, as is leaving Islam for another religion!

Yet, I had many great experiences on this trip. We had a private meeting with the Grand Ayatollah of Tehran who sat on a large pillow with about 4 aides on either side. I asked him how he developed the faith that he talked about. "Take out you cell phone," he directed me. Someone put a cell phone in my hand. "Do you see how intricate it is. It is the hand of a god." I knew the argument as a symbolic depiction of a higher power.

It never had any weight for me, as I know a cell phone to be an instrument of creative engineers. I wanted him to talk about his own life experience with faith. Just as he got going about the cell phone, I was tapped on my back. "Do not point your feet at the Grand Alatollah," I was told.

Our group also had a meeting with the Grand Ayatollah of Shiraz that was on closed circuit t.v. I asked him a question about Islam: "If Islam is a religion of love and kindness, why is it that Sunnis and Shias kill each other in places around the world?"

"Others make them do it," he said. "But they are the agents that pull the triggers on each other," I responded. Again, he said, "Others make them do it."

I knew that "Others" was President George W. Bush. So, I asked the Ayatollah what his impressions of Bush were. He said, "We respect men who are just about the boundaries of others, and do not respect those who are not." I could get what he meant, as Bush, not a student of history, often talked in ways that disrespected the Great Persian Empire.

I remember, too, the day we were taken to an ancient Zoroastrian burial site.

It was once the primary religion of Persia before Islam took over. It was a long climb up a long hill to get there. As they believe that burying the dead in the earth defiles the earth, the nude body is placed in a large circular outdoor space on the hill where vultures can eat the flesh. We were told it takes about 3-4 days for the vultures to complete the task. Ironically, the bones are left to leach into the earth.

I remember doing a stupid thing on the way into Natanz on the bus. I had brought a map with me where the Iranian nuclear sites were indicated. One of them was at Natanz. He announced that we would be passing the nuclear sight on the left and then announced, "No photos allowed. I repeat no photos allowed." It seemed strange to me that he was telling us where the site was. And there it was, surrounded by SAM missiles, ack-ack guns and large radar antennas. I couldn't believe it! So what did I do?

I was sitting in the back of he bus, so I slid the window up a little bit, stuck my camera lens into the opening and snapped a picture! I looked at the photo, and immediately realized that it was probably "hot," as it had all the features of the site. It was a perfect photo. I then deleted it. Whew!!

We were taken to a conference of doctors and other officials who wanted to tell us about the chemical warfare the Iraqis had inflicted upon them during their war.

Lots of horror photos on a big screen.

We were asked if anyone in the audience, the Americans, that is, had anything to say or to ask any question. As I had long been troubled by U.S.-Iran relations, especially their lack of real dialogue, I raised my hand. I then went over to the translator and told her I would be speaking slowly so that she could translate accurately.

"I see that your President Ahmadinejad was in America last week to speak at the United Nations. I think that our President Bush ought to visit Iran and see for himself how wonderful are the people of Iran." This was met with loud applause by the Iranian people at the meeting. And then I said, "And I wish that your president did not fly back to Iran immediately after his U.N. speech. I wish that he would have spent time talking to ordinary Americans to see how wonderful they, too, are. I wish that our two leaders would talk with each other." One could have heard a pin drop. Predictably, Bhatman got on me, big time. "Who are you to come here," he protested, "and tell our president how he should conduct his foreign policy? Who do you think you are?"

I wanted to recite Emily Dickinson's poem "I'm Nobody" to him.

He really got down on me after that. You see, my older daughter's neighbor, Sayid, was (and still is) from Iran, and he asked her if I would say hi to his parents in Tehran. He hadn't seen them in many years. As he was some kind of a big-shot at a University in Massachusetts, and seemed genuinely affectionate towards his parents, I figured there was some kind of bureaucratic reason behind his not going back. I found out later what it was. He gave his parents' phone number to me.

At the time, Bhatman was the only Iranian I knew. And, as making a phone call in Tehran was quite complicated, I asked him to call Sayid's parents to set up a meeting. Lo and behold, he did call them. He told them that I was sick and could not see them while I was in Iran. I was very angry with him, and told him that I did not appreciate his lying on my behalf. I thought I would not meet Sayid's parents.

Until another lucky meeting took place. I was asked by one of our group if I would like to meet a well-known medical doctor who was an instructor of interns at one of the universities. Apparently, the doctor and my tourist friend practiced in the same field, I think childhood diseases. Over the course of the meeting in our hotel lobby, I told the doctor about my aborted quest to meet Sayid's parents. He asked if they had ever been in trouble with the authorities. "Probably not," I said.

"If you want," the doctor said, "give me their telephone number and I will call them right now on my cell phone." He told me that he did not approve of the theocratic government in Iran but, as he said, "I don't join groups, so my disagreements are quiet and subtle. I keep my nose clean."

He made a long call to them in Farsi, the language of Iran. "They are very nice people," he said. "You are to meet them for dinner at . . . ." I did meet them, on my last evening in Tehran at a public restaurant in a hotel. Indeed, they were very nice people.

They brought along Sayid's sister who could speak English, and gave me presents, two huge packages of peanuts. I gave them less weighty gifts.

As it was, Sayid's dad was a leading cartographer for the government. He gave 3 of his maps of the city to me. I treasure them. He told me, too, to tell Sayid that he had paid the Iranian government the necessary rials (about $300 U.S.) to exclude him from military service. So that is why Sayid did not go back to Iran for all those years!

One of the powerful memories I have of this trip is having a long talk with a woman in our group who had gone to Baghdad at the outbreak of the war there to serve as a "human shield." This was a project started by those who were against the imminent war in Iraq, Bush's war. I was not a fan of Hussein, yet I knew there were no weapons of destruction in Iraq. I was especially saddened when General Powell, for whom I once had a great respect, spoke with the American people about the pipes found in Iraq as being parts of weapons of mass destruction. They were more like bathroom pipes, and I was ashamed of Powell for allowing himself to be used this way by Bush. I had once thought of him as a man of integrity. He was now using his influence to help start a war without a just cause.

I knew that this war would result in the death of many innocent people, many children. So, I decided to be a "human shield," being quite sure that the Iraqis would not ever really use us as a shield. They are not stupid. I told Sheila about my interest in doing this, and ran my plans by her, as I always do before I take a trip. It is a courtesy, a way, too, to receive her blessing on a trip I am taking without her.

"What do you think?" I asked her. She said no, she did not approve, the first and only time she has ever said no. So, I did not go.

I wish that every human would have a chance to listen to the lady who actually went to Baghdad as a human shield. Her job was to hold children tightly in her arms while the Iraqi doctors treated them, without anesthesia. She described the horror and the screaming of these poor little ones, the ones we call "collateral damage."

On one of my last nights in Iran I found a few minutes one evening to take a deep and peaceful breath. Bhatman took us to a large store that sold Persian rugs. I was really not interested in buying a Persian rug for my modest home. I asked Bhatman if I might be excused. He told me that there was a staircase that led up to the roof where I could get a good look at the city.

Indeed, it was a good look over the old city of Shiraz. The sun was going down, and so there was a beautiful aura about the city in the early evening. The Muslim prayer, "The Call to Prayer," which is said or sung five times each day, was being sung simultaneously over several loud speakers in the city. The evening aura of the city, combined with the Call to Prayer, was peaceful and beautiful, a memory I shall always hold dear.

XXX

In 2007 I had a chance to go to Iwo Jima, a WW II battle that has intrigued me even as a little boy when my father would tell me about the iconic battle. By the time of the trip to Iwo, I had read just about every book written about it. In fact, I once met a Marine who was wounded in the battle. He said to me, "You know more about Iwo Jima than I do."

Iwo Jima, which we turned back over to the Japanese in 1968, allows visitors once a year, and only for 8 hours. When I heard that a company called Military Historic Tours had scheduled a trip to Iwo, I jumped at the chance to go.

It was a long trip to get there: JFK to Houston to Guam to Saipan, all in one day!

In addition to Iwo Jima, we would visit Saipan, Guam and Tinian.

On Saipan, we visited Suicide Cliffs and Banzai Cliffs where about 10,000 civilians jumped to their deaths, sometimes clutching their babies, because they were told that U.S. Marines would kill their babies and rape their women. Frank Rappl, a Marine who received the Bronze Star for heroism on Iwo Jima (for carrying 13 wounded Marines across a minefield) and who fought in the battle of Saipan, told me as we looked over the suicide cliffs, that it was the saddest thing he saw in all the major battles he fought. He told me that Japanese interpreters begged the civilians over loudspeakers not to jump, that they and their babies would be fed and treated well. But they would not believe it, and jumped to their deaths.

We went on from there to the island of Tinian where the Enola Gay and the Bockscar took off to drop the atomic bombs on Hiroshima and Nagasaki. As I have been to Hiroshima five times, I am probably one of a select few who have visited Able Runway on Tinian where the Enola Gay's mission started and Hiroshima where it ended.

From there we flew to Guam where we had a chance to climb into a B-52 at Andersen Air Force Base. All I could think of is how the Vietcong soldiers screamed and cried as the concussion from B-52 "iron bombs," sometimes as large as 1,000 pounds, squeezed the air.

We were told a "stinky story" as we passed what was once a MacDonalds on Guam. So goes the story that 2,600 Japanese from the battle for Guam were buried in a mass grave. Years later, not knowing that this open green site was a grave, Big Mac built a big burger restaurant on it. As the years went by, more and more patrons complained about funny smells permeating the restaurant. You can see where this story is going.

And then we were readied for the trip to Iwo Jima! I remember getting more and more excited, as a childhood dream of mine was about to come true. I got up that morning about 4 a.m., ate breakfast, made sure my camera was loaded with a fresh battery and card (with extras in my backpack), and got ready for a 6:00 a.m. Continental flight to Iwo Jima. There were two groups, each going on separate flights. I was in Group Yellow and was lucky enough to draw a window seat.

The flight from Guam to the island took about 2 hours. As we approached it in the distance, I could feel the excitement in the plane – I could feel my own heart thumping in my chest. The pilot first circled the island counter-clockwise, then clockwise so as to give everyone a chance to take their first photos of the island.

We landed on the Northern Airfield, once known as Motoyama 2, one of 3 airfields on Iwo in February, 1945. We were greeted by U.S. Marines dressed in WW II uniforms and gear, a nice touch. Cameras were clicking everywhere.

There was a number of small trucks that ran along a perimeter road, making stops here and there for visitors to get off and on as they chose. I got off at a cave that was a Japanese hospital. The Marines had set up a string of battery operated light bulbs, so we could go into the cave as far as we wanted. Except for guns, there was the bric-a-brac of war in the cave, saki bottles, canteens, boots, etc. There was a "spider hole" in the cave.

A spider hole was a round hole that could be reached from inside the cave by climbing a ladder. A Japanese soldier could climb the ladder, push open the natural hole of grass and fire on a Marine, sometimes only yards away, before quickly concealing the hole with the grass cover.

Including Frank, there were 12 veterans of the battle in which 6821 U.S. Marines, Army and Navy personnel died, and some 20,000 Japanese. I got to know Frank, "Bangs," and Marion.

As you might know, it was a horrific battle that lasted from mid-February to late March, 1945. One of the American survivors said it was like running through a rainstorm, and trying to not be hit by a rain drop!

Iwo is a small island held tight by the Japanese who had spent months digging tunnels and caves that protected them from the bombs of planes and the shells from off-shore battleships. The men who fought in the battle and who were with us 62 years later said it was hard to re-picture the island as they knew it, then denuded from all the bombardments, but now overgrown by lush vegetation.

I went to the top of Mt. Suribachi where the famous Rosenthal photo of the flag was taken. As there were many Japanese visitors on the island that day, some to place a cup of water, a Japanese practice to quench the thirst of the dead at the spot where they believed their loved one died, we were asked to handle the proceedings with respect for their feelings.

A U.S. Marine, Sergeant Frisvold from Tacoma, Washington was stationed at the top of Suribachi, a few feet from where the flag was raised on the 3rd day of the battle.

I asked him if he would be willing to fly my family's American flag up the pole right where the original flag raising occurred. "Will do," he said. I have a great photo of me raising the flag, framed and hanging, in a prominent place in my study.

As the battle of Iwo Jima had always held a large place in my psyche, I felt as if I had completed a very important entry on my bucket list. Perhaps it is a feeling of completeness about the gratitude I have always felt to the men who died in this battle, a gratitude I expressed to them after I snuck out of the Japanese-American ceremony to go down to the beachhead to speak with the Marines who landed there that February day long ago. I was alone as I sat in the sand where many of them had died, most a little older than the young men I taught as a high school English teacher.

It was with a profound sense of sorrow that I could say, "Thanks, Marines." And with that a profound sense of joy and gratitude that I made it to these sands to say that.

On the following morning in Guam, the governor held a breakfast for everyone who had gone to Iwo Jima the day before. In an official ceremony, the governor called each of the 12 Marines there who had fought on Iwo Jima to come up on stage to be presented with a certificate honoring their service. I cannot tell you the confusion I felt when he called out my name.

I stood up. "There must be some kind of mistake," I said. "I have never been a Marine, and I have never served in the armed forces. My three brothers have, but I always fell in the gaps between wars." I didn't know what else to say. One of the active Marines who was in our group yelled, "Just go take it." To end the confusion and embarrassment I felt, I went up, thanked the governor and sat down.

The Marines had just made me an "Honorary Iwo Jima Marine"!

I had tears in my eyes. Of course, I was deeply honored, yet did not know why.

I went over to Colonel John Powell to ask him about this. "Sometimes the Marines just like to do nice things," was all he said. It now also hangs in my study.

XXX

Israel and Egypt:

Three times in my life I had wanted to go to Israel. As I contemplated each one of these trips, open warfare broke out between the Palestinians and the Israelis, usually an over-reactive bombing of Gaza by the Israelis after mortar fire from Gaza onto an Israeli town or city.

I waited until September of 2007 when things seemed fairly settled between the two. Lo and behold, I learned later that the Israeli air force bombed Syria on the night of September 6th, three days after I arrived in Jerusalem. The target was a suspected Syrian nuclear reactor that was being built by North Korean workers. Later, too, I learned that Israel was prepared for a Syrian retaliation that, fortunately, did not occur.

Having been brought up as a Catholic, there were many places of historical and biblical interest for me in Israel. I remember mostly going to the Yad Vashem, the Holocaust Remembrance Center. There is so much to see and we had so little time to see it. So, I decided to run through a few sections before spending most of my time at the Children's Museum, a most extraordinary museum that honors the million and a half Jewish children murdered in the Holocaust. It is a dark place that is lit slightly by one candle that is refracted in the ceiling hundreds of times. The names and ages of the children killed are called 24/7 in a steady drumbeat that takes three months to recite.

It is a very powerful experience that keeps me wondering and mystified. Again, I have written three books about it, trying to understand that which I cannot, except in a global sort of way that the perpetrators were less than human. It is no consolation as I had always thought that every person was born in goodness, truth and beauty. I no longer hold that as a given.

As I mentioned before, I think that most of organized religion is a scam, built around patriarchy, money, and power. I did, though, have a few spiritual experiences while in Israel. I went alone one day to the Garden of Gethsemane where, according to the Bible, Jesus prayed all through the night before he was hanged on the cross. During that same night he asked his apostles to pray with him. They all fell asleep, leaving him alone.

I remembered the story from the Bible, as it has always struck me as being a most human, yet indifferent, response. I actually think I could do better. So while in the Garden I said to Jesus "I would have prayed with you all night." And in a voice as clear as clarity itself, I heard a voice saying to me, "I know you would have."

Now, I do not drink. I do not smoke. I do not take drugs. I can only say the voice was real. Yes, real. I do not pretend that I am a holy person, someone that Jesus would talk to. I only know that it happened.

I walked the Via Dolorosa (Way of Sorrow) in the Old Quarter of Jerusalem that same day. It is the path where Jesus walked carrying the cross on which he soon would be crucified. According to the Bible, a man named Simon of Cyrene was forced to help a weakening Jesus carry the cross. As I thought about this, I said in my heart, "I would have helped you, Jesus. Until I died trying." And then a voice said to me, "I will help *you*." Again, the voice was clear. And it did happen.

I believe less in what I read than I do in my experiences. By the time I went to Jerusalem, Muslims in America were receiving a lot of bad press. More sophisticated writers were trying to give a balanced point of view, yet I was still a bit confused.

Beginning the afternoon when I walked through the Muslim Quarter of Old Jerusalem, I discovered first-hand in many countries, especially in Jordan where I spoke several times at universities to young doctors, that most Muslims are exceptionally kind, generous and moral people.

Let me tell you about my experience that opened my heart to investigate the accuracy of who Muslims are. I spent a little time in the Muslim Quarter trying to find a map of Old Jerusalem. I found one and paid with a U.S. dollar. As I left the store and walked down the street, I kept hearing someone yelling, "Sir, Sir." I finally turned around to see. It was the Arab man who had just sold the map to me, trying to give me one shekel, my change.

That little act, an act of justice to me, began to open my heart about Muslims.

Later in my life, I lived among them for periods of time. In the long run, I suspect that they are like the followers of every religion, most good, a small number bad.

We went to Qumran on the Judaean Desert of the West Bank to enter one of the caves where the Dead Sea Scrolls were discovered. We could not enter, as two baby ibex were sleeping in the cave. I did, though, get a few photos using my zoom.

A story that has always moved me is the story of Masada, a site high on a plateau in the hills of the Judaean Desert. We had a choice to go to the top: a two and a half hour tough up-hill hike or a cable car ride of about ten minutes. Everyone chose the cable.

The palace of King Herod which was built there in about 30 BC was overtaken by Jews rebelling against harsh Roman rule. The rebels, called the Zealots, remained there for several years until overtaken by the Roman army that built a ramp up one side of the mountain to breach the fortress. They found, it is alleged, over 900 Jews dead by suicide rather than live under Roman rule. Only two women and four children remained alive. It is a story of great courage, great conviction.

Of course, I visited the Western Wall, sometimes called "The Wailing Wall," a place of powerful spiritual and historical significance for Israelis. It is a custom to write a prayer note on a piece of small paper and to stuff it in the cracks of the wall. I wrote a few on behalf of my Jewish friends.

And then it was on to Egypt. I am sad about how chaotic things are there now. It was palpable during my trip that violence was lurking in the background, armed men everywhere. When we took a river trip down the Nile, soldiers came on board to set up a heavy machine gun on the bow of our ship.

I couldn't believe it, given this shadow hanging over us, when we were taken to a small town outside Cairo in a string of two-seater "cars" attached to each other, about 26 cars in all, through the streets. As I remember, it was a long ride and I kept on thinking how convenient this was for assassins to murder lots of tourists lined up like ducks in a row!

We visited many of the great and ancient monuments and places in Egypt: Dendera, Luxor, Kom Ombo, the Aswan Dam and, of course, the Giza Plateau, home of the Great Pyramids and the Sphinx. We also visited the Valley of the Kings and the Valley of the Queens, homes of the ancient caves that are the burial sites of consequential kings and queens. We could chose any three to enter.

My everlasting memory of Egypt is the trip down and then up the Nile. I fixed the chair in my room to face the couch under the very large window. I had many enjoyable daylight hours during our seven day Nile trip with my feet up on the couch as I watched the wonders of old and new Egypt pass in front of me, as I sometimes got up to wave to the children on the banks. They are days I shall never forget.

XXX

The Philippines

Because I am somewhat of an historian of WW II, I have always wanted to go to the Philippines. So I went there for two weeks in January of 2008 with my friend, John Collier.

It was a most extraordinary trip, as I witnessed many of the places I had previously only read about. We started by spending a few days in Manila where we visited what is called "The Intramuros," i.e., the walled inner city. It was the place of horror when MacArthur invaded Manila in 1945. 100,000 innocent people were killed by American bombardments as well as by the cruel executions of the beleaguered Japanese soldiers.

I am not sure why I visit so many battlefields. It is not that I relish seeing these places. I think perhaps I cannot fully accept that these things happened until I see them with my own eyes. I told you that I am a doubting Thomas.

We drove almost the entire length of the Bataan Death March, stopping along the way now and then to meet the locals or to buy ice cream for the children who would gather around us being assured, I guess, by their parents, that we were the "good guys."

It was always a delight to meet the Philippino people, as the stories of WW II and the American role in helping to free their country from the Japanese has obviously been passed on from generation to generation.

John asked our guide if whoever wanted to would be allowed to walk some of the Death March before entering Camp O'Donnell, one of the two largest camps that held the American and Philippino prisoners who survived the March.

We then went on to the other large prison called Cabanatuan where in January of 1945 American Rangers, Scouts, and Philippino guerrillas rescued over 500 prisoners who would then tell the world of the horrible things that Japanese soldiers did to them on the Death March and in the camp.

This knowledge enraged the American people, motivating them further to do whatever it took to end the war.

We took a ferry to Corregidor where we stayed for two days. The island is off the western coast of Manila. It is quite famous as the last outpost of MacArthur before he left the Philippines in March of 1942.

Our group spent time in the Malinta Tunnels, the place where the last of the Americans held out. It was kind of spooky to be in the tunnels, yet uplifting to know it was where the men and nurses gave a courageous stand before surrendering.

Back in Manila, we were invited to dinner by Bong Gordon who was running for President of the Philippines. We found out later that he lost.

XXX

North Korea

Later that year I went to North Korea on another diplomacy mission, one that was quite different from the one I went on to Iran.

Going to North Korea is like going to "Bizarro Land." The 14 of us had 5 minders watching our every move. Except for Mr. Sun and his assistant, they all claimed that they could not understand nor speak English. It was soon clear that they could at least understand it, as they laughed at humorous things that the Americans said, and seemed slightly startled at our stupidities.

We were not allowed to talk to a North Korean without first getting permission from Mr. Sun. I asked him once, for example, "if I could talk to that woman over there."

"Why?" he responded. I could only think of why George Mallory, when asked why he wanted to climb Mt. Everest, answered "Because it's there." It really would have been an honest answer, but I said, "Because." He spun and walked away without answering.

To show you how bizarre all of this was, if a North Korean talks to a foreigner without permission, it is a felony!

The trip itself started in a bizarre way. You see, I had already been to China four times before this trip when I had to fly to Shenyang, China, before another flight to Pyongyang, the capital of North Korea. Actually the flight from Seoul, S. Korea to Pyongyang would be about an hour, but because of the animosities between the two countries, this was not allowed.

Having been to China so many times, I did not want to get a visa to visit it again.

I thought I could simply pass through the airport in Shenyang on my way to North Korea.

Not so! I should have realized that I did not have the proper papers when the authorities at JFK did not want to allow me to get on the plane to China. I told them that I would meet an agent in China who would have the right papers for me, which was the truth. Finally, the chief of these matters allowed me on the plane, but told me that if anything went wrong, he would disavow knowing anything. "OK," I said.

When I got off the plane in China, I expected to meet the agent with the papers I needed. Alas, I wasn't allowed upstairs to get the documents because I didn't have the right papers to go upstairs!

So, I did what I do when I am in trouble abroad. I look for a friendly face. It has never failed me that a friendly face is the face of a friendly person. I looked and looked before finally finding that face. Lucky me, he spoke English and was the head of security at the airport! I explained my dilemma and asked him if he would call her cell number, which I gave to him (I did not have a cell phone at that time) and go upstairs to get the papers I needed. He was extraordinary and came back in a few minutes with the documents to freedom!

We were met in North Korea by Mr. Sun and his assistant whose English needed some work. He confused genders and gender pronouns, a fault that would soon impact my life.

I was met the next morning in the lobby by five North Korean plain clothes men.

They told me that I did not have the proper papers to leave North Korea. At that time, I still thought that the agent from Global Exchange which had arranged the trip had let me down. Given the experiences I had had with Communists, I knew that being aggressive with them was the most effective way to deal. So, I took off my back pack, knelt down to open it, and began to take out anything my hand felt.

"You have failed me," I loudly said, pointing to the man on my extreme left, while throwing onto the ground whatever was in my hand. Then I reached into the bag again, repeating the act to the second man. And on to the last of the five. I remember that the final thing I found in my bag to throw on the floor was a small pack of tissues from the plentiful supply that Sheila always insisted I take.

They looked at me dumbfounded, as if to say, "Who is this crazy American?"

I stood up and topped it off by stating emphatically, "I want this straightened out by tomorrow morning!"

I asked Mr. Sun every morning if they had gotten things straight for me. And every morning he had nothing to say to me, literally. I was patient and decided to enjoy the trip. You see, I was not anxious or worried about this, as I always feel as if there is a benevolent force watching over me. I really don't know if I think of this force as a god, a supreme being, a higher power. I just don't know. But, I am grateful

Just to finish the drama of the proper documents, they waited until we were to board the Russian Tupelov to give me the necessary papers to go home.

While all this was being processed, I became involved in a new drama of sorts.

I was eating breakfast one morning when several of the guys in black asked if they could sit with me. What was I to say?

"We have been told that the person with a pony tail has been telling the group that Kim Jong Il is dead, that the speeches he makes are made by a man that looks like him."

I was aware that this kind of talk was going around about Kim because I saw it on CNN in my hotel room. In fact, I knew who was spreading this rumor, but I would not let on to them that I knew. It was a young lady we called "The Smoking Girl," as she liked to smoke as we waited for the bus in the morning. Yes, she wore a pony tail. I had heard her telling Mr. Sun's assistant in the bus the evening before that Kim Jong Il was dead. The men in black told me that the young assistant was a delicate person, which I would later see first-hand, and was crying over the news of the dear leader's death.

"Gentlemen," I said, "you've got the wrong guy. I have been around the world, and I am not stupid. I know when to keep my mouth shut and when to open it. I will help you get this straightened out. I hope you know that this has been talked about on CNN that we all get in our rooms. So, it could be anyone."

And so I went to the Smoking Girl who always seemed quite naïve to me. I figured that she had no idea of the ramifications of saying this to a North Korean who consider Kim a god. I hoped that the men in black could see that she was an inexperienced and naïve person who meant no harm.

I told her about my plight and that I had heard her the night before tell the young assistant that Kim had died. "Would you be willing to go to Mr. Sun and tell him it was you?"

"Sure," she responded in all her innocence.

Within fifteen or so minutes she sought me out to tell me that she talked with Mr. Sun and told him that she was the one who told his assistant that their dear leader was dead, that she had seen it on t.v. I asked her if he seemed angry. "No," she said, "I guess everything's OK." And that was the end of it!

For some reason, I became friends with the young assistant. We talked about this and that and sometimes he sat next to me on the bus rides. He told me that he wanted to enter diplomacy work but the authorities would not allow that as his father was a diplomat and no two persons in a family were allowed in the same career.

He got a little angry at me one day when I asked him about the small red pin that he and others were wearing on their lapel. The image of Kim Il Sung was on it. I asked him where I could buy one. He looked at me like I had just slapped him in the face.

"Could you buy my heart?" he answered in a tone that suggested I had just insulted his dignity and that of Kim Il Sung.

I told him that I did not mean to insult him or the Great Leader, but that I simply wanted to have one as a souvenir. He then told me that only a citizen can earn the honor of wearing the pin that was given at a ceremony. It was a high honor to wear one.

He got drunk one evening at the Ari Rang or Mass Games, an extraordinary exhibition of gymnastic and dance held annually at the May Day Stadium. 100,000 citizens participate in this most skillful and colorful show that I have ever seen.

On the way back to our hotel, he sat next to me and said he wanted to tell me that one of the men in our group – "See him up there with the gray hair?" – had sung the American national anthem on the bus earlier that evening. We had gotten stuck in traffic on the way to the Mass Games and were invited to come up to the mike and sing a song.

Well, the gray haired man was once a dean at a major college.

"When the bus stops, I am going to tell him that he must find someplace to sleep

Tonight," he said.

"Do you have a grandfather?" I asked him. "Yes," he said. "And does he have gray hair?" Yes, again.

"Would you like to see your grandfather thrown out onto the street at night in a foreign country."

Without hesitation, he said "No".

"I think you're a good man," I said, "and I know you would not want to throw this old guy out onto the street. Here's what I think you should do. As soon as we get to the hotel, you should go right to your room and go to sleep. You're tired and need some rest.

Besides, it probably will not be appreciated by Mr. Sun if you embarrass this old man."

I was holding my breath as we pulled up in front of the hotel, wondering what he would do.

I followed him as he walked right past the offending American and up the the hotel staircase. He staggered up the flight of stairs, I presume to his room. Whew!

This was not the end of today's drama. I thought the old American who sang the American national Anthem in the bus was way off base and I told him so right then in the hotel lobby. "You really laid a fart in the bus by singing our national anthem. It is their 50th anniversary and you are in their country. Have some respect."

He and his wife, a noted children's author, got angry. "I am an American," he said, "and I can say whatever I want whenever I want wherever I want." I thought about the book "The Ugly American."

"Don't be so naïve," I said back to him.

I thought, for the sake of the group, I ought to clean this up as soon as possible. So, I got up early, hoping they would be at breakfast, which they were.

"May I sit with you?" I asked.

"If you want," he said coldly.

I apologized for saying that he had laid a fart.

"You have made us feel like pariahs in the group," he retorted.

"Actually, no one in the group heard what I said. So, it was between us only. I think you are both very important members of the group, and I hope you will remain so."

They seemed to be flattered by this, and remained "important members of the group."

And then I wanted to get things right with the drunk assistant from the night before.

In the morning, he walked right past me. I presumed he was embarrassed. He suddenly turned around and came up to me to shake my hand. "Thank you," he said.

"You're welcome," I retorted.

"Is there anything special you would like to do today? If so, I will make it happen," he said to me.

"Yes, there is," I said without hesitation. I would like to see the main square, the one named after Kim Il Sung." It is one of the largest squares in the world, perhaps the largest.

He came with me that afternoon on a small bus to the square. It truly is enormous, sometimes seen on American T.V. showing off their military might, the same as the Russians do in Red Square.

I had a chance for the first time to say hi to a few young Communists in training.

They wear a white blouse and a red bandanna around their neck.

Emboldened by this experience, I went to the park with the group on the west bank of the Taedong River where many of the locals hung out, and where the famous Juche Tower was. I had a clown nose that a new friend, Joseph "Fungus" Mungus, a clown, had given to me. I thought I would wear it and bring some laughter to the park.

Well it brought lots of laughter until Mr. Sun caught wind of it. He began to yell at me to put it away, that I was causing disruptions. You can see why I call this country "Bizarro-Land," as I think it strange to shut down innocent laughter. I did what he asked and spent the rest of the time seeing the Juche Tower, a large yet more decorative tower than the Washington Monument. It has an intense large artificial red flame at the top of it.

It is actually called the Tower of the Juche Idea, an idea, a symbol created by Kim Il Sung.

The word itself means "the main body," or the people. The basic idea, a ruling idea in North Korea, is that the people have the power, that the people are the masters of their own destination, that they have the power to create and develop their own destiny.

Now, this sounds sweet and empowering, right? Not really!

The idea has been translated into a political reality that allows the Kim dynasty to continue. You see, it is only by subordinating themselves to Kim Il Sung (and then to his progeny) that the masses can achieve self-reliance.

In principle, I guess it was a good idea, as its original motivation was to create an independence among the North Korean people after the Soviet Union began to cut off aid to the Kim Il Sung government. But there was a sneaky agenda attached to it and that was the subordination of the people to the Great One.

Over time, this took on the model of a loving family. The masses and their leader, Kim Il-Sung became one, he the father figure, they the children who look for assistance from him in all things.

This was reified when I was there by the many posters showing Kim Jong-Il giving "immediate assistance" everywhere – in stores, businesses, garages, the home, schools. It's an air-tight system for keeping things under control and the Kims in power in a kind of personality cult. In fact, the system resonates a religious tone.

One of its principal slogans is kind of biblical, "Kim will always be with us." They even believe that on the day that Kim Il-Sung was born a huge bolt of lightning wrapped itself around a tree in Manyongdae where he was born, a sign that he is a god. We were taken to see it and were invited to drink from the "holy well" on the property. I declined.

They picked up the intensity of the trip as the days of our stay grew thin. Their agenda began to make some in our group paranoid. When talking about going home, they wondered out loud if they had the right receipts, and no forbidden photos.

We were taken to the *Pueblo*, the American intelligence ship that was captured by the North Koreans in 1968. The U.S. denied that it had invaded their territorial waters until many years later. I think that when the North Koreans brought us down to the code machines in the Pueblo, something that not many Americans had ever seen, people began to get a little out of sorts – a not so good reminder of when we had been the bad guys.

And when they took us into a private room where there was a large statue of the Great Leader and directed us to stand in lines of three to bow to his image, some in the group started to ask each other questions – "Did you bow? How far down did you bow? Do you think they noticed if you didn't bow?" Things were getting a little jittery.

When they took us to the Victorious Fatherland War Museum, which highlighted American atrocities, I think some began to look over their shoulders. Time to go home.

When Mr. Sun took us to the Pyongyang airport, I still had not yet been told about the papers I needed to leave North Korea. I figured if they took me to the airport that things were OK. I told Fungus Mungus that I was going to make one of the military people at the airport laugh by using my red clown nose. Fungus did not like it at all. I told him if I was arrested that I'd be held for a year or so until the diplomats did their thing to free me. The North Koreans probably would take me around to be seen by the people as the enemy of the people. I'd pull out my clown nose once in a while, and when I got back to the States I would write a book and call it "Clowning Around In North Korea."

So I walked up to an officer who seemed to be taking a break, turned my back to him, put on my red nose and then turned to look directly at him. He laughed with gusto, Fungus grabbed me by the arm and led me away before I got the man in trouble – for laughing. North Korea: a place where one can get in trouble for laughing.

Mr. Sun gave me the necessary papers to go in and out of Shenyang!

XXX

Guadalcanal and Tarawa: I have always wanted to go to Tarawa to see where the famous battle took place in November of 1943. So when my buddy, John Collier, asked me if I wanted to go there I jumped at the chance, late in 2008. Added to this was going to Guadalcanal, Iron Bottom Sound, as well as Gavutu and Tulagi, part of the Florida Islands where the U.S. Marines fought savage battles.

Our visit to Guadalcanal brought us into close contact with many of the famous battles on the 'Canal that were fought from August, 1942 to February, 1943. By the time the Japanese evacuated the island, 7,000 U.S. fighting men had died, and 19,000 Japanese. It was probably the beginning of the end for the Japanese.

I remember especially going to Alligator Creek where 800 Japanese soldiers were machine-gunned to death, mainly by Al Schmid while he was blinded in one eye by a hand grenade. A movie of this event was made, starring John Garfield.

One of the men on our tour knew exactly where the machine gun was placed, as he had been there before with a man who was at Alligator Creek with Schmid. I began to dig lightly into the ground with a strong twig. I found a rusted lynchpin that would have been inserted into the tripod of a machine gun. I had to pay the government of Guadalcanal to take it home where it now rests in my study with other valuable keepsakes.

We visited many of the iconic battles such as Bloody Ridge and Mt. Austen, yet what I remember most was a trip to Gizu Village, high up in the hills where the villagers went before the Japanese manned the island in order to keep their women and children safe. They decided to stay there after the war was over.

The elected mayor, "Samson" by name, took me under his wing and showed me around the village that housed 40 families. They lived in straw huts, grew yams and ate pigs, and had a cleared soccer field. The water source was two miles away. It was the daily duty of the children who were strong enough to carry the water bags to make the round trip. The small children had natural whitish-yellow hair.

As I was not interested in looking at bullets and teeth from dead Japanese that are still decaying in the bottoms of ravines, I spent my time taking photos of the children with my clown nose on them and then letting them see themselves on my digital camera screen. The men told me later that the howls of delight from the children echoed across the hills.

We took a trip across Iron Bottom Sound where a great naval battle took place during the campaign. We mostly got our asses kicked in the this battle, as the Japanese already had radar, but our history books like to call it a draw.

There was a female surgeon, not attached to our group, who asked if she could take the trip across Iron Bottom Sound with us. She told us that she had spent many hours with government officials to locate the exact place where her brother's ship went down. It was only when Robert Ballard, the man who located the Titanic, gave her the information that she came here to place a wreath on her brother's grave. I remember that his last name was Quincy. She told us that she did three weeks a year doing *pro bono* work in the Solomons in honor of her brother. She inspires me.

We toured Tulagi and Gavutu, part of the Florida Islands located north of Guadalcanal. They are now beautiful, idyllic, something you'd see in a Bob Hope and Dorothy Lamour movie – men sleeping in hammocks, others sipping drinks on grassy lawns in front of thatch huts decorated with colorful flowers. Flowers everywhere, now a garden of Eden, yet back in the day of WW II, small islands bitterly ought over by U.S. Marines and Japanese troops.

I learned that Tulagi was a re-fueling site for Naval PB-Y's, the amphibious plane that my brother Bob flew in around these parts. In all probability, he might have flown in and out of these waters many times to re-fuel or repair. It gave me nostalgic feelings as I looked at the re-fueling station now rotted away.

And then we were on our flight north to the islet of Betio which everyone calls Tarawa, the string of islets of which Betio is one. So I will call it Tarawa rather than Betio. It is a beautiful place. What we saw from the air as we circled this spit in the sea was a progression of inky ocean, followed by light green water, then cloudy pink reefs that melded into a crystal blue lagoon. The island itself is rimmed by rock hard beach coral that has been pounded by the surf into tiny grains of pinkish tan sand. The scene reminded me of the sunny beaches of the Caribbean.

On the morning of the invasion, Higgins boats were to take the Marines into shore from about a mile out at sea. Because of a miscalculation of the tides, the boats got hung up on coral reefs that were as dry as baked leather. Hundreds of men were forced to abandon the boats and had to wade chest high into the shore while burdened by heavy back packs, grenades and weapons. Tetrahedron obstacles and barbed wire set into the the water impeded their way to safety. For two consecutive mornings, Marines were mangled in the sea.

The hard reality of those two days is that the blood of young men red-speckled the glassy waters of Tarawa, dead bodies rocked in the ebb and flow of the tide, corpses floated miles out into the black waters of the ocean.

It took the Marines three days to secure the island and the runway which enabled us to control the central Pacific. One thousand Marines and five thousand Japanese died in the three days.

As the island is about half the size of Central Park, I walked much of it in the days that we were there. One afternoon, I walked

Green and Red Beaches, the invasion designations where most of the Marines were killed. It was a strange afternoon for me. The weather was beautiful, the island peaceful. Yet the beaches were strewn with garbage of every sort, as well as human body waste, the result of the garbage disposal company pulling out years ago over a disagreement about money. As I walked, I was aware that the bodies of about three hundred U.S. Marines were buried in unidentified places around the island, and that I might be walking over some of them.

The fleeting importance of time and place became evident as I went to see the runway, the possession of which was the purpose of the battle. It was 65 years since a thousand Marines died for it, and now there were only tiny traces of it, the rest grown over by Mother Nature and tiny thatch houses.

I spent time with the children who followed us around. Their opportunities were severely limited, and they seemed destined to spend their lives on this island, or on another island of Kiribati, the motherland. It is estimated that the rising ocean waters from global warming will wash over Tarawa in about 2025. The president of Kiribati is already making plans to move the population of Tarawa before they drown.

One of the battle sites where I spent time was at a Japanese cement bunker where Lt. Alexander Bonnyman was killed while atop of it leading a group of Marines overtaking it. I listened carefully to the story of how Bonnyman, an engineer, took over to organize the group of men who captured the bunker while killing about 150 Japanese soldiers. When Bonnyman was killed at the top of the bunker, his body rolled down to the bottom. My admiration for him grew as I took a few photos of where he landed, a place now covered with garbage, including beer cans and used condoms.

I was upset by this and by the fact that his body was still missing. So I wrote to the Commandant of the Marine Corps, reminding him that "No Marine would be left behind," while asking him to support those trying to find Bonnyman and others.

I even sent him photos of the desecration. I never heard back from him. So much for "No Marine would be left behind," even Medal of Honor recipients such as Bonnyman.

As time went by, Lt. Bonneyman's body was discovered beneath a small area by a gas station. A remarkable man named Mark Noah directs an organization called History Flight which has developed underground radar. His group discovered Lt. Bonnyman's body some seventy years after his death. Under the guidance of his grandson, Clay Bonnyman Evans, his body was brought back to Knoxville, Tennessee, where he was re-buried in the family cemetery.

Here is part of a eulogy which Clay graciously allowed me to give that day:

". . . . When the fighting was over, a temporary cemetery was erected on Tarawa for some of the Marines who died there. Alexander's body, and the bodies of perhaps 300 others, was not buried in that cemetery. Its epitaph, though, was prophetic. It read:

Rest warriors, rest
Against the day of journeying forth.
Tender hands shall lift thee out
To home soil waiting.

"And now, after over 71 years lying under the sands of Tarawa, Alexander has journeyed forth where tender hands, led by those of his grandson Clay, have lifted him out to home soil waiting. He is no longer body #16 in cemetery #27. He is 1st Lt. Alexander Bonnyman, Medal of Honor.

"Today, he is home where his parents wanted him to be, resting now securely in the love of his family and friends, in the love of America. It is said that America is the land of the free and the home of the brave. Truly, Alexander has helped to keep America the land of the free, and truly Knoxville today is the home of the brave, Alexander 'Sandy' Bonnyman.

"We are often asked by the media to honor as *Hero* those who throw a ball into a hoop, or run through others with a pigskin tucked under their arms. Or rock stars whose artificial lamentations suggest an angst hardly earned. Even movie stars whose fragile glitz will surely fade against the glare of the morning sun.

"Their accomplishments, though, do not spring from nobility, courage or bravery, as do Alexander's. Indeed, we might say, in his deeds, he is a hero. He answered the call to duty and in the response gave his life. As President Truman said is the Medal of Honor citation, 'He gallantly gave his life for his country.' No greater love has any man."

XXX

Peru, the Amazon Jungle:

I have always wanted to see the Amazon Jungle. In 2009 I had a chance to be in it for a few days and to see Machu Picchu on the same trip, a wonderful double–header.

Our group immediately went from Lima onto a speedboat to a ferry on the Amazon River to Equitos to our lodge in the Amazon jungle! Our rooms were separated by thin wood, and we slept under a net. We did not have electricity at night, except for a night-light in my bathroom. And so when I awoke each morning my bathroom was covered with insects of every sort, hundreds of them. Before I could use the water to clean up and brush my teeth, I would have to spend time to rid the dead insects from my sink.

When I opened the curtain which covered a window in my room I saw that it exposed the jungle to my room. I figured I was safe, yet it came to mind now and then that a snake or who knows what could enter my room. The only thing from the jungle that entered my room, though, was a mosquito, one little mosquito in the whole time! Hardly anything to worry about as I got under my bed net.

We immediately got into our agenda, fishing in the river for piranhas.

Now, this sounds like a great and dangerous thing to do, what with all the adventure movies telling us that these fish could eat a man down to the bone in seconds.

That's how big and ferocious they are presented to us.

Well, they are not big. If I wanted, I could fit one into my hand. I did not fish, as I do not believe in killing living creatures. But I did take a photo of one up close and it does look scary with its sharp teeth showing. Our guide told us that there was so much food in the river that If I jumped in around the piranhas they would flee for their lives.

We went to a local village that was called Yangua Village. It was kind of sad to see the women, some nude from the waist up, and children dance for us. I do hope they get paid for doing this denigrating show.

The men showed us how to use a poison blow-dart gun, still a way for them to catch food. They asked me if I wanted to try to shoot a dart (not poisonous, I hope) at a target about 30 feet away. I hit the bulls eye on my one and only attempt. I guess it is silly and vainglorious of me, but I was mighty proud of that.

Our trip to have a shaman render his services to us was exciting, as I have never been in contact with one. Our meeting took place in an open field. We were each given three leaves by the shaman, and then had to give them back in a certain order to him.

He put our leaves and other natural things, such as peanuts, and wrapped them in paper into a large bundle which he tied with string before setting the bundle on fire. I remember each of us being slapped lightly by him on the head and back with a bundle of leaves.

And it was over! It was a bit of tourist razzle-dazzle, but interesting never the less.

While walking in the jungle, I was introduced to a part of the world that I did not know existed. A man named Henry who looked like Jesus, was walking near me, carrying a sort of boom-box on his shoulder. Apparently, he was talking to someone.

When he was done, I asked him what that was all about.

"It's called Skype," he said. "I was talking to my wife back in the states."

"Wait a minute now," I said. "You mean that you were actually talking to her live?"

"Yes, in Massachusetts."

"Well, I'll be darned. I live in Connecticut. Do you mean that I could actually talk to my wife on this?"

"Of course," he said, realizing, I think, that he was talking to a high-tech moron.

"What's her phone number?" he asked.

I could not believe it. "Sheila, hi! It's Jerry and I'm in the Amazon Jungle talking on a thing called Skype."

We talked for a minute, maybe two, before I told her again that I was in the Amazon. She is a tech wizard, so Skype was old stuff to her.

The Peruvians keep skulls of the dead in their restaurants and, sometimes, in their homes. On a home-hosted visit, two skulls sat on a wall board. We were served dinner in a typical home that had about two dozen guinea pigs loose on straw in the corner of their dining room. They killed one of these little guys for our dinner!

Our visit to a shanty town that held about 200 families was an eye-opener for me, an experience that certainly gave me a wider appreciation for those who live hand to mouth. If I had my way, I would have every high school student in America visit one of these shanty towns, much worse off than our poorest ghetto.

We visited Monkey Island, a most difficult place for me. Having been brought up in the city, the only monkey I ever saw was in the Central Park Zoo. On Monkey Island we were taken through a runway filled with monkeys of every size and gender. Some stood at the sides, others stood on side-bar platforms, while others walked around the floor. I especially remember a mother with five newborns clinging to her back. We arrived at a large room that had about seven or eight mature monkeys in it. They proceeded to sit in our laps and on our heads, where they, in classic monkey style, combed through our heads looking for whatever monkeys look for.

I spent the entire time avoiding them, moving from one seat to another as I saw any of them approaching me. I was getting goose pimples at the thought of one of them touching me, and was again spooked as we left, knowing that I would have to walk through that corridor one more time.

I later had the chance to hold a baby sloth in my arms. I have a framed picture of him in my study, as he has the most beautiful and happy face I have ever seen on an animal anywhere in my travels.

When we got to Cusco on the way to Machu Picchu, it was suggested that we buy coca leaves to chew as a preventative for altitude sickness. We were also made aware to rid any trace of them in our carry-on bags, as the airport police used sniff dogs that could detect the smell. The "problem" is that cocaine can be extracted from coca leaves. Without coca leaves, there is no cocaine!

We spent two days visiting Machu Picchu, one day in a group led by an expert in its history, the other on our own. It is a quite extraordinary story of the Inca Indians, so exceptional that I spent the second day by myself, with a bag of food, simply photographing and enjoying the beauty of it all, this gem sitting up high in the Andes with llamas roaming about as natural weed-wackers.

We took the Amazon Queen back to Iquitos where a real-life drama began for us.

The town was in a shambles. Many roads were closed and others were no longer passable as tires were burning in the roads. I asked questions of the guides, but they were unwilling to answer.

They hustled us onto several small craft that sped us down the river, dangerously fast I thought, to a paper mill where we walked though wood chips to busses that took us via a circuitous route to the airport. Still, no answers, though it was obvious that something bad or dangerous was going on.

It was only after I was home and put the news on my computer that I learned that 22 policemen and two natives were killed that day in the Amazon, in a dispute over land and the distribution of money.

XXX

Japan: as you know I have many friends in Japan, going back to the 1995 Hiroshima Peace Conference. This would be my 5th trip there, this time in 2009 to climb Mt. Fuji.

Fuji is a beloved symbol and place in the Land of the Rising Sun. My son, Jay, asked me if we could climb Fuji together. So, I called Noriyo Ueda, whom you have met before in this book, and asked her if she could arrange it.

She not only arranged the climb, but asked us if we would stay at her and her parents' home for a week. She already had plans for us.

The Fuji climb was a sort of disaster for me. It was on the first "Day of the Sea" national holiday in Japan to honor the sea and the fish which provide Japan with much of its food. A lovely idea, a lovely holiday.

I think half of Japan was there that day to climb Fuji. I really was not prepared. I was overweight, did not exercise, and was travel-fatigued. Making it worse was that we had to get up early the morning after our arrival to get to Fuji, another two hour bus trip from Tokyo.

It was raining that day, and I just could not make it to the top. I asked Jay and Noriyo to go on to the top and I would meet them in the morning at a spot where I would get a place to sleep in one of the many huts available, one station from the summit. "We are not going to leave you," they continually insisted. So, we got three places on wooden beds, ate a brief meal, and went off to LaLa Land.

It took us a while to get back down the mountain in the morning. Two of Noriyo's girl friends made it to the top, and made it back to the starting point in the morning. I found a place where I could sleep on a tatami while waiting for the bus to take us down the rest of the mountain.

We took the shinkansen speed train for four hours to Noriyo's parents' home in Hiroshima. It was really good again to see her dad, a most kind man who was recovering from a stroke. He left the house the next evening, the first time in two years we were told, to have dinner with his family and us. I was very pleased.

The highlight of the trip for me was that Jay had a chance, many years after he first became aware in New York City of the A-bombing of Hiroshima, to visit the Peace Museum in Hiroshima. It's a very powerful experience, and I could see that he was silent for several hours after our visit.

XXX

The High Himalayas: Nepal, Bhutan, Tibet (Mt. Everest), 2010 I always had a yearning to visit these countries, and when I found out that I could see all three and Mt. Everest in one trip, of course, I took it.

I was with a small group for the Nepal and Tibet parts of the trip, but alone with a Buddhist monk as my guide in Bhutan. I was especially lucky to have Tenzig as my guide as he got me into places where tourists are not allowed to go.

I arrived late night in Kathmandu, the capitol of Nepal. I already felt a bit ill at ease because the airplane transfers were different from what I was used to and we could not understand each others' languages. At one point, everyone got off the plane.

So I thought I'd get off, too. Everyone seemed to stay together in a large room, so I figured I ought to wait there with them. My boarding pass said "Kathmandu," so I concluded I should wait with the crowd. No one I asked about what was going on could understand me. In time, I followed the crowd back on to the plane.

Seems as if the plane had stopped to gas up again before the flight into the Himalayas.

It was very dark when the plane landed in the capitol. I mean dark as at night AND no electricity. I breathed a sigh of relief when I saw a young man holding a sign with my name on it. He, too, could not speak English so I didn't know what was going on. There were no lights on anywhere on the drive to my hotel. We seemed to be taking a route somewhere through side streets and alleyways.

For the only time in my travels, I was becoming a bit scared for my safety. I felt trapped: in a foreign land, very dark everywhere, being driven by a man who could not understand English, taking me through side streets and alleyways to who knows where.

We finally arrived at a hotel, small by our standards. When we got into the tiny lobby, there was an armed policeman standing there. I beckoned to my driver to sit and work out the arrangements for the next morning's drive to the airport. He just kept shaking his head *No*. I even offered him a large tip if he would just pick me up in the morning.

More head shakes left and right.

Finally, the policeman explained in very good English that Kathmandu was under siege by the Maoists. I could only infer from the name *Maoists* that it was some kind of Communist movement. I learned later that it had been going on for some years in an attempt to take over the government of Nepal.

It was "touch and go" in the morning. The hotel got one of its workers to walk me to the bus that went to the airport. Because of the Maoist siege, it was the only way to get to the airport. There was a large crowd waiting, mostly Russians. I used my New York City growing-up experience to slowly work my way towards the front.

Even with that, I barely made it on to the bus, and simply guessed where to get off for the airport. Our bus was surrounded by Maoists, identified by red scarves around their necks. There was lots of noise and fist-shaking. Yet, it seemed more demonstrable than threatening.

The flight was eventful as we flew through mountain passes, and sometimes our wings came quite close to touching the mountains on the way into Paro, Bhutan. I had read about these narrow passes and so the hair did not rise off my arms.

Tenzig was waiting for me. I don't know if his presence, a real Buddhist monk, or the ambience of Bhutan itself, but I immediately felt relaxed and buoyant to be there.

We did some remarkable things, including lunch at his mother's house, with its glimpse into the everyday life in Bhutan. He also took me to a school for young Buddhist monks who howled with laughter at my presence as they thought I looked like a famous wrestler named "Tapochle." They actually watch wrestling on T.V. for entertainment between lessons.

We saw the famous Tiger's Lair, and in Thimpu, the capitol, the wildlife preserve for the "takin," the national animal of Bhutan. It is an animal that has the head of a goat and the body of a cow. The King of Bhutan had recently been annoyed at the existence of the preserve, announcing that keeping animals in captivity was against Buddhist principles regarding the treatment of animals. So, the takin were immediately released.

I guess the king figured they'd head for the hills. No, they headed for the nearest town seeking food, and causing chaos. They were rounded up and placed back in the preserve until a new solution for their release could be figured out.

Bhutan has this extraordinary national active philosophy called the "Gross National Happiness" index. Perhaps its everyday implementation is the reason I felt so good every day that I was there. I felt accepted and valued, not because I was a foreigner with money, but just because I was.

The index, indigenous to Bhutan, has four main principles:

1. A sustainable and equitable socio-economic development;
2. Environmental conservation;
3. Preservation and promotion of culture;
4. Good governance.

The GNH is not a hypothetical model. It is actually endorsed and worked on by the government and the king.

A few examples: there is a Lost and Found on the national T.V. station last thing at night before signing off. I watched it one night when it cited a wallet that had been found. Another example is that of a little town I stayed in for two nights that turned on the electricity every day from 9-12 a.m. and 5-9 p.m. only. The reason? The black necked crane migrated there, and the townspeople were afraid that electrical currents were not good for them. When I was there, a movement was underway for the electric lines to be cabled underground.

I spent an afternoon in a small village called Haa. Yes, "Haa." As Tenzig wanted to see a friend, I was on my own. The highlight of my day walking around was the bakery shop where I gorged myself, and the old man who took off his shoe and sock to show me his infected foot! Where could that happen in America?

In Ganty, I had a most extraordinary experience when Tenzig took me to the funeral of a prestigious monk who had recently died. He apparently was the "re–incarnation" of the monk (Ashoka) who found the relics of Buddha, and helped to spread Buddhism across Bhutan. To be the "re-incarnation" of such a man is a big deal, so being invited into his funeral was a special experience.

We had to walk clockwise two times around the temple while fir trees burned on the grounds. The smell was evocative of many Christmases gone by. I stood in the shadows in the back of the temple while monks of every age knelt while playing musical instruments of every kind. The music was not coordinated nor modulated, so there was a discordant air about it, while another sprinkled incense about. An old monk came over to me and took me by the elbow to follow him over and around the kneeling monks to the front of the temple where the body of the "re-incarnated" one was laid. The old man gave the typical card of the dead as well as a piece of red string to me. He then escorted me out of the building. I asked Tenzig, who seemed to be very moved by being there, what the string was for. He said it was a sign of respect and mourning for the dead man and was to be worn around my neck for two weeks. It began to chafe in about a week so I took it off and gave it to a Buddhist follower back in the States.

Tenzig drove me to the airport for a sad goodbye. He is a most extraordinary man and we continue to e-mail now and then.

I joined a group of about ten people in Lhasa, Tibet, to begin a memorable Journey that began with a visit to the 1300 year old Johkang Temple. For the next two hours I felt like a sardine in a sardine can. It was so crowded inside and out that I had to shuffle rather than walk. I felt like I was a part of something old and important in the lives of the Tibetan people. I was, too, while there, very aware of the take-over of Tibet by the Chinese. Chinese statues with red paint poured over their heads was a reminder.

We drove to the Potala, the palace that was the home of the beloved (except to the Chinese) 13th Dalai Lama who left one night for his present home in India. The Potala is a most beautifully architectured palace of 13 layers, and is over 300 feet tall.

A few years ago, Sheila and I went to see him speak in the nearby town of Danbury. When he was done, I noticed that the bottle of water he had been drinking from was still on the stage, half full. I asked one of the stage workers if I could have it. He said no, but that he could wash my hands with it. I said, "Sure." Though I am not a celebrity worshipper, I thought for a guy like the Dalai Lama, "What the hell!"

And then we were off on a small bus for a long ride across the Tibetan Plateau and up to one of the base camps on Mt. Everest at 17,200 feet. The views along the way were spectacular: small villages, some covered with snow, glaciers, mountains famous to climbers. And then the base camp at Everest! I was so excited, I could feel my heart pounding.

We would sleep in a large tent with several rooms. A middle-aged woman greeted us and, with the help of our guide, Ashok, who knew English and Sherpali, showed each of us where we would sleep, when dinner would be ready, and where the bathrooms were.

Our guide told us that it was OK for the men to just tinkle on the ground in the shadows and the women could, too, if they wanted, or they could use the old wooden bathrooms which, upon inspection, seemed to be thousands of years old. And smelled it, too.

I went out in the cold darkness of night, hoping to see Everest. The light of the stars was spectacular, as they had no competition from the artificial lights of civilization.

And there it was – Everest!

Even as I think of that night today, it seems surreal to me. There I was, the Little Prince, standing three quarters of the way to the top of the highest mountain on earth. Oh, my. I had asked our guide to wake me when the sun began to come up. I was so tired in the morning, perhaps the altitude, that I told him to leave me alone.

"Get up," he insisted, knowing how much I had talked about my anticipation to see Everest.

"I don't have clothes on," I lied.

"Put some on, and get your camera. The view is spectacular, and you will never have another chance in your life to see it. Get up!"

I put on a few layers and went outside. He was right, the view was extraordinary.

The sky was blue, the mountain clearly visible. I am grateful to Ashok that he got me out of bed. In a few minutes, I clicked off about 15 shots of the sun rising on Everest.

Just to the southeast of the summit as it's seen from the Tibet side, there is a huge crater dug out of the mountain by nature. It is called the Khumbu Glacier. As the sun filled it in, it appears to the eye like a huge pot of molten gold, and came out that way in the photos.

I remember that I climbed about 30 feet just so I could say "I climbed on Mt. Everest." I have never said "I climbed Mt. Everest," only that I climbed ON it.

On the way back down in a small bus, we were beginning to get warm because we still had layers of clothing on. We were told that in a while we'd make separate stops, first for the women, then the men, to take off the layers.

In the meanwhile I had a memorable experience. A man stopped the bus, and apparently asked the driver if he could get on for the trip down the mountain. He was shy, I could tell, and I beckoned him to sit next to me. His name was, and still is, I guess, Lindu, a Sherpa coming back from a job.

In time, he took out his prayer beads. I asked him if I could hold them. He gave the beads to me. I closed my eyes while I held them and prayed for him and his family, as we had somehow established that we were both married with children. I don't know why but while I prayed I began to shed tears. I had a feeling of togetherness towards Lindu. Here we were on Mt. Everest, the two of us from very different places, and cultures, yet getting to know each other. It struck me hard that it was easy to get along as long as we tried. I gave the beads back to him. He surprised me by unbuttoning the right sleeve of my heavy shirt, and rolling up the sleeves. He then put the prayer beads on that arm, twisting and rolling them up so they fit on my arm like a bracelet. He then rolled down my sleeve to cover his beads before buttoning it once again. The beads were mine!

I was in awe as I now had a sherpa's prayer beads.

The next 10 or 15 minutes were a most pleasant surprise. I asked him if he would like the wind-breaker I wore over everything else. He shook his head No. I took it off and insisted he try it on. It fit and I could tell he liked it. "Keep it," I said as I waved my hand in some kind of universal gesture that says "Keep it."

He then took his eye bracelet off and gave it to me. These are beads that sherpas wear to keep the glare of the sun on snow from hurting their yes. They hang in my study, as do the prayer beads.

I offered him my sweat shirt, the next garment on my body. He liked it and took it without resisting. Then my hat. Sharing came to a halt when he took a handsome knife from its sheaf, which was unseen in a pants pocket, and gave it to me. It was beautiful, gold and gem stones! I could not take it. It was expensive and beyond the bounds of this spontaneous give-aways. I told him as best as I could that I would not be allowed to take it on a plane, and handed it back to him. He seemed relieved.

He got up and asked our driver to let him off. We did a "man-hug" before he got off. His wife and children were waiting for him at the doorway of what seemed to be his home. They did not move, as Lindu waited outside my window seat until the bus pulled away and we waved good-bye. It was a sad moment for me, as I had never before made a friend so easily. Our photo on the bus hangs in my study.

On the way back to Kathmandu, a very crowded city, we stopped in a small town called Tingri, with about 500 residents. I am writing about this because the stop put me in touch with what I'll call "Old Tibet." Ashok gave me a room that was old beyond old. It had a cot and two very large spiders on the ceiling. When I checked out the bathroom that was the common bathroom for the "hotel," it smelled so bad that I felt nauseated.

"Ashok," I said, "I am never going into that bathroom. Never. If you don't get me some kind of a potty for the night, my stomach will explode and you will be to blame.

You will go to jail. I know that you are married and have children. If you don't get me a potty of sorts so I can go during the night you will lose your job and go to jail. Your wife and children will then starve and you will be a very sad man."

Of course, I was kidding. But I really did not want to ever enter that bathroom.

Being the nice man that he is, Ashok brought me back within the hour a night bucket for the purpose I wanted.

In the meanwhile, I had a little talk with the two giant spiders. "Listen up, Boys," I said, "I don't believe in killing living creatures. If you two guys just stay up there on the ceiling and don't bother me during the night, I will not bother you. Now, let's hope it's a deal."

It was a deal. When I woke up in the morning, the first thing I did was to look up at the ceiling. There they were, Insy and Bitsy, still sleeping away, or whatever they do when they're like that. I did my morning ablutions, held my nose and put Ashok's bucket in the thousand year old bathroom.

The next morning, I was off to Bethel, Connecticut.

XXX

Haiti: soon after I got home from the Himalayas, a strong earthquake hit Haiti.

I got in touch with my friend Louis Elneus, whom you have already met, and went there to help him on the island of Gonave, off the west coast of Haiti. It, too, was hit, though not as badly as the main island.

As my flight flew into Port au Prince, I could see tens of thousands, maybe more, of tents. I made my way to the ferry. I sat next to a Haitian minister who was on the way to La Gonave as a go-between students there and the school at Port au Prince which they would be attending.

I remember well the thin old man on the floor next to my seat. He was breathing hard and seemed to be dying. It was a very hot day and he was wet with perspiration. I felt so sorry for him that I began to pour water into a small towel I had, sprinkling his frail body and wiping his forehead, but not before asking the minister if it would be all right to do that. He said I was an angel sent by God. First time anyone called me an angel!

I slept in a small room in the town of Anse-a-Galet where I referred to my sleep as "The Nights of the Bugs," because it was filled with flying bugs and hundreds of insects each night, one of the prices paid for no electricity.

Every morning as I made my way to my mission for the day, I was met by a little girl, probably four years old, who would give me a kiss on the cheek as her neighbors gathered around. It became a ritual. I expect that her mom dressed her in cute, colorful frocks and always with a bow in her hair. I think it was a very creative and touching way for them to say "thank you" to "Blanc" as they clapped every time I knelt on a knee for the daily kiss.

Although Louis has initiated strong ecological projects on the island, his main goal is to upgrade the educational system. He systematically gives books to schools on the island, one school at a time. He has raised the scores on state-mandated testing to the national leadership.

Teaching on the island is a fatiguing way to make a living. They work from 6 a.m. to 4 p.m. and then from 4:30 to 6 p.m. I was a teacher for many years, and could not have sustained that schedule.

One day Louis asked me if I would like to go on a "Donkey Library" mission.

"What is that?" I asked. "We will meet college students from PAP tomorrow to pack up donated books on Frederika, our donkey, and take them into the hills to a village where we will unload the books, and put them on tables for the local kids to read. We pair up the more advanced students and the college kids with the younger kids for a few hours of reading, then have some treats and chocolate milk. Unfortunately, we cannot leave the books with them.

On two other days, I went with Louis and a few others in an old truck to give out donated books in science, language, literature and math at schools in small villages.

In all, he gave out 2000 books! The kids and mothers were so very grateful.

Later, I hired a taxi and driver to take three of us around Port au Prince to see what the earthquake had wrought. Needless to say, it was terrible.

The estimates of the number of people who died in the quake goes from 100,000 to 300,000, depending on who is doing the math. I would put it somewhere around 200,000. About a quarter of a million residences were destroyed, and many damaged, including the Presidential Palace which seemed to be buckled and leaning to one side.

Construction standards are low. In fact, there are no building codes. Because of this, damaged buildings were dangerous and thus destroyed. Many of the buildings looked skeletal, once held together by metal rods. Debris was everywhere, and we could see that some Haitians continued to live in the small spaces that looked like caves in the fragile remains of homes.

One of the saddest things I saw was a boy of about 10 years old standing on top of what was once his home, now a mound of debris. He had a small kitchen pot in his hands and was digging small amounts of dirt from the top.

"What is he doing?" I asked our driver.

"He has been at it since the quake happened. He is looking for his mother buried in the debris."

The city looked like the films from WW II of Berlin wiped out from Allied bombings. It was awful.

I was glad that I could help a little. Some day, I will go back.

XXX

Vietnam Again: 2010 was a busy year of traveling for me. Just when I thought I'd be home for awhile, I was asked by a friend, Joseph "Fungus" Mungus, if I would like to join his group of clowns to visit children's hospitals in Ho Chi Minh City, Vietnam.

Most of these hospitals, he told me, were for children who were victims of agent orange, the toxic chemical dropped by the tons in order to defoliate forested lands, and crops.

The chemical causes horrible birth defects and cancers that are also inherited by offspring of both American soldiers and Vietnamese.

The only up-beat note for me re my three hospital visits was that I had to choose a clown name. So, I became "Merry Jerry."

As for the rest, quite sad. Really very sad, experiences that have affected my soul with deep scars and a hatred for war. The children I tried to make laugh had physical defects unlike any I have ever seen. Some were missing limbs, others had eyes that seemed to pop out of their heads. Others had very narrow heads that they would bang on the sides of their cribs. The doctors called these children "flatheads." I asked one of the nurses why they banged their heads. "To relieve the pain," I was told. Sometimes, I cannot get the image of these children staring at me with blank eyes. I tried speaking what I thought might be soothing words, but there was never a reaction. I asked that same nurse if she thought they understood what I was saying. "We don't know," she answered.

I told Joseph that I was finding it hard to continue trying to be a funny clown.

"You don't have to be funny," he said. "Some of the great clowns were sad. Just show up tomorrow and stand there and see what happens."

I did what he asked of me. I stood in the back, and before long there were children sitting at my feet, totally fascinated by my sneakers that Sheila made to look like clown shoes with lots of multi-colored spray paint.

The happy part of my trip was spending a few days with Thoan, my Vietnamese "grand daughter." She and her husband, Vu, live about an hour by motor bike from the tiny hotel I lived in before I went to the big hotel with the other clowns. She not only took me to many of the historic sites from the American war. She came each day to my hotel to see if I was OK.

We went to the famous Presidential Palace where the North Vietnamese crashed through the gates in tanks after the American troops left the country in April of 1975.

We went to the War Remnants Museum and to the Cu Chi Tunnels.

I wanted to go to the central highlands, where some of the fierce fighting took place. She was not comfortable with that. Instead we went to the city of Dalat, about a two hours plane ride, also in the highlands, but not devastated by the war. She was very familiar with the area, as it was in this city that she and Vu had their honeymoon.

My friend, "Fungus Mungus," who was a medic in the war, told me that he was still having trouble resolving some of the issues about his service. He had given medical aide to both American and Viet Cong soldiers, and so had a first-hand experience with suffering and death of friend and foe. It seemed to have scarred his soul.

When Thoan and Vu invited me to their apartment for dinner, I asked them if I could bring Joseph and his wife. I told them about his unresolved feelings about his participation in the war, and thought it would be a good experience for him to meet and talk with a Vietnamese couple. Joseph and his wife were happy to accept.

We had a grand time. Thoan and her mother cooked all day for a special Vietnamese meal that included bamboo soup which must boil for hours to soften it.

The taste was unlike any soup I have ever had.

I was happy to see Joseph talk so much at the dinner table. He told them that he had been a medic and asked lots of questions to Thoan and Vu, including one that meant so much to him, one that had tortured him for years: "Do you have forgiveness in your hearts for what we did to you?"

I remember that their response was so simple, so Vietnamese, so forgiving. I don't remember all the words. It was a long time ago. Their words were very re-assuring to Joseph. What they amounted to, as I remember, was "Of course we do." They went on to explain that they understood the complexities of the war, and they thanked him for helping their own, his enemy at the time.

It was obvious that their response was a soothing balm to Joseph's soul. A few days later, he told me so in as many words. I was really happy to have been a part of this.

And so, we said goodbye, Joseph and his wonderful wife, off to Texas, I to visit my son in California, Thoan and Vu to remain in Ho Chi Minh City – we all always and forever friends.

XXX

Indonesia, Papua New Guinea, and Timor-Leste in 2011. I've always wanted to go to Indonesia, mostly to see the Komodo dragons on the Komodo Islands. And then on to spend time with the Dani Indians in New Guinea. What more could a guy want on one trip? Even the short visit to Timore-Leste was an opening to my mind about the struggles that small nations have with the bigger ones colonizing them. The loss of life, of dignity, is startling, as is the courage it took over the years for the people of Timore to free themselves of bondage from Portugal at first, then Indonesia.

Bali, the first island I visited in Indonesia, is well-known to American tourists. I have little to say about it that is new. Yet, I have lots to say about Sulawesi which used to be called the Celebes, pre WW II. I had a feeling that this part of my journey would invite me to experiences I never would have imagined.

I have spent decades around high school students, so was quite comfortable starting a conversation with about 25 Indonesian students while we waited for my flight. Their flight was called first. To my surprise, they lined up to touch my hand to their foreheads before saying their goodbyes. Might I say how touching this was?

I flew into the capital Makassar, Sulawesi, with excitement as soon as we landed (incidentally, I took 17 flights on this trip which covered 30,000 miles). My new guide took me to the docks where extremely large, old-fashioned, schooners from all over the greater region were being loaded and unloaded. They were docked so close to each other that I wondered how they could separate to leave.

We took a long car ride to the village of Toraja. *Different* is an understatement.

I was taken to a remote ancient cemetery where bodies were buried high up in vertical mountain caves where their remains would be safe. The men, I was told, made their way up to the caves by connecting bamboo poles together in what must have been a dangerous job, as the caves are very high up. Sometimes, though, they would keep the mummified bodies of their loved ones for seven years in their homes before burial.

There is an ancient practice in Turaja to carve out of wood the image of a dead one and to place these wooden figures high up in the mountain for all to see. The figures are called *tau-taus*. At the bottom of the mountain skeletal pieces of the long ago dead whose caskets have deteriorated before falling from the caves can be found. Many of the skulls mouths are stuffed with cigarettes, as the Turajans believed that the dead liked to smoke on their way to their final destination.

The ground level had many caves in which the dead were buried. Tourists were allowed to enter these caves with flashlights. I chose not to, as it all kind of spooked me.

I was taken to a wooden area not far away where dead babies were interred in trees. It is a form of animism, I was told. A hole is cut into a tree, the baby, wrapped in swaddling clothes, is ceremoniously placed in the hole which is then covered by a cloth curtain which is only removed after the hole has scarred over. The belief is that as the tree grows older so does the baby.

A well-known and rich man happened to die while I was there. My guide offered to take me to his funeral, though I might not like what I would see. Hundreds of people were there, as well as dozens of cows, and smaller animals tied to poles that men would carry on their shoulders. There was music, tears and lines to see this 'n that. When it got time to see men cut the throats of the cows, I asked to leave. You see, the cows belonged to the dead man as well a to others who decided to kill their cows in honor of the dead man. As part of the ceremony, the dead cows would be cut into pieces right there, and given to the poor as a gift from the dead man and/or in honor of him.

I rented a small craft to take me across the sea of Flores to Komodo and Rinca Islands to see the dragons, after which the boat would take me to Komodo Village where I had small gifts of rubber bracelets for the children.

The trip across the sea was quite beautiful, especially watching the sun set in the evenings. The small craft had a pilot, a cook, and two deck hands. I had a very small room. I remember, too, how good the cook was, genuine Indonesian meals.

Our first stop was Komodo Island. My guide on the island gave me a short lecture regarding the do's and do nots around the dragons. They are big, about 300 pounds, and fast. He would wield a very long pole with a "V" shape at the end of it, in order to prod a dragon that might get spunky. "Do not get close and do not make sudden moves." He explained that they were very well fed by killing cows and buffalo that were plentiful.

The dragons are poisonous. They only have to bite a deer or buffalo, though it must track down the prey, as it takes weeks for the poison to take effect.

He took me to a small shed where the guides cooked their meals. It was surrounded by dragons who waited there for the excess food to be thrown to them.

I asked my guide where I could take a whiz, and he took me to a public bathroom.

A large dragon was asleep at the foot of the bathroom stairs. Momma didn't make no fool, so I used the side of the pathway, far from the sleeping giant.

My trip to Komodo Village gave me yet another experience of being on a primitive island. The men were lifting a small pre-made wooden house onto a wood floor as the women lined up with their children to get the bracelets from me. The bracelets were for their kids but, as often happens on these trips, the women also wanted them. So be it!

I remember, too, the little boy of about five years whose left leg was bandaged.

He had been bitten by a small komodo dragon a few days before. And then I was off to Papua, New Guinea, to spend a few days with the Dani Indians. I was met in Wamea, a medium size village, by my guide, a Dani Indian by the name of John who learned English to take up a career as a guide to English speaking tourists. He was extraordinary and well-respected by the Dani as one of their own.

He taught me many things about the Dani way of life. As we walked through the jungle one day, for example, to the first of several villages I visited, he showed me the leaves from a certain kind of tree that worked as a Viagra pill, though he told me that it was effective for about two years only. He showed me some white goo that was oozing out of a tree that was used as a kind of hydrocortisone for cuts.

When he told me about the custom of a woman who is related to a person who had just died having a finger cut off at the second digit in commemoration of the dead person, I was on the look-out to find such a woman. Walking though s jungle path, I found one who had four of her fingers cut off. She charged me 50 cents for a photo!

I asked John how I could say Hello to the natives. *Wa-Wa-Wa*, he answered.

So I had a lot of fun *Wa Wa Wa*-ing my way though the jungle.

When we entered a quite large village, I was greeted by bare-breasted women and men wearing penis gourds. John introduced me to the village chief, an imposing man of about six feet with bones sticking out of his nose, and hair about six inches high.

I gave him a cap I had bought in Los Angeles, but he could not wear it because of his hair being so high. I stupidly asked him why he was not wearing my gift. Duh! He said he would put it on later. John told me that the chief was elected on the basis of having killed six men in battles over women and land.

The village men put on a mock fight for me. Mock or not, it was scary. They put a spear in my hands and asked me to join them in the fight. I tried to pretend I was a warrior. I am not a warrior, so the men must have had a few good laughs when I left.

Then a young warrior who was in charge of a mummified chief from hundreds of years ago brought out the mummy for me to see. Apparently, the chief had one last wish that the village fathers build a memorial to him. Well, they did him one better: they made a memorial out of him!

John told me that they were now going to kill a pig and roast it in my honor. I asked him to explain to the chief that I did not like to kill animals and would he be offended if I left the village while they killed the little pig, walking around right in front of me. He said that would be fine. So when they bare-breasted women prepped the fire, I left the village for a while with John who told me about some of the lore that surrounded the killing of a pig: if the pig died while staggering towards the men's sleeping quarters, the next one in the village to marry would be a man. And if towards the women's quarters, a village woman would be the next. In this context of separate men and women's sleeping quarters, how they go about exercising their marital rights is both interesting and amusing.

XXX

In 2012 I went to Mongolia, a country I had always wanted to see, as it had a sort of mystical air to it. You know, the Gobi Desert, Genghis Khan, camels.

I stayed in the capitol, Ulaanbaatar, for a few days before setting out on the journey across the Gobi Desert. The city is like many other cities of the world, busy, crowded, dirty. It, too, has a main square with statues of Genghis Khan and Kublai Kahn.

The journey across the desert in a jeep type auto with two guides took about six hours. At first interesting, then quite boring as the scenery never changed. Our driver did not have a gps, and there are no roads or paths (any would be erased quickly by winds) so I have no idea how he found our home base, a place not far from the mountainous sand dunes.

About four hours into the trip, we stopped at a valley. I believe it was called the Yol Valley, a great start to the Gobi. We walked the valley for two hours or so. I must say it was intriguing with many types of animals, including wild horses, roaming about.

Our destination was a sort of tourist gathering with yurts or geres, as they are now called. These are a sort of round tent made out of sheep skin and fabric. They are decorated and quite comfortable. Besides the geres, there were separate bathroom and shower facilities and a small restaurant which served Mongolian food, including large hunks of lamb that were handed from one customer to another to cut off a piece of choice.

I got to visit a family that lived in a gere in the desert. It was a great learning experience for me about how people in other cultures live. I didn't know, for example, that a mare's milk can ferment over time. The custom, I was told, is that each family hangs a bag made from animal skin on the wall. It has a large spoon hanging next to it so that when anyone wants a mild alcoholic drink he just dips the spoon in and voila. I noticed that the teen-age son made a few trips to the bag while I was there.

I was also offered to take a sniff from my guide's small box of white powder.

Thinking it might be heroin, I politely turned it down. I found out later that the powder was an innocent concoction that was offered as an act of friendship from a small decorated box that fathers traditionally bought for their sons.

The Nadam Festival is an annual event in Mongolia that features horsemanship, wrestling and archery. I was privileged to go to one of the regional festivals. The young men who rode the horses were extremely talented. My most memorable experience of the festival was at the start of the horse competition when the riders and their horses came running towards us spectators from a far distance, picking up speed while throwing up sand and dust behind them. It was like a scene in a movie.

The wrestling was also interesting in that competitors were unevenly matched.

That is, a 230 pound brute of a man considered the best might be matched against a 90 pound weakling considered the worst. Eventually, barring a stunning upset, the biggest, strongest and most talented two would fight for the title of champion and, I was told, lots of money.

It is not an entirely stupid way to match if you want one winner only out of all the participants.

It was thrilling to take a trip to the famous sand dunes that run for miles and are some 2600 feet high, so high that you could slide down them on your back or, as some were doing, on cardboard. I especially enjoyed when my guide too photos of the large heart I drew in the sand. It said "Jerry loves Sheila." I was a kid in a huge sandbox.

The camel ride I took on the Gobi was memorable. I think it was the third time I rode a camel in a foreign country. Her name was "Brown." She was a bit feisty at first so I was sort of hanging on for dear life. I began to call her by name – *Hey, Brown, how are you today?* and *Thatsa good girl* while petting her neck. We then bonded so well that I rode Brown the rest of the way while becoming synchronize with her every motion, not even holding on to the reins. I was truly One with her. And I felt quite proud of us.

My guide took me in his jeep to what are called "The Flaming Cliffs." It got its name because when the sun shines on the cliffs they appear to be on fire. Noteworthy, though, is that in the mid 1920's dinosaur eggs and raptor bones were discovered there.

We drove to a kiosk and tent where a young married couple worked as watchmen over the cliffs against illegal digging for bones.

When I expressed and interest in the bones, the young watch man got on his motorbike and sped across the desert sand. "Where is he going?" I asked. "He's getting a surprise for you." He came speeding back about fifteen minutes later, and offered me a 60 million years old raptor bone, as big as my thumb for 5000 tugrits, about $3.75 U.S.

I tried passing this bone around at a few talks I gave, but no one would touch it, afraid that germs from millions of years ago might still be a part of it. So I boiled the bone in hot water, then soaked it in alcohol for several hours. This has now made the bone touchable, but only after I explain the two-fold treatment.

XXX

I have been to Jordan twice. The first time was in the late summer of 2013 when my friend Joseph "Fungus" Mungus called me to tell me that the famous clown, Patch Adams, a friend of his, had been reading some of my anti-war poetry at his talks, and invited me to give a presentation at a conference in Amman, and to clown with him and his followers at the Syrian refugee camps in Irbid, Jordan. I was excited, not only to meet Patch, but to give a talk I called "The Journey From Ordinary to Extraordinary."

I met many Sunni Muslims who were studying to be medical doctors. Some of them were among the founders of an organization called "The Human Doctor Project" whose main goal was to blend the clinical aspects of medical practice with the human element which they felt was absent.

The high-light of this trip was clowning at the refugee camps. I was happy to see the children so excited at our silly clown costumes and antics, and sad to see how they were so cut off from their homeland. Through an interpreter, I talked with some of the women whose husbands had been murdered by Assad's henchmen. One woman told me that her husband's throat was cut open, a way to save bullets. I felt so helpless listening to her.

An image that stands out in my mind is that of a pile of small animal bones, probably rats, in a circle of about 3x4 feet, that the refugees had cooked and eaten.

I went to a center for refugees one day and worked for an hour or so with a little girl, about four years old, trying to make a paper dog. Her name is, ironically, Ire, in English meaning "anger," something Ire was not. It is pronounced *I-ray*. It was an important time for me as I had struggled with accepting Patch's offer, including all expenses, to come to Jordan.

You see, I wondered if I could possibly make life brighter for even one child if I went there. Being a pragmatist in many ways, I kept weighing the time and effort to go to Jordan – was it worth it? I shared my misgivings with Patch who told me in his own sarcastic way that for certain I would change the lives of more than one. With that, I began thinking about my own childhood in poverty when a few people I didn't even know changed my life by giving me hope that there was a better world out there for me.

Our paper dog was a failure. As soon as we tried to stand it up, it collapsed on the table. In all the time we spent together, little Ire never expressed any emotion. When it was time to leave, I got down on one knee in front of her. "I'm sorry I couldn't make you a dog," I said as I gave her a hug. Still, no expression from her.

I got on the bus to leave and went to the back of it to take one last look at these people who had captured my heart. Suddenly, I saw this little refugee, going as fast as her tiny legs could go, running after the bus. It was Ire! Waving to me, smiling. I think she was, in her own way, saying Thank You to me.

I think of her, often.

The young doctors were so good to me. One of them took me to the site of where Jesus allegedly had been baptized in the Jordan River. There were many women going through the rituals of baptism in the river. Interestingly, not one man!

We were taken to a small apartment outside the Zataari camp, biggest Syrian refugee camp in Jordan, which a wealthy Syrian refugee family rented, to put on a Little Theater show for the children. What struck me is how frightened of us one of the little girls was. She was sobbing and visually trembling.

That is, until she began to enjoy the puppet show. A little laughter began to shine from her face, then more and more, until she was fully in a state of enjoyment, the place where every child has a right to be.

I went to this apartment in a car with two Muslim doctors, Ali and Quitaba. At some point on the way home to Amman, it was time for one of the daily prayers. Ali got out of the car, put his prayer rug on the ground and prayed. I asked him many questions about Muslim prayer. As we neared Amman, he gave his beautiful prayer rug to me as a gift. It hangs in my study as a poignant reminder of the graciousness of Muslims who practice their faith.

On our last night in Amman the young doctors held a celebration for us. The food, including the national dish called *mensaf,* was awesome and abundant. *Mensaf* is lamb cooked in the sauce of fermented yogurt from goat's milk. It is served on a bed of rice, topped with nuts and bathed in the yogurt. It is filling and delicious.

The mood was festive that night. After eating, a 10 minute walk was organized to take us to a large dance floor filled with music. I especially liked watching how the Jordanian men danced together in group of ten to fifteen.

Usually, one man would take the lead and the rest followed in a synchronized rhythm. I wanted to join in, but it was too complicated for me. I like dancing, especially at weddings.

I noticed that many of the female doctors were dancing and were not wearing their hijab, the scarf that covers the head and neck. So, I asked one of them to dance with me. She did, without any reservations. I was really curious about the seeming incongruity of their garb that night with the stereotype of a Muslim woman.

"We Americans are not used to seeing Muslim women in public not wearing the head scarf," I said to one of my dance partners. She explained, "If my mother or father was here tonight, you would not see me without my hijab." The public and the private, the old vis-à-vis the new, right there the shifting mores in the land of Islam.

Before flying home, I spent two afternoons in the shopping center of Amman.

It was an experience that broadened my horizons about the world. The shopping area is very long and wide, with stores, mostly small, and kiosks that sell everything imaginable, from shirts and shoes, scarves and burkas (the outer garment that covers a woman's body).

Houses sit high up on hills that are one side of the long main street. A few houses here and there are unoccupied, studded with the debris and scars from past wars, past bombings. As I saw these living memories of war, I thought how blessed Sheila and I are to live Bethel, our small and secure town.

XXX

I went back to Jordan again the following year, this time invited by "The Human Doctor Project," to give a few talks at the Jordan University of Science and Technology (called JUST), and Yamouk University.

A trio of doctors in their last year at JUST invited me to stay in their apartment.

I quickly accepted, as I thought it would be a great chance for me to learn about many things: Islam; the routines, both academic and practical, of doctors; what the personal lives of doctors were like. One of the three gave up his room for me, a nice, orderly, clean room with a heater.

I made the "rounds" at the hospital with Ahmad whom I knew from my first visit to Jordan. He is an extra ordinary young man, a leader in the Human Doctor Project.

On another day I was asked if I wanted to spend a morning in the endoscopy ward of the JUST hospital going to the procedure on a variety of patients with the great Dr. Bani Hani, a beloved teacher, and the students he was teaching. The procedure includes putting a scope with a small TV camera and light down into the stomach through the patient's mouth. We all crowded into a small dark room to see the live procedures on a TV. I went to nine of these, an experience I shall never forget.

I gave my talks, first on "Bedside Manners From the Point of View of a Patient."

It was well intended and I loved to be teaching again. And another talk, much needed I felt with doctors. It was called "Leading a Balanced Personal and Professional Life." I really felt my efforts were appreciated, as they did some hard listening and asked solid questions.

The Human Doctor Project had a dinner in my honor as a way to thank me for spending time with them. I felt honored at the expressions of their gratitude. It was a meal I will not soon forget.

Have you ever had a conversation that you might never forget? I had one with a young Syrian doctor named Suma. She was asked to watch over me one day at the hospital while I waited to meet a certain doctor. We talked for about an hour as she told me about how her life in Syria once was, the beauty of its ways and the love she had for her parents and siblings which were left behind. She wiped tears from her face as she reminisced, wondering, too, when she would ever see them again.

Talking with her gave new meaning to me now when I watch the fighting in Syria on t.v.

On one of the last days before I came home, a friend of my room-mates took me to the vestiges of a second century Roman city called Umm Qais. I was really impressed to see the remnants of their bathing facilities, bathrooms and how human excrement was washed away, their shops and homes, so primitive yet so practical in their function. I've read many books about these aspects of the Roman Empire, but in seeing them that day they truly came to life.

My last talk was at Yarmouk University, a huge school of 53,000 students. I remember that the dean of the medical school came to hear me speak about living a balanced life. I remember, too, how the young doctors in training and I had many laughs together that day.

Three of Ahmad's buddies drove me to the airport in Amman, but not before they took me to young Dr. Thurayya's parents' home. Her dad took her and me into the city to show me the many historical sights, including a Roman amphitheater. Our evening and my stay in Jordan ended with a meal at the restaurant where King Abdullah sometimes eats.

XXX

The Baltics, 2014.

My visit to Latvia, Estonia, and Lithuania runs deep. As deep as it was, I am going to be brief, lest I bore you with a long and maybe dreary visit to the depths of my soul.

You see, I never knew how these nations called "The Baltics" have been so brutalized for so many years by both the Nazis and then the Soviet Union. My schooling, though extensive in its own way, never included this part of the world. Academic exclusion has been one of the many motivations behind my travelling so much, as I realized I would have to discover much on my own about the geography and history of the world.

On my first day in Riga, the capital of Latvia, I hired a cab to take me to a Nazi holding and concentration camp in Salispils where 632 children were murdered. It was a profoundly moving sight with many monuments emphasizing the virtues of goodness such as kindness and generosity. I was there alone in this large camp-site for several hours, and it all struck me quite hard, especially the memorabilia devoted to the children.

I learned that approximately 250,000 Jews in Latvia were murdered by the Nazis.

On my visit to Lithuania where 200,000 Jews were murdered, I went to the Museum of Genocide Victims. The building, now a museum, is the actual place where both the Nazis and then the Soviets imprisoned Jews. I went to the execution cell to see where victims were murdered, mostly by gunshots to the head. It was one of the creepiest places I have ever been in. I find the thought of it even now as an indictment of human cruelty. As much as I try, I cannot understand it that humans settle their differences by killing each other.

XXX

My 2014 visit to the world's newest nation, Kosovo, was one filled with enthusiasm and learning for me. It was a different kind of trip in that it was arranged for me by the sister of a member of the Kosovo government. You see, Kosovars are great restauranters, and several of them owned a bagel shop in my town. As I got to know them over the years, they realized how much I loved to open new travel vistas. And so they arranged for me to go to Pristina, the capitol of Kosovo, where they also hired a guide for me to take me to see the places of war between the Serbs and the Albanians (now Kosovo).

A meeting was arranged for me with one of the great national writers, and I also gave a talk about American literature to some of the university lit professors.

I also gave a talk called "Leading a Balanced Personal and Professional Life" to cadets and officers at the new military academy. One of the talking points of the talk was "How to say No." This, of course, drew a few wide eyes.

As I walked around the city of Pristina for a few days, I began more and more to develop my sense of the world and its problems. I was almost fatigued as I saw the many places where the Serbs slaughtered the Kosovars during their war. And I met many who were grateful to America in the person of President Clinton who developed the NATO coalition to bomb the forces of Milosevic.

I remember especially an old man in the main square who discovered that I was an American and kept blowing kisses to me as I walked away from my talk with him. There is, too, a huge statue of Clinton that honors him as a sort of savior.

I had a chance, too, to talk with men gathered together under a large tent, men who were waiting for 20% of their pension from their state jobs that had now been privatized. I could only wish them well and continued steadfastness.

Outside the tent were many pictures of citizens who had been captured by the Serbs and never heard from again.

The highlight of my trip was going to Peja, about 50 miles north, to see Medina from the bagel shop who was there visiting her father who was recovering from a mild heart attack. Her dad was in charge of a Muslim mosque about 50 yards from his home.

He took me there and opened it for me. I had a extraordinary experience as he showed me the way of Muslim prayer before giving a gift to me of the white cap, called a taqiyah, or kufi in the U.S., that he wore on his own pilgrimage, called the Hajj, to Mecca. It is a very special gift that hangs in my study.

I am sad as I write this memoir that Kosovo is still a disunified country. Against the will of the vast majority of its people, the government is trying to allow the Serbs to stake out large enclaves in Kosovo, sometimes in cities, Metrovica being one example, where the Serbs took over homes from the Albanians long ago. Of course, this does not sit well with the Kosovars.

XXX

Belgium and France:

In 2015 I took a WW I trip to Belgium and France with my buddy, John Collier.

After seeing the battle of Ypres, where 90,000 men are still missing, either obliterated or buried beneath wheat fields, the vast trenches of the Somme, Belleau Wood, the Argonne, Verdun, and a few ostuaries where the unidentified skeletal remains of over 130,000 men, friends and enemies, remain, these places are no longer names in history books. They now live in my heart.

I especially remember the day I walked for several miles through a path among the wheat fields of Flanders, Belgium. As I've said, it is estimated that 90,000 unidentified soldiers are buried beneath the wheat around there and only God knows who they are. I was walking over dead men.

As the poet soldier, John McCrae, wrote of these men and others like them:

"We are the dead. Short days ago
We lived, felt dawn, saw sunset glow,
Loved and were loved and now we lie
In Flanders fields."

I think that all wars are senseless. The concept itself is empty, immature, cruel and devoid of human compassion. And I think that WW I is the most senseless of them all.

XXX

French Polynesia, 2016

I am very visually oriented, and so I have always wanted to see French Polynesia with its aqua-blue waters and rustic ambiance. Because it didn't have a practical and/or useful agenda, it was last on my bucket list of places to visit.

It took many hours in the air to get there, but it was worth it. I booked passage on the M/S Paul Gauguin cruise ship that visited Tahiti, Huahine, Bora Bora and Moorea, the island I liked most, as I had a day there to explore by myself.

There were three restaurants on the ship. Breakfasts were extraordinary, as was my waiter, Caesar, from the Philippines. I fell in with a group from Australia whose people I have always loved, and had my dinners with them. Lots of laughs. I keep up with them via Facebook, as I do with many of my international friends.

The part of the trip I most looked forward to was swimming with the sharks. It had a certain flair of danger to it, but I knew it must be safe as it would not be offered otherwise. I also checked with the concierge about it. "They are lemon sharks," he said, "quite large but in this context quite safe. You see, they have an abundance of food in the lagoons here, and have no interest in humans. You will see them zipping by you, that is all."

When the time came, I was so busy trying to keep the snorkeling parts together, I never saw one, but was told by our guide for the day that one did bump into me, though I thought it was a sting ray trying to get me to pet it. The rays were a real nuisance as they tried to wrap their two fins around the snorkelers to get a hug.

This is the point where I have decided to call a halt to writing about the particulars of my journeys, though in a few weeks I will be off to my next one.

CHAPTER 7

Looking Back

With Sheila on a lake in Alaska

**With young Communists
in Pyongyang, N. Korea**

A Sloth at Monkey Island

I'M LOOKING FOR seat 19F, a window one I think. And I'm settling into a 5 hour flight to see my college buddy, Phil McGoohan, in California.

I intend to use the hours looking back on my life, trying to isolate the most meaningful parts.

It was never easy for me to be a father, as the bar I set for my children was not always reachable. I often didn't know what to do, and would knee-jerk into a kind of hard-ass introvert, the way my father, the only model I had at the time, was. I had not yet found the man that I have become. Perhaps it is the way of many men in our culture. And so, in some ways I am still trying to become the father, and grandfather I would like to be.

I am satisfied, though, that I have "thrown my pebble into the pond." It is a meaningful expression to me, one that stands for involvement in the world. I have thought of myself specifically as a citizen of America, but generally as a citizen of the world. I think that excessive patriotism is childish because it ignores our history and the ways we can be a more noble country.

Perhaps because of the echoes of my childhood as a member of a poor, uneducated, dysfunctional and harsh family, I have always identified with children, especially those born into poverty. And so I am proud of the decades I spent raising awareness and money for these children across the globe, especially helping them have access to food.

When I left home as a rough-edged macho teen to become a monk, I had no idea where the journey would take me. In time, I knew it was taking me to the brighter side of life, to a place where I could challenge my fears which had so led me around in my life. And so I have made it a point to face every fear that comes up in me.

I have given talks and made speeches, both here and abroad, as I combated stuttering and the fear of exposing myself as not being as articulate as I'd like. I sky-dived from 12,500 feet when I was afraid of heights. I talk to women who are beautiful, sometimes just because their beauty might intimidate me. And I do not like to feel intimidated.

I talk with people of consequence because I do not want their importance to stop me from knowing them. I say yes to invitations to be on television because it scares me that many people will see me. I take a deep breath and do it.

I believe that every good gift we have has a down-side when not used for positive outcomes. Alas, I have not yet mastered the down-side of the gifts that I have been born with. As I said at the outset of this book, I came into life with a good brain, yet I am not always good at thinking. I think too much, and it causes me anxiety and sometimes confusion.

In an intense way, I would like to really believe that there is a higher power, a God. So, I often think about the possibility that there is. I justify this constant thinking because the nature of my brain is one that wants answers. If our existence ends with our deaths it all seems meaningless to me, a sign of a strange God, if one exists. Yet, hard as I might, I cannot find the presence of a God in the world.

Yet, I find in many ways that there might be a Force that has lead me forward in a positive way. Why, for example, did the pastor of my church call me into his office to tell me that he wanted to pay for my tuition to a private boys high school in New York City. I did not know him and he did not know me. Was this the hand of God in my life?

Or am I just imagining it might be? Truly, though, when the pastor reached out to me, the course of my life changed.

Why was I saved by seconds several times from death? Was there someone watching over me? I don't know. Even if there was, I wonder why me. And I think if that is so, it is not a fair God, as I want all of us to be watched over.

I wonder sometimes why people, even those in authority, are kind to me when they might be justified in being unkind. Is there someone watching over me?

I have heard the voice of God four times in my life, a voice as clear as the clearest I have ever heard in a conversation with a friend at lunch. Was it just my imagination, or was it real? I don't know.

I wonder where this God IS in the world where there is so much evil and injustice, so many leaders who are morally corrupt. I would like an answer, for example, for His absence at the Jewish Holocaust when 1,500,00 children were murdered. I know the "go to" answer is that we have free will, and that He watched it while crying. I hope I am not arrogant, but that "go to" does not cut it for me.

Yet, I wonder why there are so many tests for us to prove that we are good and not bad. It seems to be an existence of tests, big ones and small ones like pop quizzes. I wonder sometimes if God, He or She, might simply like to hang out with some of us, not because we are good but because we are interesting or funny or likeable?

When I was a monk and learning about God, I thought of Him as a negative force, powerful, vengeful, punishing. As I began to have lots of good and bad experiences in the real world after I left the monks, I could no longer bear in my soul the things I had been taught about this God. I could no longer bear organized religion. I knew that I could not love a negative force. I really could not.

I pray in a sort of strange way: "God, if you exist, would you kindly spend a few minutes with me?" And then I talk with the God of my choice, a loving God that I simply do not understand. I don't worship this God, as I do not think He needs it. Needing it would indicate that He is needy and, therefore, not a God. I just tell Him that I love Him.

I do not live in fear of this God because, if He exists, he is a loving God who accepts me as I am, a man who is trying to be in His image as much as I can in the ways that I treat others.

Perhaps, too, I end my daily prayers in a strange way: "And please take care of Yourself. We need You." I think it is a way of telling God that I love Him.

CHAPTER 8

Those to Whom I am Indebted and Love

SINCE I HAVE reached a certain maturity, I hope to have the chance before I die to tell those I love that I love them and why I love them. It is not an easy revelation, at least for me. It gets so mixed up with sexual and gender things in our culture that it is sometimes difficult to handle.

Too, my parents never said the words to me. I understand that, as it was not something that those of their generation and education said easily. I was 29 years old before anyone ever said the words to me, and 27 before I ever said it to another.

I remember the purity of the declaration when my son Jay told me one day on line at the supermarket when he was about eight, "Daddy, I love you" as he tugged at my pants. I will never forget that. I was going through a divorce and was feeling lonely, so his words sank deeply into my soul.

And the total purity of the declaration when my grand-daughter Julia called me up one day and asked me, "How long have we known each other?" I said "About four years."

"I want to say something about that," she said.

"OK."

She paused, then said, "I love you. And I am glad that I am your grand-daughter."

Her words, too, were powerful to me, and authentic which is a trait I admire when I come across it in others. She is a most extraordinary person. Her mother might have named her "Integrity." To be loved by someone like her is an extraordinary gift.

I am a lucky man now. Sheila and I never let a day pass without declaring "I love you" to each other.

Please note that I have a random abstract mind, so these people to whom I am indebted and love are not in any order of importance or degree of love.

I want to start with all those whom I have loved and are now gone. Perhaps it is a reminder that I have such a powerful love for certain people who have left us that they keep popping into my head. Albert Occelli, whose sudden death at the age of 12 pulled the existential rug from under me, often visits my brain. As does the more recent deaths of Joseph, my 92 year old friend, the template of the kind of person I would like to be when I am that old, and Ryan Kirk who left us at 34. My thoughts of his generous nature will never leave me. My sister Eileen died before I was born, yet I have always had a loving relationship with her in my soul. I hope there is an after-life, as I really want to meet her.

To those I loved and are gone, especially my brother Bob and sister Joan, thank you for being in my life.

It is said that you can tell a person by the company he keeps or has kept. In this regard, I often think of Monsignor Kelleher whom I knew once every three months for three years before I left to be a monk. He is the man who paid for me to go to a private boys' school. I did not know him nor did he know me, yet his act of generosity altered the path that the rest of my life took. Truly, his was a primary life-changing gift.

My mom and dad, Rita and George. As I have grown older and more mature, I realize that they accepted the cards they were dealt and did the best they could with them.

They both had an addiction to alcohol, so they had their faults, some grievous. Yet, I know in myself the mystery of an addiction, when it starts and where it takes us. I know now that I cannot measure or judge the intensity or negligence of their spirit. I know that they made me do the responsible things that would make my life better than theirs. And for that I am grateful.

I am indebted to and love the Christian Brothers of Ireland, the order of teaching monks I joined at age 17. I was somewhat of a punk kid and they did not have to accept me as one of them. They gave me a truly great education at Iona College. It was at the college that a life-long love for books and learning was enkindled in my spirit. It was here that the seeds of kindness, love and generosity were sown in my soul.

Mr. Tom Calabrese was the principal of Memorial Junior High School, the first school I taught in after I left the monks. The several years he was my principal were difficult years for me trying to adapt to secular life. He could have fired me many times for being late, distracted and incompetent. But he did not. I always felt that he understood the difficulties of adjustment. When he was in the hospital dying of cancer I told him that I loved him. It was the first time I ever said that to a man.

And then there were two other principals, both at Staples High School in Westport where I headed the English Department for a quarter of a century. To be sure, during a time of personal growth and professional development they both, Dr. Marv Jaffe and Dr. Gloria Rakovic, might have treated me harshly, but never did. For that I am grateful.

I am in debt to everyone who ever showed up at an AA meeting, as the very act of presence was, and is, an inspiration to me. I have always seen the evil in the world.

Without the inspiration of my fellows in AA, it might have worn me down by now.

Each of my four children, Kevin, David, Suzanne and Jay, my step-daughter, Jessica, and my grandchildren have had a profound impact on my life. Beyond all else, I wanted each of them to be a good person. None of them has failed me. I wish I had spent more time with them as they were growing up. I was too busy getting ahead on the job, and not moderate in trying to make the world a better place. I think I needed a course in Fatherhood, as the template I had in my head about that was not gracious enough.

As, too, I was not gracious enough with my first wife, as the template of Husbandhood failed me. I am, though, still friends with her, and for that I am grateful. I learned much from being with her in the years of our marriage.

Quite frankly, I don't remember by name the hundreds, probably thousands, of students I have had. I do remember, though, growing in relationship with them from a rather prescriptive teacher to a caring, loving man. I thank them for their role in the process.

I am indebted to Eileen Byrnes, and I do love her for who she is, the most extraordinary exercise instructor there possibly could be.

And my talented and compassionate dentist for many years, Dr. Deidre Condon, who teaches me the relationship between healthy teeth and a healthy body.

Since finishing his necessary medical obligation and offering his talent to the public, Dr. Sean McGrade, my family doctor, continues to be the best of the best.

It goes without saying (what a silly expression to preface a "saying") that I might not be writing this were it not for Dr. Alice Higgins, my psychologist for many years before she moved south. She never judged me. Extraordinary!

To the many friends I have: Dana, Barry, Louise, Orlando, Dean, Will, Phil, Rita, John and Caren, Tom, McG, Medina, Kate, Donna, and my sister Eileen, a most extraordinary person. There are more who if not on this paper still live in my heart.

My many friends around the world: Noriyo, Sarah, and Thoan (my Vietnamese "granddaughter"), Aline, Kangi, my many Muslim friends in Kosovo and Jordan.

And the Uedas who have always cared for me on my trips to Hiroshima. The Knights of the Oval Table (Joe, Dana, Barry, Orlando, Edwin).

I am extremely indebted to my Aunt Priscilla who was a second mother to me.

And to the Police Athletic League (PAL) officer who brought hope into my heart by giving me $.38 cents when I was about 8 or 9 years old.

Br. Carthage Ryan who miraculously cured me of stuttering. And Brs. Scanlon, Lynam, Doyle, Galway, McKenna, and Egan who taught me about sincerity.

And Mr. Cobert, an Astoria taxi driver, who taught me how to play baseball. And Kyle Pritz, USMC and Afghanistan veteran who taught me the value of prayer. Dan Sullivan, the wisest and most spiritual man I have ever known.

To Drs. Quick and Pepper (really), philosophy teachers both, whose classes at Iona College I never wanted to end. They put me in touch with the love for learning.

And to my high school history teacher, Mr. Gilson who, while sitting on his desk one afternoon at Rice H.S., almost hypnotized me with his tale about being aboard a naval vessel approaching the Hawaiian Islands at twilight. "I could see the lights on Oahu," he recalled. "They sparkled in the distance, like emeralds." Thus began my travel bug.

I am grateful to the mothers and fathers of the town of Westport, Connecticut, whose children went to Staples High School. They always respected me and allowed me to be me.

To Kiki, my childhood dog, from whom I learned much about endurance. And my cats, especially Annabelle and her daughter Chloe. As I matured and watched them, I found the deep intelligence of animals. I so love them. In many ways they have been my teachers.

The land on which we live in Bethel. We know that it is Nature's land, so when we finally paid off the house, we did not think of it as our house, or our property. Sheila and I held two ceremonies when we paid off our mortgage.

One was to thank our property, especially our trees, for allowing us to be their caretakers. We hugged them. And inside our home we poured water from the tap in the kitchen, blessed it and sprinkled it lightly about the house.

I want especially to thank John Nolan, the man who watched over me when I came out of the monks. In many ways, he taught me how to be a man.

To Sue Anderson: thanks for giving me the title to this book.

And to the dearest friends of mine for the past five years, Louise and Julia.

Louise is a remarkable mother to my granddaughter, Julia, one of the most extraordinary young ladies I have ever known. She is exceptionally bright, kind, generous, and committed to the possibilities of life. She is my hope for the future.

My wife, Sheila, as you already know, was once my student at Kings Park H.S. I never really got to know her until over thirteen years later when my former writing class held a reunion at Sunken Meadow State Park on Long Island. Three years later we got married and it is now over 30 years. I think she took a chance on me, Lucky Boy. She is my rock. I think we both learned a lot from our first marriages. We talk things out when they get a bit edgy, as we believe it is the unspoken word that causes trouble in marriages. She is a strong woman who has taught me lots about how to respect and expand the field of my emotions so I now get along better in my world than in the past.

I especially love her tireless and abiding affection for animals of every kind. She gets up at 6 a.m., snow blizzards included, to feed the deer, the birds and any other critters who shows up. Habitat for Humanity has designated our property as a Wildlife Habitat.

Sheila is a beautiful soul-mate who lives by the principles inherent in generosity and love. Indeed, Lucky Boy.

See you at the ticket counter!

APPENDIX I

Distinctions Include:

. Inducted into National Teachers Hall of Fame

. Jefferson Award, Inst. For Public Service

. Mahatma Gandhi Peace Award, Ct. Ed. Assoc.

. Elected Fellow of Society For Philosophical Inquiry

. Alumni Outstanding Achievement Award, St. John's U.

. 21st Century Ct. Educator of the Year, 1995

. Peace and International Understanding Award, Nat. Ed. Assoc.

. Honorary Degree, Gibbs College

. Br. Driscoll Award for Outstanding Humanitarian Service, Iona College

. Walt Whitman Poetry Award

. Iona College Philosophy Award

- Human Relations Award, Ct. Ed. Assoc.
- Honorary Doctor of Humane Letters, Iona College
- Gary Mintz Award in Education, St. John's U.
- Haiti Lumiere de Demain "Bearer of Light" Award
- Honorary Iwo Jima Marine

APPENDIX II

Other Books by the Author

A Gathering of Doves

Even Whispers Can Be Heard

A Quiet Conversation

The Illustrator

Dew Drops On Tree Tops: a Book of Haiku

The Jesus Ultimatum

Oh Israel, My Heart Yearns for Thee

There's a Fortune Cookie in My Turtle Soup

Looking For Light

Short Stories and Essays: the Musings of a Man Held Captive by His Imagination

Waiting for the Red Cow

Pieces of Me

Printed in the United States
By Bookmasters